# Conservation, Land Conflicts, and Sustainable Tourism in Southern Africa

## Contemporary Issues and Approaches

Edited by Regis Musavengane and Llewellyn Leonard



Routledge
Taylor & Francis Group
LONDON AND NEW YORK

earthscan
from Routledge

First published 2022
by Routledge
4 Park Square, Milton Park, Abingdon, Oxon OX14 4RN

and by Routledge
605 Third Avenue, New York, NY 10158

*Routledge is an imprint of the Taylor & Francis Group, an informa business*



*British Library Cataloguing-in-Publication Data*
A catalogue record for this book is available from the British Library

*Library of Congress Cataloging-in-Publication Data*
A catalog record has been requested for this book

ISBN: 978-1-032-03762-2 (hbk)
ISBN: 978-1-032-03770-7 (pbk)
ISBN: 978-1-003-18890-2 (ebk)

DOI: 10.4324/9781003188902

Typeset in Bembo
by Deanta Global Publishing Services, Chennai, India

# Conservation, Land Conflicts, and Sustainable Tourism in Southern Africa

This book examines the nexus between conservation, land conflicts, and sustainable tourism approaches in Southern Africa, with a focus on equity, access, restitution, and redistribution.

While Southern Africa is home to important biodiversity, pristine woodlands, and grasslands, and is a habitat for important wildlife species, it is also a land of contestations over its natural resources with a complex historical legacy and a wide variety of competing and conflicting issues surrounding race, cultural and traditional practices, and neoliberalism. Drawing on insights from conservation, environmental, and tourism experts, this volume presents the nexus between land conflicts and conservation in the region. The chapters reveal the hegemony of humans on land and associated resources including wildlife and minerals. By using social science approaches, the book unites environmental, scientific, social, and political issues, as it is imperative we understand the holistic nature of land conflicts in nature-based tourism. Discussing the management theories and approaches to community-based tourism in communities where there are or were land conflicts is critical to understanding the current state and future of tourism in African rural spaces. This volume determines the extent to which land reform impacts community-based tourism in Africa to develop resilient destination strategies and shares solutions to existing land conflicts to promote conservation and nature-based tourism.

The book will be of great interest to students, academics, development experts, and policymakers in the field of conservation, tourism geography, sociology, development studies, land use, and environmental management and African studies.

**Regis Musavengane** is a faculty member in the Department of Tourism, Hospitality & Leisure Sciences at the Midlands State University, Zimbabwe, and a Research Fellow in the School of Ecological and Human Sustainability at University of South Africa. He is a member of the IUCN's World Commission on Protected Areas (WCPA) Tourism and Protected Areas Specialist Group (TAPAS). He holds a PhD in Geography and Environmental Studies from the Witwatersrand University.

**Llewellyn Leonard** is a Professor in the Department of Environmental Sciences, School of Ecological and Human Sustainability, College of Agriculture and Environment Sciences at the University of South Africa. He holds a PhD from Kings College, University of London, and is a geographer and environmental sociologist. Before joining academia, he worked for a human rights environmental organisation working to support vulnerable communities exposed to environmental risks.

## Routledge Studies in Conservation and the Environment

This series includes a wide range of inter-disciplinary approaches to conservation and the environment, integrating perspectives from both social and natural sciences. Topics include, but are not limited to, development, environmental policy and politics, ecosystem change, natural resources (including land, water, oceans and forests), security, wildlife, protected areas, tourism, human-wildlife conflict, agriculture, economics, law and climate change.

**Is CITES Protecting Wildlife?**
Assessing Implementation and Compliance
*Tanya Wyatt*

**A Political Ecology of Forest Conservation in India**
Communities, Wildlife and the State
*Amrita Sen*

**Ethics in Biodiversity Conservation**
*Patrik Baard*

**Protected Areas and Tourism in Southern Africa**
Conservation Goals and Community Livelihoods
*Edited by Lesego Senyana Stone, Moren Tibabo Stone, Patricia Kefilwe Mogomotsi and Goemeone E. J. Mogomotsi*

**Women and Wildlife Trafficking**
Participants, Perpetrators and Victims
*Edited by Helen U. Agu and Meredith L. Gore*

**Conservation, Land Conflicts, and Sustainable Tourism in Southern Africa**
Contemporary Issues and Approaches
*Edited by Regis Musavengane and Llewellyn Leonard*

For more information about this series, please visit: www.routledge.com/Routledge-Studies-in-Conservation-and-the-Environment/book-series/RSICE

# Contents

# Illustrations

## Figures



## Tables

# Contributors

**Adrian Nel** has a PhD in Geography from the University of Otago and completed a post-doc with a dual affiliation with the Institute for Development Studies at the University of Sussex, and the National University of Science and Technology (NUST) in Bulawayo, Zimbabwe. He is currently a senior lecturer in Geography at the University of Kwazulu-Natal, and serves on the advisory collectives of the Society of South African Geographers (SSAG), and the Political Ecology Network (POLLEN). https://orcid.org/0000-0002-5924-9084

**Dzingai Kennedy Nyahunzvi** holds a PhD in Tourism and Hospitality Management from Otago University, New Zealand. He is a senior lecturer in the Department of Tourism & Hospitality Management at the Midlands State University, Zimbabwe. He is past chairperson of the department. His main research interests span tourism and neoliberalism, protected area tourism, voluntourism, pro-poor and green tourism.

**Eduard Gargallo**. PhD in Contemporary History (University of Barcelona, 2007), with a thesis on the history of the Department of Agriculture in Zimbabwe. Researcher at the Centro de Estudos Internacionais of the ISCTE-Instituto Universitário de Lisboa. Currently carrying out research on land policies and community conservation of natural resources in Namibia and Mozambique. He was Projects Director of the Centre d'Estudis Africans in Barcelona, and he has taught in African Studies courses at the University Pompeu Fabra and the University of Barcelona. He has published in the *Journal of Southern African Studies*, *Journal of Namibian Studies*, *Politique Africaine*, *Journal of Contemporary African Studies*, and *Development Southern Africa*. https://orcid.org/0000-0002-7351-1122

**Emmanuel Mogende** is a Research Scholar in natural resource governance at the Okavango Research Institute, University of Botswana. He holds a PhD in Geography from the University of Cape Town. His research focuses on the political economy of natural resources in particular wildlife conservation and development in Botswana. His doctoral thesis draws attention to processes that produce the green state in the context of Africa using the example of the shifting wildlife conservation policy and practices in post-independent Botswana (1966–2018). Recently, his work has sought to understand how Botswana has placed the environment at the centre of state-making and how political leaders have been instrumental in forging the country's green international profile. He is also interested in issues of global politics in environmental governance, transfrontier conservation areas, militarization of wildlife, and border studies. https://orcid.org/0000-0001-5832-8058

**Inocent Moyo** is a Senior Lecturer and Head of the Department of Geography and Environmental Studies at the University of Zululand, South Africa. Dr Moyo is a Human Geographer with a deep interest in the interface between people and the environment, particularly the broader fields of Political Geography, Political Economy, Political Ecology, Migration, Regional Development, Globalization and Transnationalism, Borders and Borderlands, and Urban Geography, among others. He has published and done international presentations on these topics. He is the founding Chair of the IGU Commission on African Studies (IGU CAS).

**Jona Heita** is a lecturer of tourism studies at the University of Namibia (UNAM). He holds an MA in Culture and Environment in Africa (CEA) from University of Cologne, Germany. He is currently a PhD candidate at UNAM. His PhD research is assessing factors influencing human-wildlife conflicts in communal conservancies in Namibia. Local community development and community wildlife conservation form part of major themes covered in tourism studies taught. Although not published, he participated in tourism-related research in communal conservancies in Namibia. https://orcid.org/0000-0003-0640-7234

**Jones Mudimu Muzirambi** is a PhD Alumni of the University of South Africa, as well as an Educator/ Researcher in Mpumalanga Department of Education, SA. His research focuses on community-based natural resources management, with an interest in sustainable conservation and ecotourism, protected area governance, and the politics of costs and benefit sharing. https://orcid.org/0000-0002-0749-6868

**José Mourinho** (MSc) is a teacher at the Faculty of Environmental Engineering and Natural Resources, Zambeze University, Mozambique. His area of expertise is natural resource management. Currently, he is studying the inclusion of gender in management of protected areas. https://orcid.org/0000-0002-2923-2142

**Joseph E. Mbaiwa** is the Director of the Okavango Research Institute (ORI), University of Botswana. He holds a PhD in Parks, Recreation and Tourism Sciences from Texas A&M University is also a Professor of Tourism Studies. He is widely published in areas of tourism development, community-based natural resource management, rural livelihoods, and biodiversity conservation. Prof Mbaiwa is in the editorial boards of academic journals such as *South African Geographical Journal*, *Journal of Sustainable Tourism*, and *Journal of Ecotourism*. He was a taskforce member appointed by the Ministry of Environmental, Natural Resource Conservation and Tourism to prepare a proposal dossier that resulted in the Okavango Delta being listed as the 1000th UNESCO World Heritage Site. Prof Mbaiwa is a Non-Executive Director (Board Member) of the Botswana Tourism Organisation. He is also as a member of the 2019–2021 Ramsar Convention' Scientific and Technical Review Panel for the 2019–2021 triennium. https://orcid.org/0000-0002-1757-4866

**Kevin Mearns** is a full Professor in the College of Agriculture and Environmental Sciences (UNISA), South Africa. His research interests include Sustainable tourism, Environmental management, Ecology, and Ecotourism. He is involved in a number of community projects such as Sustainability benchmarking for the South African Tourism Industry, Social ecology of conservation areas, and Climate change and tourism amongst others. https://orcid.org/0000-0001-5874-3542

**Llewellyn Leonard** is a Professor at the University of South Africa, Department of Environmental Sciences. He received his PhD in Human Geography from Kings College, University of London, School of Social Science and Public Policy. Research interests include environmental justice; human rights and ecological justice, risk communication; urban risks, climate adaptation; democracy and governance; civil society-state-industry relations; as well as industrial risks and tourism/conservation impacts. His affiliations include the Society of South African Geographers (SSAG), the International Association for Impact Assessments, and the Rotary (New Dawn) South Africa. https://orcid.org/0000-0002-6279-0373

**Luis Cristóvão** (PhD) is Assistant Professor at the Faculty of Environmental Engineering and Natural Resources, Zambeze University, Mozambique. His key knowledge and expertise include environment and natural resource management. Recently, he is studying water-food security-energy-biodiversity nexus in changing climate. https://orcid.org/0000-0003-0854-8102

**Oscar Mthimkhulu** is an Environmental Science PhD Candidate at the University of KwaZulu-Natal. He has extensive work experience conservation having served for more than 20 years at Ezemvelo KZN Wildlife; the provincial managing authority responsible for the biodiversity conservation of protected areas in KwaZulu-Natal. https://orcid.org/0000-0003-4774-1503

**Pekka Virtanen** (PhD) is Adjunct Professor at the Department of Social Sciences, University of Jyväskylä, Finland. His areas of interest include development studies, natural resource management, and democratization.

Currently he is studying local populations in protected areas. https://orcid.org/ 0000-0001-9371-2274

**Regis Musavengane** is a political ecologist and a human geographer. He is a Faculty member at the Midlands State University, Zimbabwe, Department of Tourism, Hospitality & Leisure Sciences. He is a Research Fellow at the School of Ecological and Human Sustainability, Department of Environmental Sciences, UNISA. He holds a PhD in Geography and Environmental Studies from the University of the Witwatersrand, Johannesburg, South Africa. His research interests include collaborative management of natural resources, community-based tourism, land reform, urban risk & crisis management, and inclusive tourism systems for both urban and rural spaces. His affiliation include the IUCN's (International Union for Conservation of Nature's) World Commission on Protected Areas (WCPA) Tourism and Protected Areas Specialist Group (TAPAS Group), the Society of South African Geographers (SSAG), and the Zimbabwe Climate Change Coalition (ZCCC). https://orcid.org/0000-0002-5276-7911

**Simon Naylor** is the conservation manager for &Beyond Phinda Game Reserve. He has a degree in nature conservation and has assisted in taking &Beyond's ranger training programme to East Africa communicated the &Beyond way throughout Kenya and Tanzania.

**Tariro Kamuti** is a Research Fellow at the Centre for Gender and Africa Studies of the University of the Free State, Bloemfontein, South Africa. He holds a joint PhD from Vrije University Amsterdam, The Netherlands, and the University of the Free State, South Africa. His research interests include land and environmental policy, governance issues surrounding sustainable utilisation of natural resources, the social dimensions of biodiversity conservation, sustainable rural and urban development. https://orcid.org/0000-0002-4769-9037

**Zibanai Zhou** is a lecturer and current head of the Department of Tourism & Hospitality Management at Midlands State University, Zimbabwe. His main research interests are tourism management, destination marketing, event tourism, and community-based tourism development. https://orcid.org/0000-0002-7918-2200

**Zwelakhe Thulasizwe Mascot Maseko** recently completed a Master's degree in Geography and Environmental Studies in the Department of Geography and Environmental Studies at the University of Zululand, South Africa. The focus of his thesis was on assessing the impact of natural resource conservation on the livelihoods of KwaNibela. Zwelakhe is interested in advancing his research on natural resource conservation. He has presented his work in local and international conferences and is working on getting his work on these topics published. https://orcid.org/0000-0003-1594-3178

# Acknowledgements

The editors of this book, *Conservation, Land Conflicts, and Sustainable Tourism in Southern Africa: Contemporary Issues and Approaches*, would like to thank all contributors who agreed to contribute to this volume. The issue of land is generally complex to handle in Southern Africa due to extreme social and political forces. Many scholars avoid writing about land issues in the region for this reason. We, therefore, salute the contributors for the courage and effort they took to share their knowledge in addressing the land conflicts in Southern Africa while improving the livelihoods of communities that depend on land and tourism resources. Furthermore, the chapters were written during the 3rd wave of COVID-19 under tight lockdown conditions by different governments. A number of the authors and their families contracted the virus during the writing process, but they didn't give up. You raise the flag for Africa higher, you are true heroes, and we salute you. All chapters describe the links between conflicts, tourism growth, and development trajectories in Southern Africa. We also acknowledge the input made by the three anonymous reviewers who provided insightful comments to our book proposal. Similarly, we appreciate the Taylor & Francis team, especially Hannah Ferguson and John Baddeley, for their guidance during the process.

All chapters were peer-reviewed by two reviewers, in accordance with accepted academic practices; we thank them for their time, effort, and valuable input on improving the chapters. Finally, we thank our families and friends for their love and support. For providing the spiritual sustenance needed to pursue a more just society, Llewellyn would like to thank his wife Jessica, son Udhav, and daughter Tulsi Rasa Leonard for their support. Regis would like to thank his wife Rutendo Rhoda Musavengane, his son Christian Tapiwanashe, and daughter Chantelle Ruvimbo Musavengane for their support and understanding for the work he does for the betterment of Africa.

# 1 Land conflicts in Southern Africa

## The sustainability of tourism and conservation

*Regis Musavengane and Llewellyn Leonard*

*The Law of the Land*[1]

*Now this is the law of the land, son*
*as old and as new as the hills*
*And the farmer who keeps it may prosper*
*but the farmer that breaks it, it kills.*

*Unlike the law of the man, son*
*this law it never runs slack,*
*What you take from the land for your own, son,*
*you've damn well got to put back.*

*Now we of the old generation took land on the cheap and made good*
*We ploughed, we stocked, and we burnt, son, we took whatever we could,*
*But erosion came creeping slowly, then hastened on with a rush,*
*Our rooigras went to glory, and we don't relish steekgras as much.*

*The good old days are gone, son*
*when those slopes were white with lambs,*
*The lands lie thin and straight, son,*
*and the silt has chocked our dams.*

*Did I say those days were gone son? For me*
*they are almost gone*
*But for you they will come again, son,*
*when the task I set you is done.*
*I've paid for this farm and fenced it,*
*I've robbed it, and now I unmask –*
*You've got to put it back, son,*
*And yours is the harder task.*

*Stock all your paddocks wisely, rotate them as you can,*
*Block all the loose storm-waters, and spread them out like a fan.*

DOI: 10.4324/9781003188902-1

*Tramp all your straw to compost and feed it to the soil,*
*Contour your lands where they need it, there is virtue in sweat and toil.*
*We don't really own the land, son, we hold it and pass away.*
*The land belongs to the nation, to the dawn of judgement day.*
*And the nation holds you worthy, and if you are straight and just*
*You'll see that to rob the land is betraying a nation's trust.*
*Don't ask of your farm a fortune,*
*True worth ranks higher than gold;*
*To farm is a way of living, learn it*
*before you grow old.*

*So this is the law of the land, son,*
*to take, you've got to put back.*
*And you'll find that your days were full, son,*
*when it's time to shoulder your pack.*

## Introduction

At the core of issues that matter to Africans is the governance of land and the associated natural resources. This pertains to the use, access, and sharing of land and its vast natural resources (Nelson, 2010). The livelihoods of most of the African populace hinge on the land and its associated resources. The land is central to natural resource governance. Economically, land is important in the provision of ecological services that underpin agricultural livelihoods. In addition, the tourism and conservation sectors rely heavily on wildlife resources (Muboko & Murindagomo, 2014; Stone & Nyaupane, 2018). The Southern African region has almost all the major minerals necessary to transform the livelihoods of many of its citizens, but to date, the extraction of natural resources has destroyed the land and not resulted in the wealth distribution among citizens that would enable sustainable livelihoods. In many African countries, such as Nigeria, Sierra Leone, Angola, the Democratic Republic of Congo, and Liberia, the exploitation of extractive natural resources has only contributed to increasing political instability, conflict, wars, and socioeconomic degradation (Arthur, 2014). Politically, the quest for land and the associated natural resources led to the exploitation of Africans through colonisation, which in turn framed the current conflicts. In the postcolonial era, issues regarding natural resource governance such as land tenure continue to underpin evolving relationships between states and citizens. Inequalities relating to land use and access have been and continue to be the major reason for land conflicts in Southern Africa. This consequently affects tourism development in land-contested spaces (Nelson, 2010). There are several key natural resource challenges within Southern Africa. Some of these include limitations in inclusive decision-making over land use; large-scale land acquisitions (land grabbing) that result in anti-people investment policies; marginalisation regarding the access of vulnerable peoples to common resources; lack of devolution of natural resources and insufficient transfer of power; dispossession by powerful economic interests that deploy conservation narratives driven by outsiders' innovations; and a greater reliance on biological science that excludes the majority of the population (Bugembu, 2016). Access to land use is a pivotal aspect in assuring sustainable rural livelihoods, with natural resources becoming natural 'assets' when access is guaranteed either through asset ownership or other means of securing access and control (Lee & Neves, 2009).

To consolidate the much-needed political authority and control patronage of natural resources after gaining independence, most Southern African countries maintained the centralised natural resource management (NRM) systems. This situation appears to have led to the mismanagement of natural resources due to the lack of capacity and the misaligned incentives that have culminated in the privatisation of public resources and patronage (Nelson, 2010). Resource-rich countries on the continent are among the most poorly governed. Risks related to governance issues have also hindered African countries from transforming resource wealth to production and revenues and, therefore, sustainable development. The 2017 Resource Governance Index is a tool for assessing good governance. It measures accountability and transparency rules and practices related to many issues deemed by African institutions as critical in improving benefits from resources. Generally, Africa achieves a 'poor' resource governance rating although there is variance between countries (Natural Resources Governance Institute, 2018). The centralised NRM of land and associated resources such as wildlife, forests, and fisheries allows for their exploitation due to the lack of capacity of the states to enforce policies. The centralised NRM system has evolved into a top-down management approach in which the elite bureaucrats and party loyalists who are far removed from the reality of rural life continue to dictate how rural residents should manage their natural resources (Musavengane & Simatele, 2016). This situation often results in the disgruntlement of local people because central government authorities naively believe that they are in a better position to make decisions concerning the management of natural resources (Binns et al., 2012). Harnessing the potential of natural resources is key to delivering better development outcomes for the African population, which is projected to double by 2050 (Natural Resources Governance Institute, 2018).

Central governments have been identified as key instigators of land conflicts (Arthur, 2014). Cheru (2002) opines that central governments oftentimes naively view themselves as better placed to make key decisions on NRM. Binns et al. (2012) add that such thinking and the associated practices result in poor policies and institutional failures that undermine the productivity of rural populations. The communication and knowledge gap created between the central governments and local communities creates a suitable environment for land conflict. Having gone through repressive eras under colonialism and apartheid, local people resist policies that are imposed upon them. Chirenje et al. (2013) note that while African governments have understood the need to devolve control and management of natural resources to the local communities, the latter are excluded from the planning and budgeting that is important in decision-making. Instead, communities are involved in the implementation of NRM programmes but lack ownership of the projects, resulting in poor commitment to the project development programmes and at times, hostile reactions from the communities. Community participation is effective when the local population is involved as project owners. Hence, Chambers (1994) and Child (2019) stress the need for greater civic participation in making decisions pertaining to NRM. The growth of democratic and development discourse has necessitated discussion on the inclusion of local people in decision-making processes in the management of land-related resources. Grassroots decision-making in common pool NRM enables and promotes the collective cooperation of stakeholders in devising strategies for effective resource management (Tantoh & Simatele, 2018). African governments need to secure the inclusion of communities in decision-making and not impose external solutions if NRM and land use are to be sustainable. Even international interventions to resolve land conflicts in Southern Africa will not be sustainable without the involvement of communities in decision-making processes. According to Kalabamu (2019), despite international support and a number of tenure reforms undertaken by various post-independence governments, land conflicts appear to be ongoing, with conflicts intensifying in terms of magnitude and frequency in some Sub-Saharan African countries. This has exacerbated the inequalities inherited from colonial regimes and created new platforms for social injustices and political instability, working against peace, social justice, and equality.

## International and Southern African debate on land conflicts, NRM, and tourism

Researchers across the globe have written on land conflicts in the Sub-Saharan African region (see Bansah, 2017; Berry, 2017; Boone, 2017; Fisk, 2019). The issue of land claims is rife within the continent and has attracted many authors and publishing houses. For example, *Geoforum*, a leading international and interdisciplinary journal published a Special Issue on "Claim-Making as Social Practice – Land, Politics and Conflict in Africa" (Van der Haar et al., 2021). The Special Issue focused on Sub-Saharan Africa for two main reasons. First, there are widespread concerns over the intensity of the competition around land due to the global 'land rush' and the prevalence of land tenure insecurity in Africa. The second reason is that "there is a need to bridge the scholarships around 'development' and 'conflict', a concern, we feel, is particularly acute on the African continent considering its relative underdevelopment and the violent conflicts that affect large parts" (Van der Haar et al., 2021, p. 11). This current book agrees with such sentiments and propositions; Southern Africa should not be known for grabbing the land violently and destroying any economic activity, including tourism. Hence, the book navigates the pertinent issues on the nexus between land conflicts and tourism in Southern Africa.

In September 2021, the Web of Science TITLE-ABS-KEY (land conflicts AND tourism) revealed a total of 544 documents. A further scan of these documents showed that the published documents focused on themes such as land-use conflicts and governance (Hjalager, 2020); conflict heritage tourism (Mansfeld & Korman, 2015); conflicts in tourism development (Wang & Yotsumoto, 2019); land conversion for tourism development and land rights (Duong et al., 2020); distribution of land income (Qingyun & Mu, 2020); geopolitics of tourism (Ram et al., 2017); collaborative approaches for tourism conflicts (Almeida et al., 2018); and mining and wildlife conflicts (Izquierdo et al., 2018). These themes are presented in most tourism, geography, and development journals whose focus includes conservation, land use, and tourism development. The Southern African region is no exception to these global thematic tourism conflicts. Although not regarded as a conflict per se, COVID-19 has affected the tourism sector significantly. As of 1 September 2021, 105 000 results were generated upon searching TITLE-ABS-KEY (COVID-19 AND tourism). Although it is a health-related pandemic, COVID-19 resulted in social conflicts within the tourism sector (Musavengane et al., 2020). For example, the pandemic generally resulted in the deterioration of security both inside and outside protected areas across Africa, causing loss of natural resources and loss of livelihoods for communities. COVID-19 also heightened threats of human-wildlife conflict, with 90% of the countries in Eastern and Southern Africa according high importance to managing such conflict (Waithaka, 2020). Similarly, although natural disasters cannot be construed as conflicts in absolute terms, they destabilise tourism operations and may lead to conflicts. For instance, the Zambezi River basin in Southern Africa has been prone to the risk of violent (armed) conflicts such as collective violence and popular unrest induced by climatic changes/variability. Such instances amplify the stresses on the socio-political fabric because they affect the governance of resources, including tourism, and result in economic challenges such as rising food prices (Swain et al., 2011). Thus, the chapters presented in this current book provide discussions on the issues raised in these global themes relating to land conflict and tourism.

## *Land tenure and land reform*

A closer look at land tenure in Southern Africa is needed to understand land-related conflicts. The region's land tenure has varying degrees of classification, namely freehold, which awards private titles, communal or traditional systems, public land, and squatting (Bob, 2010). To a great extent, accessibility and ownership of land have been characterised by social dimensions (class, gender, religion, and ethnicity) (Matondi, 2012). These dimensions comprise the major sources of land conflict in the region (Musavengane & Kloppers, 2020). At community, household, and individual levels, access to the land and the associated resources hinges on one's connections, power, and bargaining position (Lee & Neves, 2009). At the national level, the exogenous factors such as political forces and the quantity and quality of the land influences one's access to land and the associated natural resources. These largely influence the stability of land use and the access and sharing of the accrued benefits (Khapayi & Celliers, 2016). At local level, internal factors are more visible, and these define who accesses and controls the land. These factors are mainly demographic and include gender, age, household status, and lineage (Bob, 2010). In addition, culture appears to be a significant influencer on who benefits from the land and its resources. Culture defines the livelihoods and behaviour of most people in the Southern African region (Thondhlana & Shackleton, 2015). The sustainability of tourism in rural communities depends on how these factors are handled.

It would be incomplete to discuss land in Southern Africa without mentioning land reform. There have been growing calls for land restitution in the region to redress past injustices (McCusker et al., 2015). Land restitution has been at the centre of the conflict between the long-standing owners, who mainly consist of white people, and the majority black population comprising indigenous people (Ramutsindela, 2004). The conflicts have been extended and exacerbated by politicians, cultural leaders and conservation organisations (Ngubane, 2018). These conflicts have led to increasingly persistent calls for enhanced and effective governance processes for the collaborative management of communally owned natural resources (Musavengane & Kloppers, 2020). Collaborative management aims to facilitate the participation of community members in making decisions regarding their resources and in taking ownership thereof (Cundill et al., 2013). Co-management of common pool resources tends to lead to power sharing among actors and, to a certain extent, reduces conflicts (Musavengane, 2022). The long-standing environmental uncertainty regarding community-based NRM (CBNRM) and the social shocks due to tensions between centralisation and decentralisation forces, policy fragmentation, and the hegemony of the elite bureaucrats and party loyalists require good governance approaches including co-management (Reed et al., 2013). There is, however, need for more social-ecological approaches that can create resilient communities who are capable of managing common pool resources earmarked for sustainable tourism and improved livelihoods.

In sum, as noted in the literature, the main conflicts that exist in the Southern African region include inheritance-related conflicts among family members, conflicts between traditional and non-traditional organisations in land governance and dispute resolution, and conflicts between newcomers and long-standing residents. In addition, generational conflicts of access to land benefits, conflicts over land use, gender conflict over land access, land use, human-wildlife conflicts, and appropriation of benefits are indicated. Conflicts between households, neighbourhoods, and neighbouring communities over land rights and boundaries are prevalent in the Southern African rural spaces (Bob, 2010).

## The call to revisit land conflicts and tourism trajectories

Southern Africa is home to important biodiversity, pristine woodlands, and grasslands and is a habitat for important wildlife species. Nonetheless, it is also a land of contestation over its natural resources and is often associated with poverty. Southern Africa accounts for 9% of the extreme poverty globally despite only accounting for about 2.5% of the world population. An additional 40 million people in the region are expected to be in extreme poverty by 2040 (Porter, 2016). All countries in Southern African are expected to see an increase in absolute poverty. As in the past, the region's economic growth is not expected to reach its most vulnerable members. Unfortunately, Southern Africa has the highest level of inequality (as measured by the Gini coefficient) of any region in the world, and this will increase in years to come (Porter, 2016). To add to this scenario, natural resources associated with land and resource tenure continue to underpin evolving relations between states and citizens in the postcolonial era, with African governments largely reinforcing centralised authority over natural resources to control resources for patronage (Hwande, 2010). Postcolonial Africa has spearheaded a neoliberal development trajectory and created the unsustainable use of natural resources (Siakwah et al., 2020). This pathway has exacerbated the historical inequalities of colonial exploitation, with natural resource degradation contributing to further inequality (ISSC, IDS, & UNESCO, 2016). Notably, contestations of land span centuries and have been a source of conflict among Africans over indigenous lands (i.e. land distribution and ownership) and the white people concerned with conservation issues (i.e. issues of land restitution) (Cousins et al., 2008; Musavengane & Leonard, 2019). Between these spaces, there are also the issues of 'land grabs' by multinational corporations and governments on the continent to pursue alternative economic projects (i.e. mining, industrial development). Hence, conflict between rural populations and traditional authorities over land use ensues, with the latter entering into deals with corporations over indigenous land use that is against customary law and communal land ownership (Leonard, 2019; Rihoy et al., 2010). All of these land typologies have implications for community-based tourism and the ownership of natural resources.

Southern Africa is witnessing mixed calls for land restitution and redistribution and calls that are against land grabs by indigenous people (Matondi, 2012; McCusker et al., 2015). Politicians, technocrats, bureaucrats, traditional councils, and experts may agree on developments (in private and away from local communities) but sometimes, because of the complex nature of the issues, strongly disagree on the notions of land restitution, redistribution, and land grabs, how and if they should be done, and the time frames (Cousins et al., 2008; Kamuti, 2018). Rural communities and traditional authorities may also disagree over land redistribution and ownership of the land, which has implications for customary laws and interpretations since land restitution, redistribution, and land grabs are not mutually exclusive. In Southern Africa, tourism depends significantly on land and the related natural resources (Mbaiwa, 2005;

Musavengane, 2019). Mkono (2019) notes that "tourism in Africa is an ever-evolving tale of communities and economies striving to deliver memorable tourist experiences while optimising the gains, in the face of many challenges" (p. 1). Land restitution and redistribution, although viewed as a positive approach to redress past injustices, is also viewed as a challenge. Land conflicts (i.e. restitution, redistribution) can enrich or destroy community-based tourism in Southern Africa. Hence, there is the need for a book on community-based tourism and land conflicts in Africa with a focus on equity, access, restitution, and redistribution. A discussion on the management theories and approaches to community-based tourism in communities where there are land contestations is critical in understanding the current state and future of tourism in African rural spaces. This book aims to determine the extent to which land reform affects community-based tourism in Africa in order to develop resilient destination strategies.

## Structure of the book

This book explores three main themes. *Theme 1: Land governance and sustainable tourism managemen*t acknowledges that governance of land has implications for the sustainability of natural resources. The theme explores the broader issues pertaining to governance, including the use, access, and sharing of land and how these influence sustainable tourism development. The challenges of governance and leaderships and how these influence a more inclusive approach to sustainable tourism development are examined. In Chapter 2, Llewellyn Leonard discusses an alternative governance approach towards addressing the intersection between mining developments and the impacts on tourism and conservation sites in Southern Africa. He examines the 'resource curse' whereby multinational corporations and African governments view minerals as an opportunity for wealth generation and economic development over environmental protection. In Chapter 3, Tariro Kamuti explores the deepening challenge of governance of wildlife and land issues in the context of rising citizen participation in South Africa. He takes a close look at the conflict in the governance of the wildlife ranching sector. In Chapter 4, Oscar Mthimkhulu and Adrian Nel explore the leadership and governance complexities of communally owned protected areas in KwaZulu-Natal, South Africa. The authors investigate the case of Somkhanda Game Reserve as a communally owned protected area established in 2005 after a successful land claim by the Gumbi community.

*Theme 2: Managing natural disasters and land reform tourism crises* concedes that protected areas are arenas of conflict with contested power relations between various stakeholders that have implications for securing sustainable community-based tourism. In Chapter 5, Pekka Virtanen, Luis Cristóvão, and José Mourinho explore the complex effects of natural disasters on protected areas in Mozambique. The authors conducted a comparative analysis on the impact of Cyclone Idai in two contrasting protected areas, namely the national parks of Chimanimani and Gorongosa. In Chapter 6, Zibanai Zhou and Dzingai Kennedy Nyahunzvi examine the challenges and prospects of community-based tourism post Zimbabwe's land reform programme in the Midlands Province. The chapter makes an important contribution to the limited scholarly focus on the land reform–induced challenges on community-based tourism in this region. In Chapter 7, Jones Mudimu Muzirambi, Simon Naylor, and Kevin Mearns conduct a review of the conflicts relating to the post-restitution land rights agreement and their resolution at the Phinda Private Game Reserve in South Africa. The authors reviewed achievements and challenges regarding land ownership and community participation in management at Phinda. The authors suggest a way forward to address the challenges affecting community-based conservation and tourism in Southern Africa. In Chapter 8, Regis Musavengane examines environmental operational research for sustainable tourism and conflict management in CBNRM in South Africa. The author usefully reviews conceptual and methodological approaches for environmental operational research associated with participatory CBNRM in tribal communities and proposes alternative methodological imperatives for sustainable tourism and conflict management.

*Theme 3: Land use, access, and benefit-sharing conflicts* recognises that unequal access to land use is rife and contributes to large-scale land conflicts in Southern Africa, thus having implications for tourism development. In Chapter 9, Joseph Mbaiwa and Emmanuel Mogende examine the state of community-based tourism and wildlife user rights in tourism concessions in Botswana. The authors show that the implementation of neoliberal policies and the emergence of an elite class in the wildlife-based tourism industry have reduced local autonomy over wildlife resources and secured more power for foreign-owned multinational companies in this sector. In Chapter 10, Eduard Gargallo reflects on the COVID-19 pandemic and the socioeconomic and land-use impacts and implications for conservation and tourism in Namibia's conservancies. He analyses how the crisis in the tourism sector has affected populations in conservancy areas. In Chapter 11, Zwelakhe Thulasizwe Mascot Maseko and Inocent Moyo explore the conflicts between conservation and community at KwaNibela and the iSimangaliso Wetlands Park in South Africa. The authors present how the park conservation strategies have a negative impact on the socioeconomic wellbeing of the people in KwaNibela due to the limited access to natural resources and lack of economic opportunities of this community. In Chapter 12, Oscar Mthimkhulu and Adrian Nel examine the transformation crises in transfrontier conservation and the role of the state in the Maloti–Drakensberg Transfrontier Park, South Africa. The chapter provides insight through practitioner-critical research engagement into the successes and the existing challenges of the conservation area.

The chapters presented in this book will be of interest to students, researchers, development experts, policymakers, and academics in the field of tourism geography, development studies, land use management, and environmental management. This volume includes a variety of rich cases from Sub-Saharan

Africa and can be used as a main course textbook or a supplementary book. This volume presents important insights into dealing with and avoiding land conflicts in order to secure more sustainable tourism and conservation development. The book outlines the implications of land conflict in Southern Africa and suggests future research directions.

## Note

1 Poem by an anonymous poet found hanging on the wall in a roadside café near the small town of Heidelberg, Southern Cape, South Africa. Adapted from Swilling & Annecke (2012, p. 137).

## References

Almeida, J., Costa, C., & da Silva, F. N. (2018). Collaborative approach for tourism conflict management: A Portuguese case study. *Land Use Policy*, *75*, 166–179. https://dx.doi.org/10.1016/j.landusepol.2018.03.034

Arthur, P. (2014). Governance of natural resource management in Africa: Contemporary perspectives. In K. T. Hanson, C. D'Alessandro, & F. Owusu (Eds.), *Managing Africa's natural resources. International political economy series*. Palgrave Macmillan. https://doi.org/10.1057/9781137365613_3

Bansah, K. (2017). Governance challenges in Sub-Saharan Africa: The case of land guards and land protection in Ghana. [Doctoral dissertation, Kennesaw State University]. 14. http://digitalcommons.kennesaw.edu/incmdoc_etd/14

Berry, S. (2017). Struggles over land and authority in Africa. *African Studies Review*, *60*(3), 105–125. https://dx.doi.org/10.1017/asr.2017.96

Binns, T. A., Dixon, E., & Nel, A. (2012). *Africa: Diversity and development*. 1st ed. Routledge.

Bob, U. (2010). Land-related conflicts in Sub-Saharan Africa. *African Journal on Conflict Resolution (ACCORD)*, *10*(2), 49-64. https://dx.doi.org/10.4314/ajcr.v10i2.63310

Boone, C. (2017). Sons of the soil conflict in Africa: Institutional determinants of ethnic conflict over land. *World Development*, *96*, 276–293. https://doi.org/10.1016/j.worlddev.2017.03.012

Bugembu, B. (2016). *Natural resource governance framework challenges and opportunities in Eastern and Southern Africa*. A report for the International Union for Conservation of Nature and Natural Resources. https://www.iucn.org/sites/dev/files/content/documents/africa_5.pdf

Chambers, R. (1994). Participatory rural appraisal (PRA): Analysis and experience. *World Development*, *22*, 1253–1268.

Child, B. (2019). *Sustainable governance of wildlife and community-based natural resource management from economic principles to practical governance*. Routledge.

Chirenje, L. I., Giliba, R. A., & Musamba, E. B. (2013). Local communities' participation in decision-making processes through planning and budgeting in African countries. *Chinese Journal of Population Resources and Environment*, *11*(1), 10–16. https://doi.org/10.1080/10042857.2013.777198

Cheru, F. (2002). *The PRSP process in Ghana*. Report prepared for the second meeting of the African learning group on the poverty reduction strategy papers. UNECA.

Cousins, J. A., Sadler, J. P., & Evans, J. (2008). Exploring the role of private wildlife ranching as a conservation tool in South Africa: Stakeholder perspectives. *Ecology and Society*, *13*(2), 43.

Cundill, G., Thondhlana, G., Sisitka, L., Shackleton, S., & Blore, M. (2013). Land claims and the pursuit of co-management on four protected areas in South Africa. *Land Use Policy*, *35*, 171–178. https://doi.org/10.1016/j.landusepol.2013.05.016

Duong, M. T. T., Samsura, D. A. A., & van der Krabben, E. (2020). Land conversion for tourism development under Vietnam's ambiguous property rights over land. *Land*, *9*(6), 204. https://dx.doi.org/10.3390/land9060204

Fisk, K. (2019). Camp settlement and communal conflict in sub-Saharan Africa. *Journal of Peace Research*, *56*(1), 58–72. https://doi.org/10.1177/0022343318814588

Hjalager, A. (2020). Land-use conflicts in coastal tourism and the quest for governance innovations. *Land Use Policy*, *94*, 104566. https://doi.org/10.1016/j.landusepol.2020.104566

ISSC, IDS, & UNESCO. (2016). *World Social Science Report 2016, Challenging inequalities: Pathways to a just world*. UNESCO Publishing. https://en.unesco.org/wssr2016

Izquierdo, A. E., Grau, H. R., Navarro, C. J., Casagranda, E., Castilla, M. C., & Grau, A. (2018). Highlands in transition: Urbanization, pastoralism, mining, tourism, and wildlife in the Argentinian Puna. *Mountain Research and Development*, *38*(4), 390–400. https://dx.doi.org/10.1659/MRD-JOURNAL-D-17-00075.1

Kalabamu, F. (2019). Land tenure reforms and persistence of land conflicts in Sub-Saharan Africa: The case of Botswana. *Land Use Policy*, *81*, 337–345. https://doi.org/10.1016/j.landusepol.2018.11.002

Kamuti, T. (2018). Intricacies of game farming and outstanding land restitution claims in the Gongolo area of KwaZulu-Natal, South Africa. In F. Brandt, & G. Mkodzongi (Eds.), *Land reform revisited: Democracy, state making and agrarian transformation in post-apartheid South Africa*. Brill.

Khapayi, M., & Celliers, P. R. (2016). Factors limiting and preventing emerging farmers to progress to commercial agricultural farming in the King William's Town area of the Eastern Cape Province, South Africa. *South African Journal of Agricultural Extension*, *44*(1), 25–41. https://dx.doi.org/10.17159/2413-3221/2016/v44n1a374

Lee, D., & Neves, B. (2009). *Rural poverty and natural resources: Improving access and sustainable management*. ESA Working Paper No. 09-03. http://www.fao.org/3/ak422e/ak422e.pdf

Leonard, L. (2019). Traditional leadership, community participation and mining development. *Land Use Policy*, *86*, 290–298. https://dx.doi.org/10.1016/j.landusepol.2019.05.007

Mansfeld, Y., & Korman, T. (2015). Between war and peace: Conflict heritage tourism along three Israeli border areas. *Tourism Geographies*, *17*(3), 437–460. https://dx.doi.org/10.1080/14616688.2015.1036916

Matondi, P. B. (2012). *Zimbabwe's fast track land reform*. Zed Books.

Mbaiwa, J. E. (2005). Wildlife resource utilisation at Moremi game reserve and Khwai community area in the Okavango Delta, Botswana. *Journal of Environmental Management*, 77(2), 144–156. https://doi.org/10.1016/j.jenvman.2005.03.007

McCusker, B., Moseley, W. G., & Ramutsindela, M. (2015). *Land reform in South Africa: An uneven transformation*. Rowman & Littlefield Publishers.

Mkono, M. (2019). Positive tourism in Africa: Resisting Afro-pessimism. In M. Mkono (Ed.), *Positive tourism in Africa* (*Contemporary geographies of leisure, tourism and mobility*) (pp. 1–7). Routledge.

Muboko, N., & Murindagomo, F. (2014). Wildlife control, access and utilisation: Lessons from legislation, policy, evolution and implementation in Zimbabwe. *Journal for Nature Conservation*, *22*(3), 206–211. https://dx.doi.org/10.1016/j.jnc.2013.12.002

Musavengane, R. (2019). Land reform and the promotion of collaborative community-based ecotourism at Somkhanda Game Reserve, South Africa. In M. Mkono (Ed.), *Positive tourism in Africa (Contemporary geographies of leisure, tourism and mobility)* (pp. 23–35). Routledge.

Musavengane, R. (2022). Collaborative management. In D. Buhalis (Ed.), *Encyclopedia of tourism management and marketing*. Edward Elgar Publishing. https://dx.doi.org/10.4337/9781800377486.collaborative.management

Musavengane, R., & Kloppers, R. (2020). Social capital: An investment towards community resilience in collaborative natural resources management of community-based tourism schemes. *Tourism Management Perspectives, 34*, 100654. https://dx.doi.org/10.1016/j.tmp.2020.100654

Musavengane, R., & Leonard, L. (2019). When race and social equity matters in nature conservation in post-apartheid South Africa. *Conservation & Society, 17*(2), 135–146. https://dx.doi.org/10.4103/cs.cs_18_23

Musavengane, R., & Simatele, D. (2016). Community-based natural resource management: The role of social capital in collaborative environmental management of tribal resources in KwaZulu-Natal, South Africa. *Development Southern Africa, 33*(6), 806–821, https://dx.doi.org/10.1080/0376835X.2016.1231054

Musavengane, R., Leonard, L., & Mureyani, S. (2020). Doing tourism in Southern Africa amid the coronavirus pandemic: Navigating political, socio-economic and environmental inequalities. *Development Southern Africa*, 1–17. https://dx.doi.org/10.1080/0376835X.2020.1829459

Natural Resources Governance Institute. (2018). *Key facts: Governance of natural resources in Africa*. https://resourcegovernance.org/sites/default/files/documents/key-facts-_governance-of-natural-resources-in-africa.pdf

Nelson, F. (2010). Introduction: The politics of Natural Resource Governance in Africa. In F. Nelson (Ed.), *Community rights, conservation and contested land: The politics of natural resource governance in Africa* (pp 1–31). Earthscan.

Ngubane, M. (2018). "Disrupting spatial legacies": Dismantled game farms as success stories of land reform? In F. Brandt, & G. Mkodzongi (Eds.), *Land reform revisited: Democracy, state making and agrarian transformation in post-apartheid South Africa* (pp. 246–269). Brill.

Porter, A. (2016). *Extreme poverty set to rise across Southern Africa*. Institute for Security Studies. https://issafrica.org/iss-today/extreme-poverty-set-to-rise-across-southern-africa

Qingyun, P., & Mu, Z. (2020). Evolutionary game analysis of land income distribution in tourism development. *Tourism Economics, 27*(4), 670–687. https://dx.doi.org/10.1177/1354816619898078

Ram, Y., Isaac, R. K., Shamir, O., & Burns, P. (2017). Geopolitics of tourism and academia in the Holy Land. *Tourism Planning & Development, 14*(3), 411–429, https://dx.doi.org/10.1080/21568316.2016.1243354

Ramutsindela, M. (2004). *Parks and people in postcolonial societies: Experiences in Southern Africa*. Kluwer (Springer). http://link.springer.com/book/10.1007/1-4020-2843-1/page/1.

Reed, M. G., Henderson, A. E., & Mendis-Millard, S. (2013). Shaping local context and outcomes: The role of governing agencies in collaborative natural resource management. *Human Dimensions of Wildlife, 18*, 292–306. https://dx.doi.org/10.1080/10871209.2013.801003

Rihoy, L., Chorozva, C., & Anstey, S. (2010). People are not happy: Crisis, adaptation and resilience in Zimbabwe's CAMPFIRE Programme. In F. Nelson (Ed.), *Community rights, conservation and contested land: The politics of natural resource governance in Africa* (pp 174–201). Earthscan.

Siakwah, P., Musavengane, R., & Leonard, L. (2020) Tourism governance and attainment of the sustainable development goals in Africa. *Tourism Planning & Development*, *17*(4), 355–383. https://dx.doi.org/10.1080/21568316.2019.1600160.

Stone, M. T., & Nyaupane, G. P. (2018). Protected areas, wildlife-based community tourism and community livelihoods dynamics: Spiraling up and down of community capitals. *Journal of Sustainable Tourism*, *26*(2), 307–324. https://dx.doi.org/10.1080/09669582.2017.1349774

Swain, A., Swain, R., Themnér, A., & Krampe, F. (2011). *Climate change and the risk of violent conflicts in Southern Africa*. Global Crisis Solutions.

Swilling, M., & Annecke, E. (2012). *Just transitions: Exploration of sustainability in an unfair world*. UCT Press.

Tantoh, H. B., & Simatele, D. (2018). Complexity and uncertainty in water resource governance in Northwest Cameroon: Reconnoitering the challenges and potential of community-based water resource management. *Land Use Policy*, *75*, 237–251. https://doi.org/10.1016/j.landusepol.2018.03.044

Thondhlana, G., & Shackleton, S. (2015). Cultural values of natural resources among the San people neighbouring Kgalagadi Transfrontier Park, South Africa. *Local Environment*, *20*(1), 18–33. https://dx.doi.org/10.1080/13549839.2013.818950

Van der Haar, G., van Leeuwen, M., & de Vries, L. (2021). Claim-making as social practice: Land, politics and conflict in Africa. *Geoforum*, *109*, 111–114.

Waithaka, J. (2020). *The impact of Covid-19 pandemic on Africa's protected areas operations and programmes*. UCN-WCPA Paper. https://www.iucn.org/sites/dev/files/content/documents/2020/report_on_the_impact_of_covid_19_doc_july_10.pdf

Wande, W. (2010). Window of opportunity or exclusion? Local communities in the Great Limpopo Transfrontier Conservation Area, South Africa. In F. Nelson (Eds.), *Community rights, conservation and contested land: The politics of natural resource governance in Africa* (pp 147–173). Earthscan.

Wang, L., & Yotsumoto, Y. (2019). Conflict in tourism development in rural China. *Tourism Management*, *70*, 188–200. https://dx.doi.org/10.1016/j.tourman.2018.08.

# Part 1

# Land governance and sustainable tourism management

# 2 An alternative governance approach towards addressing the intersection between mining developments and impacts on tourism and conservation sites in Southern Africa

*Llewellyn Leonard*

## Introduction

Approximately 30% of all global mineral resources are located in Africa (United Nations Environment Programme, 2021), and this has, therefore, attracted much attention from both developed and developing countries (e.g. Australia, Brazil, Russia, India, and China) for mining investment and development (Edwards et al., 2014). Although some of the world's richest mineral deposits are found in Southern Africa, none of the countries in the region have the necessary domestic capacity and automated mining technology. Therefore, the region has turned to importing capital from countries such as the United States, China, Sweden, Canada, and Croatia (World Bank, 2019). The expansion in African mining since the turn of the century has attracted billions of dollars in investment (Janneh & Ping, 2011; Standing, 2007). However, with investment has come environmental destruction together with loss of conservation and tourism development since foreign mining companies in Southern Africa develop infrastructure in exchange for access to natural resources (World Bank, 2019). The destruction of natural resources is partly linked to corruption. For example, Leonard (2017b) investigated mining developments that occurred in a tourism destination in Dullstroom, Mpumalanga, South Africa and revealed collusion between government and mining conglomerates. This in turn has had implications for local communities, including their benefits from tourism developments. Human Rights Watch (2017) notes that generally, countries with mineral resources, including oil-rich countries, struggle with corruption and the lack of benefits for local communities. For example, the life expectancy and infant mortality rates in Equatorial Guinea, an oil-rich country, are below the Sub-Saharan African average, with roughly half the population lacking access to basic needs such as water. Therefore, although countries may be rich in mineral resources, the equal distribution of wealth is a problem and populations continue to suffer. Similarly, Nigeria and Angola

DOI: 10.4324/9781003188902-3

provide examples of the devastating effect of corruption in the oil sector with citizens living in poverty.

The African Union (AU) was formed in 1963 to promote the unity and solidarity of African states and to achieve a better life for the peoples of Africa, with 54 member states joining by July 2011 (United States Agency for International Development, 2017). However, despite its promotion of equitable, broad-based development through careful use of the continent's natural wealth (Ushie, 2017), there is growing recognition that the process of mining in developing countries is having a profound impact on the natural environment and on the rights of marginalised indigenous groups (Standing, 2007). In general, African countries have benefitted minimally from mining developments, with profits being shifted abroad or squandered, leaving many people in poverty (Kimani, 2009). This questions the Southern African governance mechanisms that are used to make decisions and monitor mining developments. For example, in the Democratic Republic of Congo (DRC), governance to combat mining impacts on tourism has been limited, generating the abuse of human rights by multinational conglomerates. From 1999 to 2002, the Kabila regime moved ownership of at least 5 billion USD of assets from the state-mining sector to private companies under its control with no compensation or benefit for the State Treasury (Monks, 2018). In 2004, owing to no local benefits, a small, mostly civilian group took over a mine operated by the Australian firm Anvil Mining in the Kilwa village, protesting that the company was making huge profits without rewarding the local workforce (Monks, 2018). Despite the vast natural resources of the DRC, 63% of the 75 million Congolese citizens were living below the poverty line of less than one dollar per day in 2012 (Extractive Industries Transparency Initiative (EITI), n.d.). This suggests that the governance approaches were traditional and hierarchical with no consideration of local communities. This has, however, been the pattern for mining conglomerates (e.g. Anvil Mining) whose activities have been implicated in environmental destruction, human rights abuses, and displacement across Africa and Southern Africa (Fitzgibbon et al., 2015). This poor governance approach and the mining activities also have implications for tourism and conservation development. As Ushie (2017) notes, the prevalence of conflicts linked to natural resources is now more than five times the level it was a decade ago.

Globally, limited studies regarding the mining impacts on tourism have been conducted (Leonard, 2016; Leonard, 2020). Hence, an exploration of this and the governance to combat the mining impacts on the natural resources of Southern Africa is needed. Some studies exploring the impact of mining on tourism have been conducted for Australia (Dwyer et al., 2014; Pham et al., 2013), for Peru in examining the growing imbalance between the livelihoods of local residents and the livelihoods of those in mining and tourism (Steel, 2013), for South Africa in exploring the impacts of mining on tourism and conservation (Leonard, 2020), and for China in exploring mining impacts on tourism in biodiversity hotspots (Huang, 2008; Huang et al., 2011) in addition to how deep sea mining is influencing Fiji's tourism industry (Folkersen et al., 2018). Surprisingly, although mining operations are affecting nature tourism sites and sustainable tourism development (Leonard, 2020), the scientific and academic literature on mining and biodiversity is scarce, with less than 1% of papers in leading conservation journals referring to mining-related threats (Sonter et al., 2018). Other authors have confirmed that little research has attempted to understand the mining impacts on specific protected environments and tourism sites (Leonard, 2017b, 2018, 2020; Leonard & Langton, 2016). The reasons for the high levels of environmental pollution caused by mines in pristine environments demand investigation but more importantly, the governance mechanisms that have been put in place to combat mining impacts on tourism and conservation sites in Southern Africa must be determined. This chapter attempts to establish the new modes of governance that are required to address the mining impacts on tourism and conservation sites and the associated land conflicts, especially in Southern Africa, in order to secure environmental justice and developments that benefit all people whilst conserving natural resources.

Good governance considers it important to manage industrial risk (i.e. mining) and the impacts on the environment (Leonard & Lidskog, 2020). An essential component of good governance is the ability to enable citizens to make their opinions known and to act and facilitate those opinions through citizen participation (Orr, 2002). According to Stirling (2006), there are two types of governance, 'unreflective governance', which denotes limited instrumental-driven decision-making processes, and 'reflective governance', which involves more critical attempts to manage the side effects and to garner a multitude of perspectives in order to implement sustainable practices. Contemporary approaches to governance are generally understood as the inclusion of the non-state stakeholders in decision-making (Van Marissing, 2005), with the emphasis on accountability, transparency, fairness, rule of law, and ethical considerations by the state (McNutt & Rayner, 2010) without relying on technocratic and bureaucratic processes to manage development (Wesselink et al., 2011). This collective understanding of modern governance can be grouped together under reflexive governance (Voß & Bornemann, 2011). Reflexive governance as a new mode of governance is viewed as organising a response to the risks by replacing hierarchical governance approaches with a more reflexive, flexible, and interactive approach (Bäckstrand et al., 2017; McNutt & Rayner 2010; Weiland, 2012), thus leaning towards the construction of a collective vision of sustainability (Sonnino et al., 2014).

Within this context, this chapter examines Southern African cases via secondary data on governance, mining developments, and contestations over land use. The chapter aims to provide insight into the unreflective governance mechanisms that may fuel land conflicts and favour a capitalist mining political economy over tourism and the protection of land-use conservation. Limited empirical data was also drawn from South Africa, the powerhouse of Africa, to clarify governance and land-use conflicts due to mining development. The chapter is divided into six sections. Section 1 comprises this introduction. Section 2 outlines the link between capitalist political economies, mining, and tourism/conservation impacts. Section 3 examines the governance of mining and the tourism/conservation impacts in Southern Africa. Section 4 explores mining conglomerates, corruption, and state governance and the implications for reflexive governance. Section 5 explores ecological reflexivity and governance potentially to address the intersection of capitalist political economy, mining developments, and the impacts on tourism and conservation sites in Southern Africa. Section 6 concludes the chapter with discussions, conclusions, and recommendations.

## Capitalist political economies, mining, and tourism/ conservation impacts

Mining development within a neoliberal paradigm has caused social and environmental harm for local communities living next to mining sites, thereby negatively affecting tourism and conservation resources (Leonard, 2016; Leonard & Lebogang, 2017). Market-based neoliberalism in Southern Africa escalated in the 1990s from a state corporatist system towards market-based neoliberalism, moving from Keynesian economic policies towards a 'free' market system. Although the process of decolonisation in Southern Africa began in the 1960s, the legacy of settler colonialism continues with the persistence of extractive and export-orientated economies based on mining (Webster, 2013). Unfortunately, the embedding of neoliberalism in transformed state institutions generally results in neoliberalisation, becoming a state logic rather than an actual policy choice, thereby strengthening the power of corporate sectors with little discussion of how power is shared or regarding issues of equity and sustainability-related outcomes (Kashwan et al., 2019). This has contributed to poor enforcement and weak state-society linkages (Campbell & Hatcher, 2019). Neoliberal market economies continually create ecological and social harm through increasing rates of production and consumption (Campbell & Hatcher, 2019). For example, Huang (2008) examined the environmental and socioeconomic impacts of mining and tourism industries in the Yunnan Province in Southwest China. The results indicated that mining activities had a negative impact on tourism and the environment and caused loss of income.

Similarly, Leonard (2016) investigated whether the tourism or the mining sector in the tourism area of Dullstroom, South Africa was more sustainable for employment and local social development. The research concluded that mining should not be allowed in conservation and tourism areas since mining has a detrimental impact on the natural environment used for conservation/tourism and thus contributes to job losses. Similarly, another study determined that mining had been proposed in the Eastern Cape Umgungundlovu community in Xolobeni, Wild Coast, South Africa against local community wishes. In 2005, Grant Thornton, an independent advisory firm, was contracted by the Department of Environmental Affairs and Tourism to conduct research on conservation and sustainable development of the Wild Coast. The firm found that the benefits of tourism overshadowed those of mining in terms of job creation and sustainability of the sector. The report indicated that tourism would create 281 direct employment opportunities and contribute R28 million of investment into the area in its first year, increasing to R50 million annually by the year 2022. Conversely, mining would last for 22 years and create 200, mainly non-local jobs, over the 22-year life cycle of the mine (Bennie, 2019).

Mining political economies seem to develop at the expense of workers, their social benefits (i.e. wages), and the environment, transforming natural resources into commodities (Kashwan et al., 2019) with state-led reform efforts seeking to enhance market 'efficiency' by transferring resource access and control (e.g. land, water, minerals) to capital interests (Wilshusen, 2010). Ostry et al. (2016) in the Research Department of the International Monetary Fund note that neoliberalism has increased inequality, with low-income developing countries witnessing a sharp economic downturn (Ostry et al., 2016). The impact of neoliberalism in Africa, as in Latin America, has been the debilitation of the welfare state, leaving the social security of its citizens to the free market whilst proliferating macroeconomic risks and inequality (Dagkas & Tsoukala, 2011), thus having implications for governance and impacts on tourism and conservation sites (Leonard, 2020). Although Hanusch and Baskaran (2019) resolved to estimate the benefits and costs of mining and to understand how they are distributed across a variety of stakeholders in Southern Africa, data was sparse. The reason for this is that many countries are part of the global Extractive Industries Transparency Initiative (EITI), which was created to reduce information irregularity by requiring disclosed information of "how revenues make their way through the government, and how they benefit the public". The EITI (n.d.) notes that a country's natural resources belong to its citizens. The EITI seeks to strengthen public and corporate governance, promote understanding of natural resource management, and provide the data to inform reforms for greater transparency and accountability in the extractives sector. Unfortunately, this has not been the case, as noted in the DRC. Surprisingly, the DRC is noted to have made meaningful progress[1] on the EITI website.

Issues of governance-beyond-the-state have become a problem (especially in Southern African states) whereby external international private economic factors such as the European Union, the World Bank, and other international factors are given greater power and control by the state for institutional arrangements of 'governing' and for policy-making, administration, and implementation (Swyngedouw, 2005). Thus, because of capitalist political economies that favour a reduced role of the state in governance and proliferating mining development on tourism and conservation sites, such mining activities can contribute to land pollution, affect local agriculture and heritage tourism, and disrupt local economies and ecosystems (Leonard & Langton, 2016). Mining can also lead to divisions within communities between those who support mining due to the derived economic benefits (e.g. traditional leaders being bribed by mining companies and local residents employed by mining companies) and those who want to preserve their lands for their cultural heritage and ancestral worship (Leonard, 2019a, b; Leonard & Lebogang, 2017). Leonard (2019b) investigated the case of traditional leaders and mining in KwaZulu-Natal, focusing on the rural community of Fuleni that borders the important tourist Hluhluwe–iMfolozi nature reserve. Fuleni is being targeted for mining development by the mining company Ibutho Coal, with the community opposing planned mining development in the area due in part to the neighbouring community of Somkele already having mining operations that are negatively affecting the community. Most traditional leaderships in Fuleni and Somkele are in collusion with mining companies to get mining developments approved due to the personal benefits that can be secured from the mining industries. A civil society informant cited in Leonard (2019b) noted:

> The corruption that was then part of the Somkele community now operates with … some traditional leaders benefitting, with the majority of people, particularly those who have lost their land to the mine, being really tragically disadvantaged and much poorer … it happens in all of these places where the traditional leaders end up being bribed quite substantially by the mining companies. It's quite cleverly done such that suddenly they are all driving new cars … so it's not in the form of hard cash … they are benefitting to be on the side of the mine …

## Governance of mining and tourism/ conservation impacts in Southern Africa

The governance of mining development in Southern Africa and the protection of conservation and tourism resources are of concern. For example, the Zimbabwean government previously granted coal-mining concessions to several Chinese companies in the Hwange National Park. The decision drew widespread criticism from environmentalists who now fear the coal-mining activities will harm the environment and worsen human-wildlife conflict as animals change location to escape the disturbances to their habitats. However, there have been calls by civil society for government to prioritise tourism and wildlife conservation in the park rather than mining activities (Karombo, 2020). These have been effective, with the Zimbabwean government announcing a ban on all mining in the park (*BBC News*, 2020). In South Africa, despite environmental regulatory interventions since the new democracy, there remains a disconnection between environmental regulations and how they work in synergy against mining and for environmental and tourism protection (Leonard, 2017b). Although legal frameworks were developed to prevent and manage environmental contamination by mines, their implementation has been largely unsuccessful. Even environmental impact assessments have been unsuccessful since these have been used as tokenistic tools to approve mining developments rather than to engage genuinely with the concerns of interested and affected groups (Leonard, 2017a). Mining pollution continues post-1994 to affect people and the environment negatively (Leonard, 2017b). For example, the Mineral Petroleum and Resources Development Act (MPRDA), No 28 of 2002 regulates the prospecting for and optimal exploitation of minerals in the country. According to Leonard (2017b), there is inconsistency between the National Environmental Management Act (NEMA) and the MPRDA since the former strongly promotes environmental and tourism protection while the latter promotes the 'optimal' exploitation of environmental resources and hence tourism/conservation destruction.

Tourist sites and pristine areas have been targets for the majority of mining developments in post-apartheid South Africa. For example, the Xolobeni mining development has threatened to destroy the tourism development in Pondoland, KwaZulu-Natal. The coastal Amadiba community has struggled for more than 10 years against repeated mining applications by Transworld Energy and Minerals (TEM), a South African subsidiary of an Australian mining company, to mine titanium on a 22-km stretch of the Wild Coast coastline (Pearce, 2017). According to Malherbe and Segal (2001), South African legislation attempted to sharpen corporate accountability for corporate actions post-1994; however, government institutions have not actively and publicly monitored corporate governance. For example, about a third of the 476 mines audited since 2015 by the Department of Water and Sanitation have failed to comply with the conditions of their water use licences, with 155 mines scoring 50% and thus indicating an unacceptable level of compliance (Bega, 2021). Unfortunately, regulation of the environment is fragmented, with functions divided among national departments, nine provincial departments, and specialised regulatory bodies. Politically, the environment is given limited attention by the ruling party, and there is a general failure to integrate environmental concerns into mainstream planning, development, and macroeconomic policy (Fig, 2005).

Generally, there is limited African governance capacity to deal with the scale and speed of the present wave of mining development and investments (Edwards et al., 2014). Although governance is important for sustainable development and to ensure the protection of social and environmental issues generally, governance may be subject to a number of constraints. These include how to treat and deal with the state's power and the fading role of the state (Voß & Bornemann, 2011; Santos, 2020), which may lead to technocratic approaches to governance and give rise to institutions that generate instability, ignore environmental externality impacts (Pickering, 2019), and lack the capacity to co-ordinate collective inputs to inform development decisions (Weiland, 2012). This is especially the case for mining developments where the state, especially African states, may be ineffective in holding mining companies accountable for social and environmental abuses and/or for not following proper procedure for mining applications (Leonard, 2017b). However, recent events in South Africa suggest that local communities and civil society provide a promising medium, serving as watchdogs against poor governance and corruption linked to mining and aiding procedural democracy. For example, the Eastern Cape Umgungundlovu community in Xolobeni fought against the mining giant TEM and the national government Department of Mineral Resources (DMR) and won a court victory that communities must be consulted and must give approval before mining rights are decided, setting a precedent for all mining-affected communities nationwide (Wicomb, 2018).

## Mining conglomerates, corruption, and state governance: Implications for reflexive governance

Within a capitalist political economy, mining is more prone to corruption and bribery, particularly in Southern Africa (Human Rights Watch, 2017). This is especially the case where a lack of legal frameworks and government capacity to enforce regulations governing the mining sector exacerbates the opportunity for private gain by corrupt individuals at the expense of the environment and the people (Van der Walt & Potgieter, 2020). Inequality is also high in many Southern African countries, suggesting that mining has not translated into inclusive growth (World Bank, 2019). African countries are generally characterised by a poor history of democratic governance, relative dependence on natural resources for wealth creation, and worsening levels of corruption (Standing, 2007). Regarding mining and land corruption in Africa, Knutsen et al. (2017) investigated mining-affected local corruption in Africa by connecting 92 762 Afrobarometer survey respondents to spatial data on 496 industrial mines. The authors found that mining increased bribe payments. Whilst mines may be initially located in less corrupt areas, these mining areas become more corrupt after the mines open, with mining income motivating and enabling the local officials already present to demand more bribes. This has implications for the governance of mining developments. For example, at the turn of the century, Angola's development indicators were among the worst in the world, while 4.2 billion USD in oil revenues illegally bypassed Angola's central bank and disappeared without explanation between 1997 and 2002. This is roughly equal to all foreign and domestic social and humanitarian spending in Angola over that period (Human Rights Watch, 2017).

The Organization for Economic Co-operation and Development (2014) previously noted that corruption remains a serious problem in South Africa, with mining identified as one of the high-risk sectors with a number of high-profile domestic corruption allegations (i.e. unveiled contracts being awarded on the basis of bribery, personal connections, or officials holding simultaneous business interests). Similarly, the Corruption Perceptions Index of Transparency International (2016) indicated that countries in Sub-Saharan Africa comprised 17 of the 30 most corrupt governments and 0 of the 30 least corrupt. The publication of Transparency International (2019), *Combatting Land Corruption in Africa*, notes that in Sub-Saharan Africa, one in every two people pay bribes to access land; this is known as 'land corruption'. Whether it is an opaque deal between private investors and local authorities, citizens having to pay bribes during land administration processes, or customary laws that deny women their land rights, land corruption hits the poor and marginalised the hardest. The results of research conducted by Leonard (2018) on mining and government corruption in South Africa revealed that the mining corporations and government (national and local) had a close relationship, with the former entity influencing the latter on how mining developments occurred. Mining corporations also strategically employed government officials in order to get mining developments approved in natural areas (Leonard, 2018). This close collaboration between the mining industry and government was found in Dullstroom, Mpumulanga, where there have been applications for mining in this pristine conservation environment. According to Dullstroom Interviewee B (Interview, 4 October 2013), who is interested in biodiversity protection,

> [The mining applicant] is connected with somebody within the government or within the DMR, I can promise you … So if they [the government] now start saying 'No, no, no, no, Steenskampsburg is out; I'm not going to allow you to do it [to mine]', they going to be pissing off somebody [mining connection] … We were at the cuff of having such a meeting in 2008 [to proclaim a protected area] … where agriculture, ourselves, Environmental Affairs, Water Affairs, DMR, labour, Premier's office, everybody would sit around the table and draw up these maps and identify priority areas, and it was cancelled two days before. There is no political will to do it … they all said, 'We agree with you 100% but if you implement it, I will be without a job'.
>
> (Leonard, 2018)

Because of the generally poor governance and corruption, there is a tension between the governance of capitalist political economies and how this governance intersects with environmental protection and land use, resulting in conflict between communities and civil society and government and multinationals. For example, Leonard (2017b) asserts that corporate influence over government in South Africa has generally swayed state decision-making over mining in tourism and conservation areas. This is reinforced by Leonard (2018) in noting the very close relationship between mining conglomerates and government in South Africa. Mining companies have strategically taken advantage of weak local governance to influence decision-making over development. Khan (2003) as cited in Vaughn and Ryan (2006) asserts that South African companies have been unwilling to divulge which political parties they have financed, and the primary sources of political subsidy remain anonymous. This attained industrial capital causes a likely conflict of interest. As Hallowes and Munnik (2006) highlight, local officials are wined, banqueted, and reminded of business contributions to government coffers. This signifies the sway that large corporations (especially regarding mining) have on democracy to act in the interests of citizens. According to groundWork (2003), the South African environmental justice and human rights organisation, government has consistently failed to ensure compliance in terms of existing rules and permits through prosecution or active sanctions, instead choosing to negotiate with industry the terms of sustained noncompliance. It is, therefore, questionable how negotiation may unfold between government and industry and on whose terms. Furthermore, this indicates that despite reflexive governance and its modern approaches to address developmental issues and impacts on tourism and conservation sites, reflexive governance may spiral into technocratic approaches to governance and overlook environmental externality impacts due to issues such as corruption. The following section explores the concept of ecological reflexivity to reveal the potential to improve reflexive governance.

## Ecological reflexivity and governance

Ecological reflexivity is considered an important concept that can enable inclusive environmental governance. Ecological reflexivity involves the capacity of social-ecological systems to reconfigure themselves in response to reflection on their performance (Dryzek & Pickering, 2017). The concept suggests that modern approaches to reflexive governance may spiral into technocratic governance approaches and overlook environmental and social external costs, as highlighted in South Africa. According to Pickering (2019), reflexivity refers to the capacity of an agent, structure, or process to change in response to reflection on its performance. Attempts to solve the issue of technocratic governance could be tackled with 'ecological reflexivity', which deals with recognition, rethinking, and response, thereby transforming the values and practices of such governance. In the first stage (i.e. recognition), an agent must recognise and be aware of the impacts on socio-ecological systems and must monitor past and current impacts and anticipate future impacts. In the second stage (i.e. rethinking), an agent should learn from past successes and failures, critically reviewing core values and practices and envisioning possible futures. In the final stage (i.e. response), an agent must rearticulate core aims, values, and discourses and reconfigure functions and practices.

Ecological reflexivity is thus equipped to take account of political contestation over the nature and direction of the change that is required to respond to ecological risks such as the impact of mining on tourism/conservation sites. According to Pickering (2019), in order to qualify as minimal reflexivity, institutions (e.g. government and industry) must show all three components of reflexivity to some degree. This understanding can assist in detecting shortfalls in reflexivity and unveil non-reflexive and reflexive institutions. For example, a government entity will be considered non-reflexive if it recognises the impact of mining on tourism or conservation job losses and fails to rethink activities and enforce environmental regulations or engage in genuine consultation with local communities. The combination of reflexive governance with ecological reflexivity in reflexive governance approaches will ensure that there is more explicit emphasis on the recognition of problems so that systems can be reformulated to avoid negative impacts and appropriate actions and responses can be taken that are sustainable for people and ecological systems. This means that mining industries must also recognise their impact on social-ecological systems and must be reflexive in rethinking their practices rather than aiming for short-term financial gains, which is not holistically sustainable for society. Such an approach entails more open, transparent, and inclusive governance.

## Discussion and conclusion

Despite the rich mineral resources in Sub-Saharan Africa that have attracted mining development and that have had implications for environmental destruction and loss of conservation and tourism development, there has been limited research in this area, with less than 1% of papers in leading conservation journals referring to mining-related threats. This chapter questioned the environmental pollution caused by mines in pristine environments and discussed the conflicts over natural resources between communities and government and industry. In addition, the governance mechanisms that are in place to combat the mining impacts on tourism and conservation sites in Southern Africa were probed. The chapter highlighted unreflective governance approaches across Sub-Saharan Africa that demonstrate limited attempts to manage the side effects and garner a multitude of perspectives via participatory mechanisms to implement sustainable practices.

Reflexive governance as a new mode of governance is viewed as organising a response to the risks by replacing the traditional, hierarchical, and deterministic governance approach with a more reflexive, flexible, and interactive approach that is transparent and draws on diverse knowledge systems. However, as witnessed in South Africa and as this chapter highlighted, capitalist political economies can influence governance processes via bribery and corruption, self-regulation of industry, and the provision of less power to the state to enforce regulations. This can cause social and environmental harm for the local communities living next to the mining sites and detract from conservation and the protection of tourism resources. This chapter highlights that a move towards an ecological reflexive governance approach with civil society pressure on unreflexive governance could potentially address the issues of capitalist political economies that have an impact on the tourism and conservation sites on which communities are dependent.

The chapter highlighted that whilst principles of good governance may be lacking within Sub-Saharan African states, the power of local communities and civil society is key in holding government/s accountable for poor governance and corruption and to push for an ecological reflexive governance approach. As was witnessed in the Eastern Cape Umgungundlovu community in Xolobeni, residents and civil society fought a legal case against the mining giant TEM and the national government DMR and won a court victory that communities must be consulted and give approval before mining rights are decided. The power of civil society and communities to ensure good governance is key in ensuring that government will eventually adhere to principles of ecological reflexive governance. An ecological reflexive governance approach has the potential to ensure that governments recognise their limitations and shortcomings. Thus, strong opposition is required from communities and civil society to unreflexive governance approaches so that governments can rethink their systems and the way in which they operate and consequently respond appropriately and in line with elements of participation and transparency with regard to civil society.

International institutions can also assist in enabling an environment for ecological reflexive governance approaches. The Organisation of African Unity (OAU), now the African Union (AU), centres on Pan-African ideals for unity, being in control of one's own destiny, and recognising equality and justice together with the communal characteristic and drive to embrace Africa's culture and common heritage (African Union [AU], n.d.). Hence, the AU can serve as a key component in enabling Sub-Saharan member states to adhere to an ecological reflexive governance approach and to ensure that governments align with its purpose to defend sovereignty, territorial integrity, and independence away from the control of multinational mining conglomerates. Such an ecological reflexive governance approach can protect the heritage of African spaces to enable the protection of natural resources and defend the collective interests of people. This chapter highlighted that mining has not been peaceful but has rather proliferated undemocratic processes that have not respected local communities and their cultural heritage or tourism and conservation development. This contradicts the aims of the AU to accelerate the political and socioeconomic integration of the continent, to promote peace, security, and stability, and to promote democratic principles and institutions, popular participation, and good governance. It is only by ecological reflexive governance that governments can apply the principles of recognition and rethinking and respond accordingly in order to promote good governance and align with the AU vision. Indeed, this may be a solution towards addressing the intersection of capitalist political economy, mining developments, and the impacts on tourism and conservation sites in Southern Africa.

## Note

1 In order for the EITI Board to conclude that a country has made meaningful progress, validation needs to demonstrate that significant aspects of certain requirements (i.e. contracts and licences, production, revenue collection and allocation, social and economic spending) have been implemented and that the broader objective of the requirement is being fulfilled.

## References

African Union (AU). (n.d.). *About the African Union*. [Online]. Available from: https://au.int/en/overview [Accessed: 18 April 2021].

Bäckstrand, K., Kuyper, J., Linnér, B. & Lövbrand, E. (2017). Non-state actors in global climate governance: From Copenhagen to Paris and beyond. *Environmental Politics*, 26(4), 56–579.

BBC News. (2020). Zimbabwe bans coal mining in Hwange and other game parks. *BBC News*, 9 September. [Online]. Available from: https://www.bbc.com/news/world-africa-54085549 [Accessed: 17 June, 2021].

Bega, S. (2021). Sisulu: Third of audited mines violate conditions of water use licence. *Mail & Guardian*, 5 January.

Bennie, A. (2019). Mining will not bring jobs to Xolobeni. *Daily Maverick*, 15 January.

Campbell, B. & Hatcher, P. (2019). Neoliberal reform, contestation and relations of power in mining: Observations from Guinea and Mongolia. *Extractive Industries and Society*, 6(3), 642–653.

Dagkas, A. & Tsoukala. K. (2011). Civil society, identity, space and power in the neoliberal age in Latin America and Greece. *Synergies*, 3, 105–113.

Dryzek, J. & Pickering, J. (2017). Deliberation as a catalyst for reflexive environmental governance. *Ecological Economics*, 131(C), 353–360.

Dwyer, L., Pham, T., Jargo L., Bailey, G. & Marshall, J. (2014). Modelling the impact of Australia's mining boom on tourism: A classic case of Dutch disease. *Journal of Travel Research*, 55(2), 233–245.

Edwards, D., Sloan, S., Weng, L., Dirks, P., Sayer, J. & Laurance, W. (2014). Mining and the African environment. *Conservation Letters*, 7(3), 302–311.

Extractive Industries Transparency Initiative (EITI). (n.d.). *Countries: Implementation status*. Oslo, Norway: EITI. [Online]. Available from: https://eiti.org/countries [Accessed: 13 February 2021].

Fig, D. (2005). Manufacturing amnesia: Corporate social responsibility in South Africa. *International Affairs*, 81(3), 599–617.

Fitzgibbon, W., Hamilton, M., Gallego, C. & Lindenberg, F. (2015). *Australian mining companies digging a deadly footprint in Africa*. Washington, DC: International Consortium of Investigative Journalists, 8 July. [Online]. Available from: https://www.icij.org/investigations/fatal-extraction/australian-mining-companies-digging-deadly-footprint-africa/ [Accessed: 11 July 2020].

Folkersen, M., Fleming, C. & Hasan, S. (2018). Deep-sea mining's future effects on Fiji's tourism industry: A contingent behaviour study. *Marine Policy*, 96, 81–89.

Hallowes, D. & Munnik, V. (2006). *Poisoned spaces: Manufacturing wealth, producing poverty*. groundWork report 2006. Pietermaritzburg, South Africa: groundWork. Available from: http://www.groundwork.org.za/reports/gWReport2006.pdf [Accessed: 15 June 2016].

Hanusch, M. & Baskaran, G. (2019). What is the contribution of the mining sector to Southern African economies? *World Bank Blogs*, 29 July. Available from: https://blogs.worldbank.org/africacan/what-contribution-mining-sector-southern-african-economies [Accessed: 19 December 2020].

Huang, G. (2008). *Mining and tourism: Comparing spatial patterns, socioeconomic contributions, and environmental impacts in China*. Doctoral dissertation, University of Vermont. [Online]. Available from: http://scholarworks.uvm.edu/graddis/113 [Accessed: 16 August 2014].

Huang, G., Zhou, W. & Ali, S. (2011). Spatial patterns and economic contributions of mining and tourism in biodiversity hotspots: A case study in China. *Ecological Economics*, 70(8), 1492–1498.

Human Rights Watch. (2017). *Africa's natural resources: From curse to a blessing*, 21 April. [Online]. Available from: https://www.hrw.org/news/2017/04/21/africas-natural-resources-curse-blessing

Janneh, A. & Ping, J. (2011). *Minerals and Africa's development*. Addis Ababa: United Nations Economic Commission for Africa. pp. 2–66.

Karombo, T. (2020). Zimbabwe has okayed a Chinese coal-mining pact at its top game reserve, even as elephants die. *Quartz Africa*, 3 September. [Online]. Available from: https://qz.com/africa/1899381/zimbabwe-okay-chinese-coal-mining-in-hwange-park-as-elephants-die/ [Accessed: 25 March 2021].

Kashwan, P., MacLean, L.M. & García-López, G.A. (2019). Rethinking power and institutions in the shadows of neoliberalism: (An introduction to a special issue of World Development). *World Development*, 120, 133–146.

Kimani, M. (2009). Mining to profit Africa's people: Governments bargain for "fair deals" that enhance development. *Africa Renewal*, April. [Online]. Available from: https://www.un.org/africarenewal/magazine/april-2009/mining-profit-africa%E2%80%99s-people [Accessed: 4 October 2017].

Knutsen, C., Kotsadam, A., Olsen, E. & Wig, T. (2017). Mining and local corruption in Africa. *American Journal of Political Science*, 61(2), 320–334.

Leonard, L. (2016). Mining and/or tourism development for job creation or sustainability in Dullstroom. *Local Economy*, 31(1–2), 249–263.

Leonard, L. (2017a). Environmental impact assessments and public participation: The case of environmental justice and mining development. *Environmental Assessment Policy and Management*, 19(1), 1–25.

Leonard, L. (2017b). State governance, participation and mining development: Lessons learned from Dullstroom, Mpumalanga. *Politikon*, 44(2), 327–345.

Leonard, L. (2018). Mining corporations, democratic meddling, and environmental justice in South Africa. *Social Sciences*, 7(12), 1–17.

Leonard, L. (2019a). Examining civil society social capital relations against mining development for local sustainability: The case of Dullstroom, Mpumulanga, South Africa. *Sustainable Development*, 27(3), 289–295.

Leonard, L. (2019b). Traditional leadership, community participation and mining development: The case of Fuleni, Saint Lucia, KwaZulu-Natal. *Land Use Policy*, 86, 290–298.

Leonard, L. (2020). How mining is threatening the sustainability of the South African nature tourism sector and civil society response. In: Rogerson J. & Visser G. (eds.), *New directions in South African tourism geographies* (pp. 317–335). Switzerland: Springer.

Leonard, L. & Langton, A. (2016). Challenges facing tourist attractions due to acid mine drainage in the West Rand, Gauteng. *African Journal of Hospitality, Tourism and Leisure*, 5(1), 1–12.

Leonard, L. & Lebogang, T. (2018). Exploring the impacts of mining on tourism growth and local sustainability: The case of Mapungubwe Heritage Site. *Sustainable Development*, 26(10), 206-216. https://doi.org/10.1002/sd.1695.

Leonard, L. & Lidskog, R. (2021). Industrial scientific expertise and civil society engagement: Reflexive scientisation in the South Durban Industrial Basin, South Africa. *Journal of Risk Research*, 24(9), 1127–1140. https://doi.org/10.1080/13669877.2020.1805638

Malherbe, S. & Segal, N. (2001). Corporate governance in South Africa. In: Policy Dialogue Meeting on Corporate Governance in Developing Countries and Emerging Economies, OECD Development Centre and European Bank for Reconstruction and Development, Misty Hills, Muldersdrift, Johannesburg, April 23–24.

McNutt, K. & Rayner, J. (2010). Valuing metaphor: A constructive account of reflexive governance in policy networks. Paper presented at the 5th International Conference on Interpretative Policy Analysis, SciencesPo. Grenoble, France, 23–25 June.

Monks, K. (2018). Why the wealth of Africa does not make Africans wealthy. *CNN*, 2 January. [Online]. Available from: https://edition.cnn.com/2016/04/18/africa/looting-machine-tom-burgis-africa/index.html [Accessed: 28 September 2021].

Organization for Economic Co-operation and Development. (2014). *Phase 3 report on implementing the OECD anti-bribery convention in South Africa.* Available from: http://www.oecd. org/daf/anti-bribery/SouthAfricaPhase3ReportEN.pdf [Accessed: 24 October 2014].

Orr, R. (2002). Governing when chaos rules. *Washington Quarterly*, 25(4), 139–152.

Ostry, J.D., Loungani, P. & Furceri, D. (2016). Neoliberalism: Oversold? *Finance and Development*, 53(2), 38–41.

Pearce, F. (2017). How a proposed strip mine brought conflict to South Africa's Wild Coast. *Yale Environment 360*, 13 March.

Pham, T., Bailey, G. & Marshall, J. (2013). *The economic impact of the current mining boom on the Australian tourism industry.* Canberra: Tourism Research Australia. [Online]. Available from: https://www.tra.gov.au/ArticleDocuments/185/Economic_Impact_of_the_Current_Mining_Boom_on_the_Australian_Tourism_Industry_FINAL.pdf.aspx?Embed=Y [Accessed: 14 April 2015].

Pickering, J. (2019). Ecological reflexivity: Characterising an elusive virtue for governance in the Anthropocene. *Environmental Politics*, 28(7), 1145–1166. https://doi.org/10.1080/09644016.2018.1487148

Santos, T. (2020). Confronting governance challenges of the resource nexus through reflexivity: A cross-case comparison of biofuels policies in Germany and Brazil. *Energy Research & Social Science*, 65, 101464.

Sonnino, R., Torres, C. & Schneider, S. (2014). Reflexive governance for food security: The example of school feeding in Brazil. *Journal of Rural Studies*, 36, 1–12.

Sonter, L.J., Ali, S.H. & Watson, J. (2018). Mining and biodiversity: Key issues and research needs in conservation science. *Proceedings of the Royal Society B*, 285(1892), 20181926. https://doi.org/10.1098/rspb.2018.1926

Standing, A. (2007). Corruption and extractive industries in South Africa: Can combatting corruption cure the resource curse? *Institute for Security Studies Papers*, 2007(153), 1. [Online]. Available from: https://www.files.ethz.ch/isn/98941/PAPER153.pdf

Steel, G. (2013). Mining and tourism: Urban transformations in the intermediate cities of Cajamarca and Cusco, Peru. *Latin American Perspectives*, 40(2), 237–249.

Stirling, A. (2006). Precaution, foresight, sustainability: Reflection and reflexivity in the governance of science and technology. In: Voß, J.P., Bauknecht, D. & Kemp, R. (eds.), *Reflexive governance for sustainable development*, (pp. 225–272). Cheltenham: Edward Elgar.

Swyngedouw, E. (2005). Governance innovation and the citizen: The Janus face of governance-beyond-the-state. *Urban Studies*, 42(11), 1991–2006.

Transparency International. (2016). *Corruption perceptions index 2016.* Berlin: Transparency International. [Online]. Available from: https://www.transparency.org/news/feature/corruption_perceptions_index_2016#table [Accessed: 11 February 2021].

Transparency International. (2019). *Combatting land corruption in Africa: Good practice examples.* Berlin: Transparency International. [Online]. Available from: https://images.transparencycdn.org/images/2019_Guide_CombattingLandCorruptionAfrica_English.pdf [Accessed: 13 February 2021].

United Nations Environment Programme. (2021). *Our work in Africa.* [Online]. Available from: https://www.unep.org/regions/africa/our-work-africa [Accessed: 1 June 2021].

United States Agency for International Development (USAID). (2017). The organization of African Unity and the African Union. [Online]. Available from: https://www.usaid.gov/african-union/history [Accessed: 12 February 2021].

Ushie, V. (2017). *From aspiration to reality: Unpacking the Africa mining vision.* Oxfam briefing paper. [Online]. Available from: https://www-cdn.oxfam.org/s3fs-public/bp-africa-mining-vision-090317-en.pdf [Accessed: 12 February 2021].

Van der Walt, J. & Potgieter, H. (2020). How to stifle corruption in the mining sector. *Daily Maverick*, 4 February.

Van Marissing, E. (2005). Citizen participation in the Netherlands: Motives to involve citizens in planning processes. In: ENHR conference 'Housing: New Challenges and Innovations in Tomorrow's Cities', Reykjavik, Iceland, 29 June–3 July.

Vaughn, M. & Ryan, V. L. (2006) Corporate Governance in South Africa: A bellwether for the continent, *Corporate Governance*, 14(5), 504–511.

Voß, J. & Bornemann, B. (2011). The politics of reflexive governance: Challenges for designing adaptive management and transition management. *Ecology and Society*, 16, 9.

Webster, E. (2013). Zambia, mining, and neoliberalism: Boom and bust on the globalized Copperbelt. *African Affairs*, 112(448), 521–523.

Weiland, S. (2012). Reflexive governance: A way forward for coordinated natural resource policy? In: Hogl, K., Kvarda, E., Nordbeck, R. & Pregernig, M. (eds.), *Environmental governance: The challenge of legitimacy and effectiveness*. Cheltenham, UK: Edward Elgar Publishing.

Wesselink, A., Paavola, J., Fritsch, O. & Renn, O. (2011). Rationales for public participation in environmental policy and governance: Practitioners' perspectives. *Environment and Planning A*, 43(11), 2688–2704.

Wicomb, W. (2018). Xolobeni judgement is vital to land debate. *News 24*, 24 November. Available from: https://www.news24.com/news24/southafrica/news/xolobeni-judgment-is-vital-to-land-debate-20181124 [Accessed: 25 February 2021].

Wilshusen, P. (2010). The receiving end of reform: Everyday responses to neoliberalisation in southeastern Mexico. *Antipode*, 42(3), 767–799.

World Bank. (2019). *Digging beneath the surface: An exploration of the net benefits of mining in Southern Africa*. Washington, DC: World Bank. Available from: https://openknowledge.worldbank.org/bitstream/handle/10986/32107/Digging-Beneath-the-Surface-An-Exploration-of-the-Net-Benefits-of-Mining-in-Southern-Africa.pdf?sequence=1&isAllowed=y

# 3 The deepening challenge of governance of wildlife and land issues in the context of rising citizen participation in South Africa

*Tariro Kamuti*

## Introduction

Wildlife ranching brings together the wildlife and agriculture sectors, as they are all based on land whose resources need to be sustainably utilised to meet a broad spectrum of needs for the diverse South African population. In the world, South Africa ranks highly in terms of biodiversity conservation, with most of that conservation happening on privately owned land coupled with the small proportion (5%) of land covered by statutorily protected areas (Cousins et al., 2008). Part of this private land falls under the wildlife ranching sector, which has experienced rapid growth since the 1990s but has also come with its governance challenges (Kamuti, 2014; Spierenburg & Brooks, 2014; Kamuti, 2017; Sommerville et al., 2021). Some of these governance challenges converge with challenges related to the broad and topical land question in South Africa manifesting itself through some conflict, some of which is the subject of this chapter. For instance, since the dawn of democracy there has been slow land reform which of late has instigated citizens to use different means and platforms to call on the government to promptly act. The argument is that increasing calls from the citizenry for the transformation of the economy to empower the previously disadvantaged majority population is being felt through the deepening challenge of the land question at a local level which, in this case, can be seen in the conflict over land under private wildlife ranching.

This chapter therefore problematises the governance of the wildlife ranching sector in South Africa, which is based on private ownership of land and thus draws together stakeholders from the wildlife ranching sector, the state, and citizens. The persistently skewed ownership of land within the post-1994 democratic dispensation justifies the questioning of the role of the state in confronting those challenges of social justice, and transformation within the broader economy. These challenges associated with structural inequality in the ownership of land through race are also causing deep concerns among citizens and thus prompting their active participation to demand redress. These governance challenges are a reflection of the enduring institutional processes

DOI: 10.4324/9781003188902-4

which are the basis of this analysis of the conflict experienced at the nexus of wildlife and land issues. The use of Critical Institutionalism (CI) that follows in the next section will help to analyse and explain these governance challenges.

Using an institutional approach that is inherently linked to governance, the paper draws from secondary information, broadly referring to the country followed by examples using empirical evidence gathered in KwaZulu-Natal Province, South Africa. The idea is to contextualise the land conflict happening at the local level as part and parcel of the effect of broad institutional processes at the national level. These national-level processes have an impact on the lower tiers of governance that include the provincial and local government levels, as this is how the country is administratively structured. So, there is a look at critical institutions and stakeholders centred around the processes of governance triggered by land conflict in private wildlife ranching, using the case of KwaZulu-Natal Province.

At the local level, the chapter cites first the land conflict over the idea of establishing a grand game reserve ahead of the need for land by recipients of land restitution and, second, the sporadic targeting of farms by local residents and others from far afield for hunting opportunities in the KwaZulu-Natal Midlands, a region in KwaZulu-Natal. In-depth interviews with key stakeholders within the wildlife ranching sector in KwaZulu-Natal Province (with a special focus on the Midlands) were the major source of information for the empirical component (which is included in the latter part of this chapter). Fieldwork was undertaken intermittently for the period 2011–2019 as part of a broad research project dealing with the governance of private wildlife ranching in the province. While the local level bears the mark of top-down policy and regulatory influences, there are nuances of local contingent factors which also need to be contextualised. Overall, this funnel approach will assist to bring a holistic view of the conflict occurring over privately owned land that has been either earmarked for or is already under wildlife-based production.

The unequal distribution of land in South Africa, for instance, historically came into being through the dominance, subjugation, and deprivation of a majority African population by a minority settler community. This inequality has left an enduring legacy that has been perpetuated even in the current democratic dispensation. That is why today we have increasing citizen participation to resist and seek redress of the land ownership imbalances that persist and cause tension in privately owned wildlife ranches. To shed more light on this tension, the chapter will proceed by giving a historical background of the challenge of skewed land ownership inherently associated with wildlife resources which are all anchored in private property rights and thus affecting their accessibility by different sections of the South African population. Then, there is a treatise of the slow pace of the land reform programme shown by the continuation of inequitable land distribution in the democratic dispensation which has triggered so much consternation, judging from the developments going on in this arena, and forming a significant part of current public debates. These debates need to be contextualised within the intractable and persistent levels of inequality entrenched in the South African economy through its neoliberal positioning. This will be followed by a snapshot of the wildlife-based production at a national level to accentuate the scene of the tension that is experienced in the sector in KwaZulu-Natal Province. The tension is over the proposed Gongolo Wildlife Reserve and also due to illegal hunting on private wildlife ranches in the KwaZulu-Natal Midlands (study area). The chapter then draws on all this information to discuss the ramifications associated with the governance of the wildlife ranching sector, which will lead to the concluding remarks. However, in the meantime, let us look at the institutional approach, which is inherently linked to governance, as experienced in wildlife ranching.

## The critical role of institutions in wildlife ranching

The chapter adopts Frances Cleaver's conceptualisation of CI in trying to understand the challenges faced in the governance of wildlife ranching in South Africa concerning the other demands placed on land occupied by the sector. The approach has been chosen mainly because of its particular focus on the governance of natural resources, which is appropriate for this chapter in dealing with both wildlife and land as natural resources that are controlled by different authorities and involving stakeholders who are generating tension that needs to be resolved. Cleaver (2012) highlights an intention to look at the means through which institutions arbitrate the relationships between people, natural resources, and society. Cleaver also hopes to enliven theory by exploring the interface between social structure and individual agency using institutions. The interest is in understanding the functioning of institutions in specific contexts, and why the outcomes favour certain people while sidelining others (Cleaver, 2007). CI places emphasis on the complicated institutions that are enmeshed in daily social life, their evolution, and the interaction "between the traditional and the modern, formal and informal arrangements" (Cleaver, 2012, p. 8) where regulations and processes guiding institutional arrangements are not clear-cut. There is an acknowledgement of how "people's complex identities and unequal power relations shape resource management arrangements and outcomes" (Cleaver, 2012, p. 9). The CI approach emphasises how local-level decision-making is entangled with national- and global-level issues, and it is being deployed here to gain insight into the different levels of the private wildlife production systems in their overall governance context. CI is associated with the nature of the institutions, institutional emergence and evolution, and the nature of human behaviour (Cleaver, 2012).

The institutions dealing with the management of natural resources, Cleaver argues, are not necessarily designed for that purpose because they are often vague, have multiple functions, are ever-changing, and are less susceptible to intentional crafting (Cleaver & Franks, 2005; Cleaver, 2012). The institutions are more appropriately viewed as a blend of the dichotomies; thus, they assume many characteristics at the same time such as being formal and informal, multi-purpose, short-lived, or more or less transparent in their operation (Cleaver,

2003, 2012). This implies that the access and use of natural resources can be arbitrated by many institutions at the same time. Thus, instead of the narrow approach and the construction of design principles, CI gives more weight to "the non-comparability of various 'messy' contexts, the inter-relating of global and local factors and the impact of social and economic changes over time" (Cleaver, 2012, p. 14; see also Ostrom, 2015; de Koning, 2011). CI has been used to analyse the institutional arrangements that mediate the utilisation of common property water resources in rural villages in Zimbabwe and Tanzania (Cleaver, 2012; Cleaver & de Koning, 2015).

Critical Institutionalists propose that the formation and development of new institutions happen through daily practices, standards, and associations such that they can fade, or can be simultaneously irregular and strong. There is also 'institutional blending', which happens "when, for example, 'informal' or customary institutions emulate state bureaucracies (adopting 'official' stamps and constitutions) and when 'formal' institutional arrangements become blurred when operationalised through social relationships and practices, such as patronage" (Cleaver, 2012, p. 14; Hall et al., 2014). This shows that the processes of institutional formation and development are not as straightforward. This 'post-institutionalist thinking' gives some understanding of "the 'messiness' of local institutional arrangements" and the formation of new institutions due to processes of bricolage (Cleaver & Franks, 2008, p. 163). There is a need, therefore, to look at the contingencies associated with the crafting of institutions entrenched in particular social contexts. Cleaver's work, which is inspired by Marxist geographers like David Harvey, "raises the questions we need to ask if institutions tasked with natural resource management are also to promote equity to access and distribution, to further social justice" (Cleaver, 2012, p. 1). The variability of circumstances that happen from one place to the other is not just a product of differences in the occurrence of natural resources but rather is caused by the unequal manner of access and control mediated by skewed interactions between stakeholders (Harvey, 2003).

## The chequered past of unequal land distribution

In the eighteenth and especially nineteenth century, South Africa was regarded as suitable for settlement by several colonial powers, notably the Dutch and the British. European settlers with the support of whites-only governments took control of vast expanses of land from Africans before and after the Natives Land Act of 1913 (Fraser, 2007; Ngcukaitobi, 2018). This Land Act apportioned 7% of the land to the "native reserves" and prohibited Africans from buying land elsewhere (Francis & Williams, 1993; Fraser, 2007). Other Africans had their land confiscated, and/or were forced to pay taxes in cash, and so took up wage labour in the mining sector. The situation of Africans in South Africa was worse than in many other African countries, in the sense that those who lost their land and were forced into wage labour in South Africa were prohibited from permanently settling in the cities (Fraser, 2007).

The state established a group of 'native reserves' (later referred to as 'homelands'), occupying about 13% of the land area by 1936, from which Africans would then migrate to the cities to work under controlled conditions (Fraser, 2007, p. 839). The National Party came to power in 1948, and that was the beginning of apartheid in South Africa, which had its ramifications concerning the land question and the lives of Africans. The process of establishing the homeland areas involved massive forced removals, through which as many as 3.5 million people were relocated or dislocated from their land in various ways. In the homeland areas, traditional leaders were given enormous powers concerning land, labour, and gender relations (Fraser, 2007). The growth of commercial agriculture controlled by the minority white population was propped up by discriminatory laws, favourable policies, state subsidies, and the exploitation of African labour following the forced acquisition of land from the African population and their subsequent displacement (Fraser, 2007). South Africa passed through phases of marginalisation of the majority African population to the benefit of the minority white population (O'Laughlin et al., 2013).

Agriculture in the country has undergone deregulation, a process completed by the post-apartheid government (Fraser, 2007). The empowerment of agribusiness has been one result in this neoliberal period as the state reorients and "acts exclusively in the interests of the corporate-financial elite" (Prabhat, 2014, p. 10). Francis and Williams (1993) wrote about the transition to democracy as it occurred, which was characterised by the abolition of racially based land measures and the enactment of new legislation such as the 1991 Land Act, which provided the legal basis for the transformation of South African agriculture to new forms of capitalism. They pointed out the dissonance between the principle of prioritising individual property rights against other forms of rights in land, while simultaneously trying to regulate the division and use of land for conservation and commercial development (Hamilton, 2006). According to these scholars, underlying these policies was an assumption that Africans were not capable of farming. The new laws in effect entrenched the position of land-owning whites, in that they worked against the broadening of access to rights in land that was for a long period reserved for them. In the same vein, Francis and Williams (1993, p. 381) pointed out that in 1993, the government according to the new laws ruled out "any form of redistribution of agricultural land whether by confiscation, nationalisation or expropriation" pending the development of a coherent land reform policy. However, due to rising concerns about the handling of land reform by the African National Congress (ANC), government has led to a push for the expropriation of land without compensation to speed up the land reform process.

## The continuation of inequitable land distribution under democratic South Africa

The skewed land ownership in South Africa is still persisting well after the 1994 dispensation of multi-party democracy. During the transition from

1990 to democratic elections in 1994 up to the adoption of the South African Constitution in 1996, the question of property rights was highly contested. In retrospect, Claassens (1993, p. 422) seems to have foreseen the challenges associated with the way the issue of property rights was handled by arguing that "in constitutionally entrenching existing property rights there is an inherent danger of entrenching the results of past apartheid land policies and racial dispossession". The country's land reform programme was formulated taking into account the unequal distribution of land in South Africa, where whites, who comprise 5% of the population, possess (together with large commercial interests) about 87% of the land (Manji, 2001; Department of Rural Development and Land Reform, 2013). It is in this context that discourses on land reform now revolve around interrogating the willing seller, willing buyer model of land redistribution to current perspectives of expropriation of land without compensation.

While these and other factors like corruption, inadequate or misguided macroeconomic and fiscal policies, and incompetent management may have contributed to slow land reform, Hamilton (2006, p. 133, p. 136) proposes that "the real problem is the constitution ... [and that] the devil is not in the detail, but rather in the framework". The fundamental challenge that remains unresolved is "how to organise economic and political institutions to determine and satisfy the needs of citizens" (Hamilton, 2006, p. 134). The final 1996 Constitution has a set of rights, and safeguards or guarantees which are entrenched for all South Africans, while simultaneously stipulating measures to remedy and redress the injustices of the past (Walker 2005; Hamilton, 2006; Cousins, 2007; Moseley, 2007). Significantly, the Constitution includes a property clause that guarantees private property rights (Bond, 2005). Of particular interest is the facilitation of the entrenchment of agricultural capital during the transition period in South Africa hitherto (Bernstein, 2013).

The contention has been that the 'land question' is still a highly contentious issue (Cousins (2009: 421; see also Du Toit, 2013) given the promises by the ANC leadership to revisit the willing seller, willing buyer principle upon which land acquisition is based, and to address the failure of land reform. Land activists from NGOs as well as social movements such as the Landless People's Movement (LPM) have been very vocal on matters concerning the need to address the land question (Hall, 2004). Violence targeting both farm workers and owners has also been connected to access to land (Hall, 2004). There is also evidence of loss of production on some of the land that has been transferred to Africans (Marketplace, 2009). So land reform is confronted with the dilemma of proceeding in a way that does not compromise agricultural production for food security and meeting other critical needs. The conversion of livestock farms to game farms, that is, wildlife-based production, has further ramifications for this dilemma.

Given this background, there has also been a build-up of a populist movement within the ANC in conjunction with labour and minor opposition parties underpinned by what has been termed "radical economic transformation".

This has been based on a broad consensus that the economy is not serving the majority, and hence there is a need to implement radical economic policies which will speed up the economic empowerment of the previously disadvantaged masses. This explains the 2013 rise of the Economic Freedom Fighters (EFF), a political party led mainly by former ANC youth leaders riding on the agenda of the nationalisation of key sectors like mining and financial institutions, together with the expropriation of land without compensation. With the EFF gaining traction in the 2014 and 2019 general elections and the 2016 local government election, they have pushed the ruling ANC party to rethink and refocus some of its policies. A landmark development in this respect was when the ANC and the EFF voted together in Parliament on a motion to amend the Constitution to pave the way for the expropriation of land without compensation. This has caused much consternation within the country and abroad as the consequences of such a policy change became glaringly evident. It is, therefore, no wonder that there have been moves to repeal some of the legislation which deals with the expropriation of land for the public good.

The purpose of land reform was "to redress the imbalances of apartheid, foster national reconciliation and stability, underpin economic growth and, lastly, improve household welfare and alleviate poverty" (Manji, 2001, p. 330). The country's land reform programme set a target to redistribute 24.6 million hectares (30%) of commercial agricultural land (which is mostly in the hands of whites) up to 1999 (Hall, 2004; O'Laughlin et al., 2013). However, the land reform programme has been progressing at a snail's pace (Hall, 2004; O'Laughlin et al., 2013). Walker (2005) contends that by 2005, the restitution, redistribution, and tenure programmes cumulatively gave a total of some 2.8 million hectares, or 3.4% of commercial farmland, which was then handed over to black beneficiaries between 1994 and mid-2005. For the period up to the close of 1999, an amount of land below one million hectares (1.2%) under white ownership had been redistributed, prompting the target of 30% to be postponed to 2014 (O'Laughlin et al., 2013). This was far below the target. O'Laughlin et al. (2013, p. 8) further state that "by March 2011, however, only 7.2 per cent (6.3 million hectares) had been transferred, and the official target date for achieving the 30 per cent target has now been set at 2025". Failures in land reform are regarded as a blot on the accomplishments of South Africa's democracy and policymakers are still faced with the critical question of the role of land as a basic source of livelihood in the fight against poverty (Cuthbertson, 2008, p. 297).

## South Africa's neoliberal positioning that entrenches inequality

Many scholars argue that a major result of the South African government's neoliberal positioning, as well as the terms of the negotiated democratic Constitution, is that the extent of social and material change is not sufficiently transformative (Harvey, 2005, 2006; Fraser, 2007, p. 843; Kahn, 2007; Walker, 2008; Atuahene, 2011; Büscher & Dressler, 2007). This positioning also includes a property clause in the Constitution that guarantees white farmers' "'veto' over land reform" (Fraser, 2007, p. 842). The narrow definition of institutions based on the private property rights of landowners (Atuahene, 2011) is exclusive to the extent of impeding broad participation and achievement of conservation goals (Edwards & Sharp, 1990; Ngcukaitobi, 2021). The land redistribution programme is based on the World Bank's model of negotiated land reform, which relies on the voluntary sale of commercial farms at fair market value (Moseley, 2007; Bernstein, 2013). Bond (1999, 2002, 2003, 2004, 2005) articulates the influence of the World Bank in the adoption of a neoliberal South African macroeconomic policy and criticises both the Bretton Woods institutions and the South African government (see also Patnaik, 2012).

The issue of land juxtaposes conservation and agriculture, and other social, political, and economic issues from different perspectives. For instance, wildlife ownership is tightly connected to land ownership and now the promotion of the wildlife economy is entrenching this stronghold over land (Gray & Teels, 2006; Snijders, 2012; Kamuti, 2020). One could also argue that the associated practices of neoliberal commodification hinder the process of transformation (Büscher & Dietz, 2005; Büscher, 2010) and this is evident in the wildlife sector. A study by Josefsson (2014) argues that the conversion from cattle farming to game farming contributes to the perpetuation of what Fraser (2007, p. 840) calls the "colonial present" by inhibiting socioeconomic transformation in rural areas.

This chapter places the role of the state in the spotlight as the guardian of society through its governance mechanisms. The South African government is confronted with a context in which the status quo of the prosperity of the middle classes under neoliberal policies is pitted against the urgent need to improve the material wellbeing of the poor majority. Unless such issues are addressed, it will continue to undermine democracy as a participatory social force (Cuthbertson, 2008). The skewed ownership of land within the post-1994 democratic dispensation justifies questioning of the role of the state in confronting those challenges of social justice and transformation within the broader economy. The lack of a pro-poor agricultural policy is a reflection of a broader trend in Africa (Jara & Hall, 2009; Poulton, 2014).

## Wildlife-based production in South Africa

A glimpse into wildlife-based production in South Africa can help to shed light on its significance in the subsequent governance challenges that are inherently experienced at the interface of land and wildlife resources. The extent of the wildlife-based production is difficult to ascertain due to the lack of accurate records on the diverse forms through which it occurs, while the sector occupies a sizeable amount of land in the country. There are game farms that constitute "private land from which domestic stock has been removed and replaced with 'game' and sometimes there can be 'mixed farms' which refer to 'private land on which combined game and stock farming are practised'" (Smith & Wilson, 2002, p. 2). Based on the ways through which these entities generate income, there are private nature reserves that rely on ecotourism and commercial game reserves which have tourism and/or function as a hunting/breeding farm. In 2000, there were around 5000 fenced game ranches and 4000 farms of mixed game and livestock occupying a proportion exceeding 13% of the total land area of the country with more properties being converted into an integrated game and livestock production system (Hearne et al., 2008). So, around 2003, there were an estimated 9000 commercial game-fenced farms in South Africa occupying about 17 million hectares (Reilly et al., 2003). The sector uses about a third of the country's available grazing land for its purposes (Cloete et al., 2007).

The establishment of game ranches is a trend that spread around the country over a long period since the 1960s and gained momentum from the 1990s after the passage of the Game Theft Act No. 105 of 1991, which gave rights to farmers to own game when they provide adequate fencing (Child, 2009; Snijders, 2012). This had the effect of changing the status of wildlife from direct state control into private ownership, thus effectively taking the resources from the commons into exclusive spaces for the benefit of landowners who also have exclusive access to land protected by property rights enshrined in the Constitution. The wildlife ranching sector has become a formidable economic subsector and is increasingly being recognised as an agricultural enterprise, given the rise in the areas under game fence enclosures and the huge wildlife market through wildlife that is traded privately and at auctions (Reilly et al., 2003; Davies-Mostert, 2014; Kamuti, 2014). There has been a decline in cattle numbers with game ranching taking over as a formidable presence in the agricultural sector. So, within the broad agrarian reform question lies this issue of wildlife ranching, which is manifesting itself through the tension that has been experienced between those who hold the land and its wildlife resources on one side and those who lay claim to the same and resources on the other hand.

## Wildlife-based land conflict in KwaZulu-Natal, South Africa

### *Institutions and stakeholders in wildlife ranching in KwaZulu-Natal*

At the provincial level, some critical institutions and stakeholders were identified to be linked and involved in issues of land- and wildlife-based production, which are at the centre of the tension that has been witnessed in the selected cases in the province. Institutional processes are meant to regulate how stakeholders own and access natural resources in a just and equitable manner. One may say that some of the conflicts have been instigated by the failure of institutions in mediating the conduct of various stakeholders in owning and accessing natural resources. In the South African context, some institutional mechanisms have been put in place to promote transformation through the redress of imbalances inherited from the past, for instance, through the land restitution process. So, some of the challenges associated with land restitution can be attributed to the conflict that has been witnessed amongst stakeholders who have been brought together by the nexus between land and inherently wildlife resources.

The stakeholders in the province were mainly state organs, private landowners, farm dwellers, surrounding communities (including traditional authorities), conservation organisations, and non-governmental organisations (including farmers' and local associations). In delivering their services, state departments administer various statutes which are used to regulate the sustainable utilisation of natural resources. The state organisations included provincial offices of national departments. For example, at the time of the study, there was the consolidated KwaZulu-Natal Department of Agriculture and Environmental Affairs, and the Department of Land Reform and Rural Development. Now there is the KwaZulu-Natal Department of Agriculture and Rural Development and the KwaZulu-Natal Department of Economic Development, Tourism and Environmental Affairs. These changes however also come with their capacity and efficiency challenges which affect service delivery. Some of these challenges are evident when we look at the tension arising from the interactions of stakeholders brought together by land and wildlife-based production. Ezemvelo KwaZulu-Natal Wildlife (EKZWN) is the provincial statutory body that oversees nature conservation, including wildlife on private land. The Regional Land Claims Commission together with the provincial- and district-level offices dealing with land reform and rural development has been instrumental in facilitating land restitution. However, the processes of land restitution have not been smooth as they have been riddled with tension amongst key players, mainly previous landowners, local communities, and state agencies, amongst others.

### *Tension over the proposed Gongolo Wildlife Reserve*

Land reform policies and programmes have three facets (Walker, 2005; Hamilton, 2006; Moseley, 2006, 2007). These are land redistribution, land restitution returning land (to those who were dispossessed), and tenure reform, intended "to secure and strengthen the land rights of both farm workers and residents of 'communal areas'" (Cousins, 2009, p. 422). In this case, land that was successfully claimed under the land restitution programme has not been handed over to the beneficiary communities in the Gongolo area of KwaZulu-Natal Province. The Gongolo area, covering close to 40 000 hectares of land, straddles the three local municipalities of Umtshezi, Okhahlamba, and Mpofana while bound by the towns of Estcourt, Mooi River, and Weenen in the Midlands region of the province (Kamuti, 2018). Some of the previous landowners bought into the idea of forming a grand wildlife reserve with the anticipation that they would lease the land from the government, which would compensate the communities with land elsewhere, as that is permissible under the land restitution programme.

The local communities constitute land claimants and farm dwellers (comprising of former labour tenants and workers), who are all entitled to land through provisions of the land restitution programme. The land claimants lodged their claims before the 31 December 1998 deadline under two traditional authorities, and their issues were handled by the Regional Land Claims Commission, while issues relating to labour tenants were handled by the offices dealing with land reform and rural development in the province and respective district. Communities were against the idea of being with land elsewhere and they organised themselves to present their grievances against being moved away. The wrangle has continued for a long time with parties taking each other to court and the issue going as far as Parliament. While broadly speaking there are questions around the strategy of market-based agrarian reform (Borras, 2003; 2009; Patnaik, 2012), land restitution has also been criticised for the manner in which it has been conducted (Walker, 2008). In many instances, land beneficiaries have been forced into partnerships with white-owned agribusinesses (for example, see Shaker, 2003). This has been the case with land beneficiaries in Gongolo who were being sold the idea of a grand game reserve.

Unlike game farmers in some other provinces, many game farmers in KwaZulu-Natal have been directly affected by land reform, as many game farms have been claimed and transferred to land beneficiaries (either through labour tenant claims or restitution claims). The Gongolo Wildlife Reserve example is instructive in this regard as it shows how these processes are working out at the local level, at what has been termed the "game farming/land reform nexus" (Kamuti, 2018). Different groups have different world views based on their practices and beliefs of how to use wildlife resources found on land which is inequitably distributed. So, there was a need to unpack the idea of competing needs over land and how the government has fared in that respect as hinted by Jones (2006). The enduring contest for land in the Gongolo area has pitted various role players against each other with no workable solution in sight. The government's position appears to have been one complicit with private capital, as there was a dragging of feet in settling land claims resulting from the history of land dispossession in the area. In this case, "the strength of the state has become contextual and entrepreneurial rather than, as was the previously the case, something derived from constitutional and legal strength of the state institutions" (Pierre & Peters, 2000, p. 194).

On the other hand, private capital is frustrated because it seems the 'dream' of the grand nature reserve might slip away due to land reform. In the process, everyone including game farmers, farm dwellers, and land reform beneficiaries are feeling ignored or marginalised by the government. For game farmers, the context of 'radical uncertainty' over land related to the tensions in the country is also suggested by their perceptions of government actions, evident in statements like, "the government does not need us" (Interview with a Game Farmer, September 2011, Estcourt), or "this is Africa, what do you expect" (Interview with a Game Farmer, 7 March 2013)

### *Illegal hunting on private wildlife ranches in the KwaZulu-Natal Midlands*

Some game farms in the KwaZulu-Natal Midlands area have endured the wrath of two groups of people who engage in various kinds of dog hunting. Traditional dog hunting is illegal. One group is made up of people who come from surrounding communities and trespass into privately owned land and hunt with dogs. In conversations with game farmers, they indicated that some of these people sometimes cause property damage. In certain instances, farmers retaliate and shoot the dogs that they come across on their land, while there can also be attacks and counter-attacks between the people who trespass on the private land and the landowners. The other group of hunters engages in what is called taxi hunting; this also involves dogs, but the hunters are generally wealthy individuals who drive to the farms with their dogs in vans (also called taxis in South Africa).

In all these cases, there is a need to look at the issue of illegal hunting and how it came into being. European hunting has a history of being regarded as a noble sport, while dog hunting which was practised by Africans has been viewed as poaching, and this provided the root of some of the current hunting regulations. It can be seen therefore that institutions for access to natural resources have been crafted in a way that favours one group while sidelining another. This is not an instant development but a practice that had found its way onto the African continent and was finally etched into the statutes as we have them today. Motivations for people to use dogs for hunting are varied even though the practice is regarded as illegal. The question is whether the available mechanisms used to control the practice are effective for the sake of peace and order in the affected communities.

The fact that in some cases game farmers have been held to ransom by people who wish to continue with their traditional dog hunts on their farms, and do so through threats of arson, shows the extent of the deepening challenge of governance of the entangled wildlife and land issues. That illegal dog hunting appears widespread provides evidence against normative institutional principles, for instance, of clearly defined boundaries and clearly defined user groups (Cleaver & Franks, 2005). This shows the blurring of formal institutional arrangements. Dog hunters, who are not included in institution-making processes, appear to be offering a 'radical challenge' to private property rights in the countryside. The state is lagging behind in regulating the wildlife ranching industry, as the policy or regulation regime is not adequately responding to the new circumstances prevailing in the sector. This gives credence to Harvey's (2003, p. 91) assertion that states do not always respond in the right way and when they do respond, the outcomes are determined by forces of capital pulling the strings behind government decisions. The available regulations need to be streamlined and integrated within one lead department to allow clarity of mandates among different structures and levels of organisation of government departments and agencies. However, power politics is crucial in directing the process of policymaking (Wagner, 2001).

## Ramifications of the governance of the wildlife ranching sector

It is important to reflect on the means through which institutions arbitrate the relationships between people, natural resources, and society, using the cases of tension arising out of the demand for land associated with wildlife-based production by local communities in the KwaZulu-Natal Midlands. These communities are using the different means available to them to forge ahead with their interests, thereby exploring the interface between their social structure and agency using institutions. For example, land restitution is a formal process whose institutional arrangements have been intended to redress the long-existing imbalances in land ownership and access. In the Gongolo case, one would have thought that the completion of the formal processes of the land claim would have led to the handover of the land to the claimants. This has not happened because the land claim process took a new twist and it has taken a long time for the available institutional arrangements to resolve the new challenges arising from the further dragging out of the process that the communities did not anticipate. This is a case where regulations and processes guiding institutional arrangements are not clear-cut, as the land conflict has not been resolved. This may be taken to mean the functioning of institutions in these specific contexts, and also why the outcomes favour certain people (those who are holding onto the land) while sidelining others (local communities). These two cases of conflict in the KwaZulu-Natal Midlands also show that the variability of circumstances that occurs from one place to the other is not just a product of differences in the occurrence of natural resources but rather caused by the unequal manner of access and control mediated by skewed interactions between stakeholders.

There has also been an acknowledgement of how people's different identities and unequal power relations influence resource management mechanisms and outputs. Two different kinds of people have been identified, for instance, in those who target farms that are under wildlife-based production for hunting opportunities in the KwaZulu-Natl Midlands region. One group is made up of ordinary citizens who look for opportunities and subsequently participate in dog hunting on wildlife ranches. Their motivations that are mainly for subsistence are different from the second group that is made up of people who drive for long distances and get to the same farming areas and engage in dog hunting for pleasure as they put bets. Unequal power relations also exist amongst these two groups in their pursuit of hunting opportunities against that of the landowners, who end up losing their animals to dog hunting. The idea behind dog hunting, which is an activity that is not allowed under the law, shows the clash between the traditional and the modern ways of life and also the disjuncture between formal and informal arrangements. One would look, for instance, at one group favouring private property, while another favours common property resources. This clash can be contextualised in the conflict witnessed in sub-Saharan Africa arising from the competition between traditional and contemporary institutions of land tenure pursued by different stakeholders that end up affecting agriculture-related business (Effossou & Cho, 2021). This is how CI also places emphasis on the complicated institutions that are intertwined in daily social life, their interaction, and subsequent development. For instance, people involved in dog hunting justify it on the grounds of it being part of their tradition and culture and hence part of their identity. The institutions designed to deal with such practices are not all appropriately structured to handle them. The convergence of different social practices with formal institutional arrangements cause blurred or fuzzy outcomes which determine the development of new institutions dynamically, a process that has been referred to as institutional blending (Cleaver, 2012).

## Conclusion

This chapter has tried to put the conflict occurring over land that is under private wildlife ranching into the context of the enduring and deepening challenges of property rights that remain unresolved. Land that is under private wildlife ranching in South Africa constitutes a considerable proportion of all the land in the country, which was historically acquired through forcible means from the African population. That is the same land that is subject to issues related to the broad questions of land reform, just like any land that is privately owned by the minority population in the country. Therefore, a broad historical reflection on these issues helps to put the governance of land under wildlife ranching into its proper context. Also, the continuation of the inequitable ownership of land and its inherent resources like wildlife is happening today in a democratic dispensation. Thus, the conflict witnessed in the wildlife ranching sector also provides some nuance to the broad agrarian question in South Africa.

Due to its particular focus on the governance of natural resources, CI has been used to show how institutions arbitrate the relationships between people, natural resources, and society. We have seen the functioning of institutions in specific contexts, and why some outcomes favour certain people while sidelining others due to different power relations, as shown by the different parties involved in the conflict in the wildlife ranching sector. Complicated institutions have also been seen to be enmeshed in daily social life, that is, how people interact in their quest to promote their own interests. The deepening challenge in the governance of the wildlife sector shows that in natural resources management, institutions are not necessarily designed for that purpose because their description can often be vague and they also have multiple functions. This shows that the problematic processes of institutional formation and development are not as straightforward and that is why some of the tension is intractable.

Rising tension on the back of the populist citizens' call for rapid economic transformation is deepening the challenge of land and wildlife governance in South Africa, especially in the rural spaces that bear the remnants of historical processes that have alienated the majority population from their land and wildlife resources. The conflict over land and wildlife resources under private ownership is a microcosm of the tension that is worsening in the economy as structural inequality persists coupled with slow economic growth, which significantly hinders the absorption of the youthful population into the economy.

The national government faces several key imperatives in the current era related to addressing the negative legacies of apartheid, coupled with current challenges that include aspects such as job creation, poverty reduction, land redistribution, and social cohesion. In addition to these political pressures, the national government has to grow the economy and ensure food security by not taking radical decisions and thus is certainly open to arguments presented to it by organised agriculture (including wildlife-based production), which flexes its muscle through capital investment.

## References

Atuahene, B. (2011). Property rights and the demands of transformation. *Researching Law*, 22(1). Retrieved from http://scholarship.kentlaw.iit.edu/facschol/824

Bernstein, B. (2013). Commercial agriculture in South Africa since 1994: 'Natural, simply capitalism'. *Journal of Agrarian Change*, 13(1), 23–46.

Bond, P. (1999). Basic infrastructure for socio-economic development, environmental protection and geographical desegregation: South Africa's unmet challenge. *Geoforum*, 30, 43–59.

Bond, P. (2002). *Unsustainable South Africa*. Pietermaritzburg, South Africa: University of KwaZulu-Natal Press.

Bond, P. (2003). *Against global apartheid: South Africa meets the World Bank, IMF and International Finance*. Cape Town, South Africa: UCT Press.

Bond, P. (2004). From racial to class apartheid: South Africa's frustrating decade of freedom. Retrieved from http://ccs.ukzn.ac.za/files/BondMonthlyReviewMarch2004.pdf

Bond, P. (2005). *Elite transition: From apartheid to neoliberalism in South Africa*. Pietermaritzburg, South Africa: University of KwaZulu-Natal Press.

Borras Jr., S.M. (2003). Questioning market-led agrarian reform: Experiences from Brazil, Colombia and South Africa. *Journal of Agrarian Change*, 3(3), 367–394.

Borras Jr., S.M. (2009). Agrarian change and peasant studies: Changes, continuities and challenges: An introduction. *Journal of Peasant Studies*, 36(1), 5–31.

Büscher, B. (2010). Anti-politics as political strategy: Neoliberalism and transfrontier conservation in southern Africa. *Development and Change*, 41(1), 29–51.

Büscher, B. & Dietz, T. (2005). Conjunctions of governance: The state and the conservation development nexus in southern Africa. *The Journal of Transdisciplinary Environmental Studies*, 4, 1–15.

Büscher, B. & Dressler, W. (2007). Linking neoprotectionism and environmental governance: On the rapidly increasing tensions between actors in the environment-development nexus. *Conservation and Society*, 5(4), 586–611.

Child, B. (2009). Private conservation in southern Africa: Practice and emerging principles. In: Suich, H. & B. Child. (Eds.), *Evolution and innovation in wildlife conservation: Parks and game ranches to transfrontier conservation areas* (pp. 103–111). London, UK: Earthscan.

Claassens, A. (1993). Compensation for expropriation: The political and economic parameters of market value compensation. *South African Journal on Human Rights*, 9, 422–427.

Cleaver, F. (2003). Reinventing institutions: Bricolage and the social embeddedness of natural resources management. In: Benjaminsen, T.A. & C. Lund (Eds.), *Securing land rights in Africa* (pp. 11–30). London, UK: Frank Cass.

Cleaver, F. (2007). Understanding agency in collective action. *Journal of Human Development*, 8(2), 223–244.
Cleaver, F. (2012). *Development through bricolage: Rethinking institutions for natural resources management*. London, UK: Routledge.
Cleaver, F. & de Koning, J. (2015). Furthering critical institutionalism. *International Journal of the Commons*, 9(1), 1–18.
Cleaver, F. & Franks, T. (2005). *How institutions elude design: River basin management and sustainable livelihoods*. Bradford Centre for International Development (BCID) Research Paper Number12, Bradford, UK: University of Bradford.
Cleaver, F. & Franks, T. (2008). Distilling or diluting? Negotiating the water research-policy interface. *Water Alternatives*, 1(1), 157–176.
Cloete, P.C., Taljaard, P.R., & Grove, B. (2007). A comparative economic case study of switching from cattle farming to game ranching in the Northern Cape Province. *South African Journal of Wildlife Research*, 37(1), 71–78.
Cousins, B. (2007). More than socially embedded: The distinctive character of 'communal tenure' regimes in South Africa and its implications for land policy. *Journal of Agrarian Change*, 7(3), 281–315.
Cousins, B. (2009). Review essay: Land reform in South Africa. *Journal of Agrarian Change*, 9(3), 421–431.
Cousins, J.A., Saddler, J.P. & Evans, J. (2008). Exploring the role of private wildlife ranching as a conservation tool in South Africa: Stakeholders perspectives. *Ecology and Society*, 13(2), Retrieved from: Retrieved from http://www.ecologyandsociety.org/vol13/iss2/art43/
Cuthbertson, G. (2008). South Africa's democracy: From celebration to crisis. *African Identities*, 6(3), 293–304.
Davies-Mostert, H.T. (2014). Overcoming barriers to understanding the biodiversity contribution of private ranchlands. *Animal Conservation*, 17, 399–400.
de Koning, J. (2011). *Reshaping institutions: Bricolage processes in smallholder forestry in the Amazon*. Wageningen, the Netherlands: Wageningen University.
Department of Rural Development and Land Reform. (2013). *Land audit*. Retrieved from http://www.dla.gov.za/phocadownload/CadastralSurveymanagement/Booklet/land%20audit%20booklet.pdf
Du Toit, A. (2013). Real acts, imagined landscapes: Reflections on the discourses of land reform in South Africa after 1994. *Journal of Agrarian Change*, 13(1), 16–22.
Edwards, V.M. & Sharp, B.M.H. (1990). Institutional arrangements for conservation on private land in New Zealand. *Journal of Environmental Management*, 31, 313–326.
Effossou, K.A. & Cho, M.A. (2021). Land tenure conflict and agribusiness development in sub-Saharan Africa. *South African Geographical Journal*, Retrieved from https://doi.org/10.1080/03736245.2021.1941218
Francis, E. & Williams, G. (1993). The land question. *Canadian Journal of African Studies*, 27(3), 380–403.
Fraser, A. (2007). Land reform in South Africa and the colonial present. *Social and Cultural Geography*, 8(6), 835–851.
Gray, R.L. & Teels, B.M. (2006). Wildlife and fish conservation through the Farm Bill. *Wildlife Society Bulletin*, 43(4), 906–913.
Hall, K., Cleaver, F., Franks, T. & Maganga, F. (2014). Capturing critical institutionalism: A synthesis of key themes and debates. *European Journal of Development Research*, 26, 71–86.
Hall, R. (2004). A political economy of land reform in South Africa. *Review of African Political Economy*, 100, 213–227.

Hamilton, L. (2006). Human needs, land reform and the South African constitution. *Politikon*, 33(2), 133–145.

Harvey, D. (2003). *The new imperialism*. Oxford, UK: Oxford University Press.

Harvey, D. (2005). *A brief history of neoliberalism*. Oxford, UK: Oxford University Press.

Harvey, D. (2006). Neo-liberalisation as creative destruction. *Geografiska Annaler: Series B, Human Geography*, 88(2), 145–158.

Hearne, J.W., Santika, T. & Goodman, P. (2008). Portfolio selection theory and wildlife management. *Orion*, 24(2), 103–113.

Jara, M. & Hall, R. (2009). What are the political parameters? In R. Hall. (Ed.), *Another countryside? Policy options for land and agrarian reform in South Africa* (pp. 206–243). Cape Town, South Africa: Institute for Poverty, Land and Agrarian Studies.

Jones, S. (2006). A political ecology of wildlife conservation in Africa. *Review of African Political Economy*, 33(109), 483–495.

Josefsson, J. (2014). Safe-guarding the colonial present: Game farms on the frontier in KwaZulu-Natal's 'Battlefields Route'. *Journal of Contemporary African Studies*, 32(2), 258–274.

Kahn, N. (2007). Land and agrarian reform in South Africa. *Policy: Issues and Actors*, 20(12). Johannesburg, South Africa: Centre for Policy Studies. Retrieved from https://citeseerx.ist.psu.edu/viewdoc/download?doi=10.1.1.464.8365&rep=rep1&type=pdf

Kamuti, T. (2014). The fractured state in the governance of private game farming: The case of KwaZulu-Natal province, South Africa. *Journal of Contemporary African Studies*, 32(2), 190–206.

Kamuti, T. (2017). The changing geography of wildlife conservation: Perspectives on private game farming in contemporary KwaZulu-Natal Province. *New Contree: A Journal of Historical and Human Sciences for Southern Africa*, 79, 39–64.

Kamuti, T. (2018). Intricacies of game farming and outstanding land restitution claims in the Gongolo area of KwaZulu-Natal, South Africa. In: F. Brandt & G. Mkodzongi (Eds.), *Land reform revisited: Democracy, state making and agrarian transformation in Post-Apartheid South Africa* (pp. 124–148). Leiden, the Netherlands: Brill NV.

Kamuti, T. (2020). Wildlife Economy and its significance in KwaZulu-Natal, South Africa. In: Murphy, D. & E. Mason (Eds.), *Africa: Economic, political and social issues* (pp. 145–172). New York: Nova Science Publishers.

Manji, A. (2001). Land reform in the shadow of the state: The implementation of new land laws in sub-Saharan Africa. *Third World Quarterly*, 22(3), 327–342.

Marketplace (2009, April 21). *Black South Africans may lose farms*. Retrieved from http://www.marketplace.org/topics/world/black-south-africans-may-lose-farms.

Moseley, W. (2006). Farm workers, agricultural transformation, and land reform in Western Cape Province, South Africa. *Focus on Geography*, 49(1), 1–7.

Moseley, W.G. (2007). Neoliberal agricultural policy versus agrarian justice: Farm workers and land redistribution in South Africa's Western Cape province. *South African Geographical Journal*, 89(1), 4–13.

Ngcukaitobi, T. (2018). *The land is ours: South Africa's first black lawyers and the birth of constitutionalism*. Cape Town, South Africa: Penguin Books.

Ngcukaitobi, T. (2021). *Land matters: South Africa's failed land reforms and the road ahead*. Cape Town, South Africa: Penguin Random House.

O'Laughlin, B., Bernstein, H., Cousins, B. & Peters, P.E. (2013). Introduction: Agrarian change, rural poverty and land reform in South Africa since 1994. *Journal of Agrarian Change*, 13(1), 1–15.

Ostrom, E. (2015). Design principles of robust property-rights institutions: What have we learned? In: D.H. Cole & M.D. McGinnis (Eds.), *Elinor Ostrom and the Bloomington school of political economy: Resource governance* (pp. 215–248). Washington, DC: Lexington Books.

Patnaik, U. (2012). Some aspects of the contemporary agrarian question. *Agrarian South: Journal of Political Economy*, 1(3), 233–254.

Pierre, J. & Peters, B.G. (2000). *Governance, politics and the State*. Basingstoke, UK: Macmillan.

Poulton, C. (2014). Democratisation and the political incentives for agricultural policy in Africa. *Development Policy Review*, 32(S2), s101–s122.

Prabhat, P. (2014). Imperialism and the agrarian question. *Agrarian South: Journal of Political Economy*, 3(1), 1–15.

Reilly, B.K., Sutherland, E.A. & Harley, V. (2003). The nature and extent of wildlife ranching in Gauteng Province, South Africa. *South African Journal of Wildlife Research*, 33(2), 141–144.

Shaker, M. (2003). Restructuring of state assets in Limpopo. *Service Delivery Review*, 2, 73–77.

Smith, N. & Wilson, S.L. (2002). *Changing land use trends in the thicket biome: Pastoralism to game farming*. Report Number 38. Port Elizabeth: University of Port Elizabeth Terrestrial Ecology Research Unit.

Snijders, D. (2012). Wild property and its boundaries: On wildlife policy and rural consequences in South Africa. *Journal of Peasant Studies*, 39(2), 503–520.

Sommerville, M., Khumalo, L., Kamuti, T. & Brooks, S. (2021). *Game on! Understanding the emerging game meat value chain in South Africa*. Boston, MA: Tiny Beam Fund.

Spierenburg, M. & Brooks, S. (2014). Private game farming and its social consequences in post-apartheid South Africa: Contestations over wildlife, property and agrarian futures. *Journal of Contemporary African Studies*, 32(2), 151–172.

Wagner, F.H. (2001). Freeing agency research from policy pressures: A need and an approach. *BioScience*, 51(6), 445–450.

Walker, C. (2005). The limits to land reform: Rethinking 'the land question'. *Journal of Southern African Studies*, 31(4), 805–824.

Walker, C. (2008). *Landmarked: Land claims and land restitution in South Africa*. Athens, OH: Ohio University Press.

# 4 Leadership and governance intricacies in Communally-Owned Protected Areas

## The case of Somkhanda Game Reserve, KwaZulu Natal, South Africa

*Oscar Mthimkhulu and Adrian Nel*

### Background and introduction

Protected area management in Southern Africa has transitioned from a preservationist and protectionist approach towards integrated biodiversity conservation management (Nyambe, 2005). Within the South African context, there has been a growing recognition in conservation that protected areas cannot be managed without considering the socioeconomic requirements of the adjacent local communities (Knieter, 2014). Alternative protected area management models for Communally-Owned Protected Areas (COPAs) have had to be established to adapt to the reality of community members being able to initiate, develop, and manage their protected areas. Moreover, the governance of protected areas that were successfully claimed through the national land reform programme tends to be predicated upon co-management agreements between the claimants and state conservation agencies (Cundill et al., 2013).

The concept of collective proprietorship underpins communal rights for use and beneficiation from natural resources (Jones, 2004). However, despite the promises of democratically informed management, co-management has preserved the *status quo* in terms of conservation practices, with limited material benefits for land reform beneficiaries who have limited decision-making functions (ibid). Research indicates that most COPAs fail to meet the expectations of their proprietors due to a lack of capacity, accountability, and a conflict of interest amongst beneficiaries, including traditional authorities (Sebola, 2014). The involvement of traditional authorities in rural land restitution cases has created two centres of power wherein traditional authorities contend for power and governance of restored land and its resources. These challenges are compounded by the underutilisation of the restored lands, the structure of the communal groups, and a lack of post-transfer support and access to markets (Sebola, 2014; Tekié, 2016). The establishment of COPAs created high expectations for the generation of substantial economic benefits for land reform beneficiaries as they also served as a politically motivated transformation agenda. However, as stated by Tekié (2016), these communally owned

DOI: 10.4324/9781003188902-5

entities do not always generate the intended benefits. Perhaps this is an area that requires further research.

Somkhanda Game Reserve (SGR) has received increased attention from various scholars interested in community-based ecotourism, community-based natural resource management (CBNRM), and wildlife economy investments (Musavengane & Kloppers, 2020; Musavengane & Simatele, 2016). SGR is a proclaimed protected area of 164 882 hectares, located approximately 50 km south of the Swaziland border, northwest of Mkhuze. SGR forms part of the Magudu Conservancy and is located within the Maputaland-Pondoland-Albany Global Biodiversity Hotspot (Musavengane & Kloppers, 2020). SGR is touted as a flagship community conservation and land reform project (Musavengane et al., 2019) whereby in 2005, the Gumbi community in the Zululand District Municipality in northern KwaZulu-Natal, represented by the Emvokweni Community Trust (ECT), successfully claimed large tracts of land that was mostly under conservation through the land restitution programme (Musavengane & Kloppers, 2020). A consolidated game reserve was thereafter established in the form of SGR (Musavengane, 2019) and is co-managed by the ECT and Wildlands Conservation Trust (WCT) – a prominent nature conservation nongovernmental organisation (NGO) in KwaZulu-Natal.

SGR is of particular interest as the landowning ECT is a recognised management authority for the Reserve and equally serves on a Joint Management Board with the WCT. Leadership and governance intricacies at SGR are complicated by the fact that the Reserve is an 'island' surrounded by the Gumbi Traditional Authority rural land. This resulted in the contestation for management and control of SGR and its resources by the ECT and the local iNkosi (Chief) of the Gumbi Traditional Authority. Various institutions contributed to the establishment and growth of SGR throughout the years, including the Department of Environmental Affairs, the World Wide Fund (WWF) for Nature, Ezemvelo KwaZulu Natal KZN Wildlife, and the Wildlife ACT Fund Trust..The role of these institutions in SGR is discussed in subsequent sections of this chapter.

This chapter presents the institutional support structures and the leadership and governance intricacies at SGR. It is based on the findings of an empirical qualitative study on SGR. The Structuration Theory and Theory U framework underpinned the study as theoretical frameworks. The Structuration Theory identifies structure as both a constraint and a product of human action (Barley & Tolbert, 1997). It displays a mutual dependence between structure and agency wherein agency is improved by seizing control over resources, and the control is exercised by following the system's practices or rules (Whittington, 2010). The Theory U framework is based on understanding different levels of perception and change (Senge et al., 2005). Theory U has been extensively applied for learning and leading change in individuals, groups, and organisations (Scharmer, 2010). The Framework uses the letter 'U' to distinguish between different depths of perceiving reality and the levels of action that follow. These two theoretical insights are utilised to evaluate the progress and outcomes at SGR.

Literature on protected area governance and leadership will first be presented, followed by an outline of the methodology used for the study. Then the following section will introduce the study area, followed by a discussion and analysis of the findings.

## Protected area governance and leadership

Protected area governance in COPAs includes various role players such as the landowning community trust, NGOs, state conservation management authorities and, in some instances, traditional authorities. The inception of COPAs within the post-apartheid South African conservation space dates back to 'contract parks', with the Makuleke region of the Kruger National Park being a prime example. Contractual parks have been touted as an unconventional kind of CBNRM which, according to Reid and Turner (2013: 225), has the potential "to be a win-win CBNRM that profits both the community owners and conservation agencies through collaboration with the communal landowners and joint management of natural resources". Reid and Turner (2013) further opined that, through joint management and contract parks, the landowning communities might achieve significant institutional and social empowerment from their role in co-management agreements, and they may also achieve higher economic benefits from contract parks compared to alternative management arrangements. However, various institutional, leadership, and governance dynamics to COPA activities highlighted in the literature will be covered in this review.

According to Borrini-Feyerabend and Hill (2015), governance refers to a process that is politically embodied in conservation management systems. Good governance is about people expressing their values, rules, self-determination, and direction towards improving their livelihoods (Kauzya, 1998). However, good governance can be obstructed by the abuse of power and authority bestowed upon leaders. The International Union for Conservation of Nature (IUCN) distinguished between governance by government and governance by indigenous and/or local people (Borrini-Feyerabend & Hill, 2015). This study specifically focused on governance by a range of non-state actors, including local people. Local communal governance is believed to be the oldest form of governance primarily based on collective natural resource governance and management (ibid).

The term 'capacity building' is often unclearly defined, but it is strongly linked to good governance. According to Kauzya (1998), capacity building includes full-range participation and embraces transparency, accountability, and equity. Effective governance requires efficient capacity-building programmes to empower all stakeholders, including local communities. It should also focus on socio-politico-economic participation. Stakeholders need to be capacitated for effective and responsive governance. Responsive governance is about community active participation, caring for the needs, priorities, and well-being of local people (Kauzya, 1998), and this implicates leadership to a significant degree.

Schuller (1983) defined leadership as the force that propels one's endeavours to success. Drawing from Senge et al. (2005), the Theory U framework identifies several attributes that define leaders, namely people who recognise and understand their ability to lead and are cooperative and tolerant with others through becoming aware of their shortcomings. Case et al. (2015) argue that environmental leadership is underappreciated as a complex balancing act where leaders are expected to reconcile divergent and equally potent societal motives and objectives across differentials of social stratification, knowledge, and power. Bennis (2007) believes that good leaders are characterised by wisdom and awareness of common good and moral values, while Cameron (2013) suggests that real leaders put the interests of a group or society ahead of their own. Irrespective of leadership attributes, with prevailing environmental challenges, leadership is critical in resolving the 'governance crisis' facing global natural resource systems (Case et al., 2015: 2).

Change in any system or governance setting is inevitable, and institutions, as well as leaders, need to anticipate change to adapt and stay ahead of the growth curve (Dibella, 2007). From the structuration and Theory U perspectives, leadership represents an arena where agency and structure interplay to determine whether an entity or community remains rigid against prevailing environmental and changing socio-political dynamics or is able to change and adapt through foresight and application (Barley & Tolbert, 1997; Kolzow, 2014). Change in this respect is fostered as a process of learning and adaptation (Kolzow, 2014) and is an unfolding and reflexive process. Theory U – a model which emphasises repeated stages of learning and adaptation (Senge et al., 2005) – is thus appropriate to explore leadership processes in the often-controversial management of natural resources. Theory U is a foundation process based on action research. Figure 4.1 annotates the Theory U pattern of change, which depicts the level of coherence, performance, and desired change against time.

An institution such as the ECT can be analysed through the Theory U pattern of change – wherein the U shape starts at a relatively high level of coherence, and thereafter inevitable pressures, triggers, and disturbances occur and are met with resistance and avoidance (see point 1 on Figure 4.1). Short-term improvements may be deployed in reaction to the triggers and disturbances, but the organisation spirals downwards towards a bifurcation point (see point 2 on Figure 4.1), which is the 'edge of chaos' that occurs when assumptions have been exposed, prompting the 'letting go of the previous order'. The bifurcation point becomes a turning point whereby a creative learning space is created, and new possibilities emerge. The institution remains on a regression path until new leadership or order leads to the emergence phase, which is an upward movement that goes through prototyping, testing, and calibration of the emerging innovations. However, if the institution remains static and does not emerge from the edge of chaos, it is not inevitable that learning will occur,

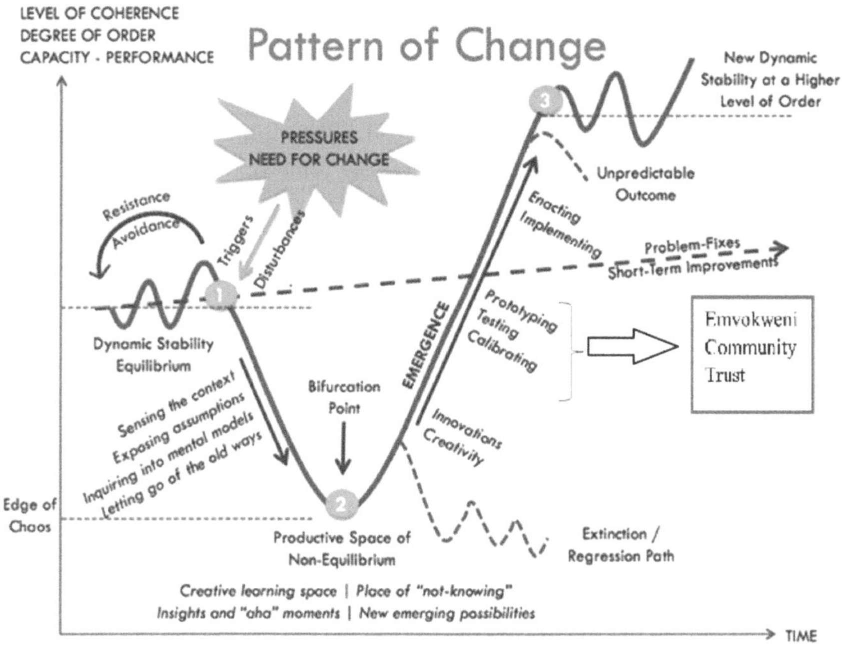


*Figure 4.1* Pattern of change @ 2015 Beatrice Ungard, PhD (Leadership in Complex Environments presented to Kinship Conservation Fellows in 2015)

and the model needs to account for this. The outcome is often a new dynamic and stability in the system.

The evolution of the ECT through the Theory U pattern of change will be discussed, situating the Trust on the emergence slope of the U-shaped pattern of change, and progress at SGR will be evaluated against the Theory U model.

## Methodology

### *Research design*

A qualitative case study design was adopted for the study. Yazan (2015) indicated that case studies are one of the most frequently used research methodologies for investigating, analysing, and understanding the complexities of an entity. According to Stake (1995), case study research studies the uniqueness and complexity of a single case to understand its workings. SGR was chosen for a case study due to the uniqueness of its institutional arrangements with the landowning community trust appointed as a management authority. Other COPAs in the province do not have landowners as the designated management authority (Mthimkhulu & Nel, upcoming). This made SGR ideal for the study based on leadership and governance as it introduced community trusts as new leaders and managers of COPAs.

## Data collection and analysis

Qualitative research methods were adopted for the study. Merriam (2002: 6) defines qualitative research as "an attempt to understand and make sense of a phenomenon from a participant's perspective". It is a holistic approach to research that unfolds in a natural setting and assists the researcher to understand the meaning of experiences and human dimensions concerning their social world (Williams, 2007). Qualitative research can also be used to investigate how social and political elements influence peoples' reality (Merriam, 2002). This made qualitative research appropriate for research at SGR (see Figure 4.2) due to the inherent socio-political forces at play in SGR as a reserve that is a product of land reform.

Before data were collected, permission to engage the local community was sought and obtained from the Gumbi Traditional Authority. Permission was also obtained from ECT to engage the land reform beneficiaries, and from Ezemvelo KZN Wildlife and WCT to engage the relevant staff. Community

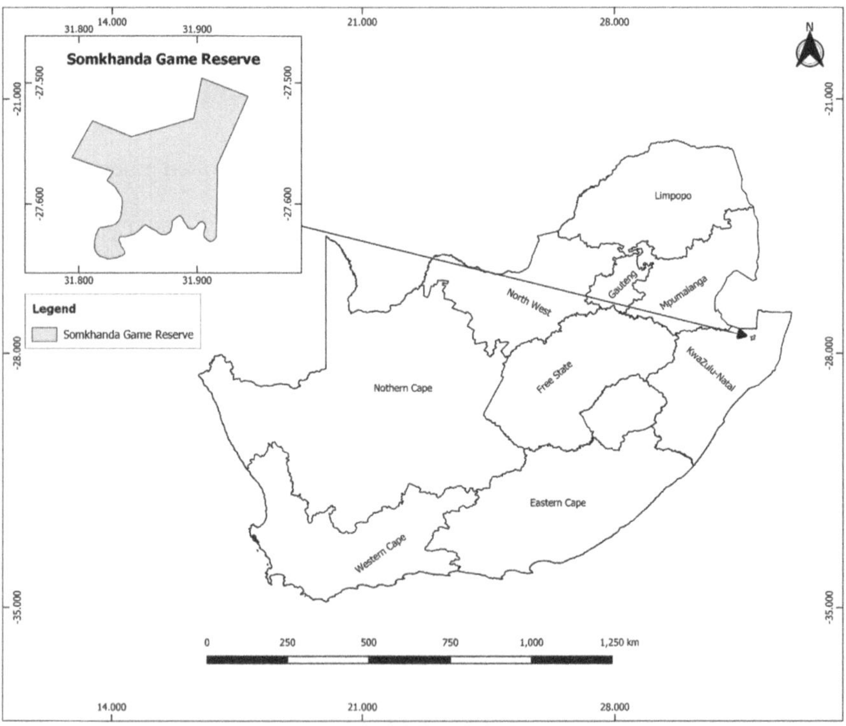


*Figure 4.2* Map of SGR in northern KwaZulu-Natal, South Africa (Olivier, 2021)

members residing in Bethel, Cotlands, and Hlambanyathi (settlement areas abutting SGR) were identified as ECT beneficiaries and former labour tenants. The researcher presented the research objectives to the relevant structures and institutions. A reconnaissance study was done in October 2017 at SGR and the surrounding communities. Data collection through fieldwork at SGR began in March 2018, and the study was concluded in June 2021. Data was not collected in 2020 due to travel restrictions and mandatory health precautions in response to the global COVID-19 pandemic.

Primary data were collected through semi-structured interviews and focus group meetings using a questionnaire guide that sought to obtain information regarding the leadership and governance intricacies at SGR, leadership experience and selection processes, beneficiary participation and beneficiation, conflict resolution within governance structures, and the enforcement of rules. A total of 91 respondents were interviewed, including members of Ezemvelo KZN Wildlife and WCT, members of the ECT, key informants, members of the Gumbi Traditional Authority, and the former Regional Land Claims Commissioner (2000–2005). Focus group interviews were conducted with members of the local community and ECT beneficiaries. All the semi-structured interviews were based on a questionnaire guide. The focus groups varied in size, with the largest group consisting of 46 participants (former labour tenants) and the smallest of four participants (see Table 4.1 below). The questionnaire was theme-based and questions were categorised according to different research aspects such as land tenure, leadership, governance, beneficiation, and conflict resolution at SGR. Individual interviews were more fruitful than focus group meetings as the respondents were more forthcoming when interviewed individually. Focus groups were prone to dominant voices overshadowing the insight of more introverted participants; the last-mentioned were more likely to agree with the collective without voicing their own opinions or going against the *status quo*.

*Table 4.1* List of interviewed respondents and their affiliation

| *Respondents' affiliation* | *No. of respondents* |
|---|---|
| African Insight | 4 |
| ECT beneficiaries | 27 (approx. 40 households) |
| ECT (trustee) | 1 |
| Former KZN Regional Land Claims Commissioner | 1 |
| Ezemvelo KZN Wildlife | 3 |
| Legal advisor – previously involved in SGR | 1 |
| WCT | 4 |
| Gumbi Community (former labour tenants) | 46 |
| SGR (enclave) | 1 (3 households) |
| Gumbi Traditional Authority | 1 |
| South African Wildlife College | 1 |
| Founder – SGR | 1 |
| **Total** | **91** |

Data were collected through purposive sampling once relevant and knowledgeable persons had been identified. Snowball sampling – wherein the researcher was referred to other persons by the initial respondents – was also employed. All the research interviews were transcribed, and the content was allocated according to the research themes. The allocation of information from interviews into research themes was done by categorising interview data based on the predominant subject matter that arose from the interviews. This was in keeping with the practice noted by Neuman (2000), who indicated that similar sets of texts can be analysed through content analysis by comparing various texts. The data collected from the fieldwork were compared to current literature, and the content of interview transcripts was analysed qualitatively. Text with more pertinent content was chosen selectively and separated into research themes.

Theory U framework and structuration theory were applied to identify transition processes and relationships between human agency and structures. The structuration theory was applied concerning the governance roles of ECT, WCT, and the Gumbi Traditional Authority. Theory U was applied to identify the levels of action and learning by the stakeholders involved at SGR.

The following section presents results and a discussion regarding leadership, governance, security of land tenure, livelihoods, beneficiation, institutional support, and capacity building.

## Findings and discussion of analysis: Leadership and governance intricacies at Somkhanda Game Reserve

Current protected area management practices are ostensibly centred around all-inclusive good governance and accountability. However, irrespective of leadership style, leadership and governance are characterised by the need for power (Jones & George, 2011; Maxwell, 2013). Power asymmetries tend to develop when power interplay results in the establishment of dominant and submissive subjects aligned to institutions or through competing institutions/entities in governance settings. Power is also at play in individual agencies, which can cause disruptions in initiatives. We will cover how each of these dynamics played out at SGR in turn.

## Institutional friction

During the research period of 2017 to 2021, power wrangling between the Gumbi Traditional Authority and the ECT over the management of SGR and influence over their constituents was evident. The two structures draw authority and power from their respective governance mandates, and they are legitimised by their constituencies. However, what happens in case of an overlap where members of the Traditional Authority are also beneficiaries of the landowning ECT? iNkosi Gumbi indicated the following regarding leadership and governance at SGR in 2017:

> The Trust has full financial control and power, whereas the Traditional Authority and the community do not receive any benefits from SGR. The iNkosi should be the chairperson of the Trust as a representative of the community. The community follows the leadership of the Traditional Authority ... The Trust does not work with the Traditional Authority because it claims that it owns SGR whereas it is the community that owns SGR.
>
> (iNkosi Gumbi, 2017)

The institution of traditional authorities has a long and complicated history in South Africa. The ECT argued that the iNkosi has no authority over land reform beneficiaries or SGR, which is regarded as private property. However, iNkosi Gumbi is also a land reform beneficiary of SGR, and therefore an ECT beneficiary. In June 2021, a learning exchange interaction session was held between ECT and the Makuleke Communal Property Association (CPA). The session provided an opportunity to present different elements of the conservation economy to the new ECT trustees and a potential structure for SGR. Notably, Hosi Makuleke is elected ex officio to the Makuleke CPA to ensure CPA alignment with the traditional authority. A similar arrangement was suggested to ECT to allow iNkosi to play an oversight role on the board of trustees to ensure effective communication between the CPA, the traditional council, and the broader community.

The establishment of community trusts through the land reform programme has created two centres of power in rural areas, as is the case at SGR with the Gumbi Traditional Authority and ECT. In most cases, COPAs in rural areas that were acquired through the land reform programme are essentially pockets of privately owned land within traditionally administered land. SGR is surrounded by settlement areas inhabited by ECT beneficiaries and former labour tenants who were excluded from the ECT beneficiary list.[1] However, both the former labour tenants and the ECT beneficiaries that reside within the jurisdiction of the Gumbi Traditional Authority are subjects of the Traditional Authority.

The former labour tenants indicated that they should have been included as ECT beneficiaries and provided the same status as the land restitution beneficiaries because they also lived on historically white-owned farms in the KwaGumbi area. This has created tension between the land restitution beneficiaries and the former labour tenants. The power wrangling between the ECT and the Gumbi Traditional Authority has caused frustration and anger for the beneficiaries and former labour tenants.

> The Department of Land Reform's policy says that you can incorporate labour tenants with the land restitution claimants because usually, the labour tenants are fewer than the land restitution claimants
>
> (Thabi Shange, 2019)

## Agency and leadership clashes

The structuration theory suggests that agency (people) and structures have an interactive relationship whereby one can influence and constrain the other. At SGR, the WCT and ECT community facilitators had collectively identified an individual to succeed the reserve manager of that time. However, upon the election of new ECT trustees, the decision was overturned, along with other critical decisions. Decisions were overturned by agencies within the structure (ECT), consequently changing the overall structure and instilling new ideologies and rules.

Internal conflict amongst the ECT trustees has also crippled the governance of SGR. During one of its terms, the ECT had 11 trustees, but in February 2014, all its trustees resigned due to internal conflict, and a lengthy legal process ensued to invalidate the resignations. Eventually, a decision was made to replace all the trustees through an election process which was also tainted by various issues such as mistrust amongst the beneficiaries. iNkosi Gumbi was initially a trustee of the ECT but was not a trustee during the subsequent term, although he was again voted back after a one-term hiatus.

Unfortunately, the leadership at SGR lent itself to power wrangling at the expense of the beneficiaries' needs and aspirations. At one point, the internal conflict amongst the ECT trustees resulted in the suspension of the Trust's bank account and all the community benefits were also suspended. Tekié (2016) attributes the failure of most communal projects to decision-making, governance, and resource management.

Previous events at SGR indicate that iNkosi Gumbi has more influence over the community members than ECT, and his legitimacy as a traditional leader provides him with authority and dominance over his subjects. Both the ECT trustees and Gumbi Traditional Authority exerted power and authority over their shared constituencies to be recognised as legitimate structures. However, the main challenge with this is that both structures exist within the same geographic space.

> The trustees are unaccountable, and they have no ties to the community. They also do not recognise traditional leadership and do not respond to community requests for meetings … We are thrilled that their time as trustees has lapsed so we can appoint new trustees. In order to avoid having unaccountable trustees again, we decided to appoint iNkosi as the chairperson of the Trust.
>
> (Induna Buthelezi, 2018)

The relationship between the Gumbi Traditional Authority and the ECT is severely strained due to contestation over ECT trusteeship, limited access for the Traditional Authority to resources generated from SGR, and continuous litigation between the two structures. However, the Traditional Authority generally has a good relationship with the residents of the Gumbi community as they report their dissatisfaction with the ECT and occurrences at SGR to the iNkosi – oblivious of his limited power and influence at SGR. The relationship between the ECT and its beneficiaries is also strained due to poor communication and what is perceived as inadequate beneficiation from SGR.

> There is absolutely no communication between us and SGR … We do not know anything about the Trust, but we are the very same people who elected the trustees
>
> (Induna Buthelezi, 2018)

The effects of institutional friction and competing agency/leadership at SGR can be summarised as follows: ECT as the landowning community trust has metamorphosised through various phases since inception and has operated both in conflict and in harmony with the local traditional authority. iNkosi Gumbi has served for two terms as a trustee – the first as an ordinary trustee and the current one as the chairman of the Trust. His one term of absence on the Trust caused turmoil between the Trust and the Gumbi Traditional Authority. His appointment as the chairman later appeased this. The contestation between trustees and the traditional authority, amongst other factors, resulted in the ECT going through the Theory U pattern of change. Drawn-out litigation between the ECT trustees and iNkosi Gumbi, the resignation of trustees, former labour tenants challenging the ECT beneficiary list, refusal of the Dlamini family to vacate from SGR, and the misappropriation of Trust funds, which resulted in the suspension of the Trust's bank account, caused pressure and disturbance. This plunged the Trust into the edge of chaos, and stability came with the new trustees, who reinstated iNkosi Gumbi as the chairperson of the Trust – thus quelling the discord between the Trust and the traditional authority. Concerning Theory U, ECT is at the 'emergence phase' (see Figure 4.1); new leadership has emerged with new possibilities, charting a new course of action to establish new leadership prototypes.

Having discussed institutional challenges, the following section will focus on security of tenure and livelihoods.

## Land conflicts: Security of tenure and community livelihoods

The variety of land tenure systems around SGR complicates the governance of the Reserve. Collective title, natural resource management, a dispute over wildlife conservation, and conflicting property rights affect community livelihoods (Naughton-Treves & Sanderson, 1995). In South Africa, rural black Africans were evicted from their communal areas for the establishment and expansion of protected areas and white designated areas (Keep, 2004; Skelcher, 2003). The beneficiaries of SGR are land restitution claimants, but former labour tenants also have land rights on land they historically worked as labour tenants. However, former labour tenants are not on the ECT beneficiary list. The land reform programme has invariably privileged the claims of those who were dispossessed (land restitution) over the rights of those who managed to remain on land (labour tenants) designated for 'whites'. Former labour tenants seek to upgrade the status of their land rights to ownership and claim for the restitution of their rights of tenure. It is ironic that those who historically remained on white-owned farms as labour tenants find themselves excluded and classed as secondary citizens by the land reform programme due to the prioritisation of land restitution claims. This is even though evictions from farms still occur at an alarming rate.

> the community trust excluded us when the land was restituted. We were excluded from the beneficiary list. They found us living here in KwaGumbi ... Anything regarding the Game Reserve and the community trust excludes us. They keep telling us that we are not on the beneficiary list although our forefathers also lived in this area. We have no voice in the matters of SGR because we are not beneficiaries.
>
> (Former labour tenant, 2018)

Despite SGR being a success story of a COPA and land restitution project, it has not been immune to the challenges of CBNRM and balancing conservation against the rights of local people. Collective ownership relies on consensus for decision-making, but the consensus amongst a collective is not easily earned. The Dlamini family are beneficiaries of the ECT, and their household is located within SGR. Negotiations between the Dlamini family and ECT broke down when they could not agree on a resettlement fee. As such, to date, the Dlamini family still resides within SGR. The Dlamini family and the ECT have been involved in numerous drawn-out litigations to evict the Dlamini family, but the courts have recognised the Dlamini family's right of tenure at SGR. This speaks to sentiments by Bond and Frost (2005) that the pressure from those previously evicted and displaced communities to make way for national parks and wilderness areas have, over the years, forced a rethink in the appropriateness of the fortress approach.

> Our local municipality ward had electricity installed and we were also earmarked to have our households installed with electricity. The trustees intercepted the process and made sure that our households within the Reserve do not get electricity. They once received a court order and evicted us. We challenged the eviction and the court granted that we could move back into our households.
>
> (Dlamini family, 2018)

Elements of the fortress conservation management approach are still at play at SGR. Fortress conservation retards neighbouring community development by alienating local people from important resource areas (Adams & Hulme, 2001). The management of protected areas is seen to be at odds with the economic interests of local people. Essentially, insensitive leadership by the ECT and a strained relationship with its beneficiaries resulted in a stalemate between ECT and the Dlamini family. Dissenting voices regarding the lack of substantial benefits also reverberated amongst community members, hence the following section on economic benefits.

## Economic benefits from SGR: An elusive dream

The recent paradigm shift in protected area management in KwaZulu-Natal has created expectations to promote conservation by considering the socio-political and economic factors, encouraging communal ownership, and the provision of substantial economic benefits. However, the communal leadership and governance structures are perceived to be inadequately responsive to community needs and aspirations.

The matter of collective beneficiation from COPAs is akin to that of the 'tragedy of the commons' whereby a few elites squandered common resources for personal gain at the expense of the commons. These are some of the sentiments shared by respondents regarding the SGR beneficiation model. Essentially, land claim beneficiaries are lured and locked into conservation land use on the basis that the current protected area management practice is underpinned by the sustainable utilisation of resources for consumptive and non-consumptive use. This is guided by a sustainable development framework that should be supported by appropriate leadership and governance structures. However, due to financial irregularities, the ECT's business bank account was suspended, and this disrupted the flow of benefits to their beneficiaries. The sustainability of benefits to the beneficiaries was threatened by the poor management skills of the ECT. ECT is currently economically not self-sustained.

> The length of the agreement must be practical to allow the intended objectives to be met ... SGR currently operates at a loss, with 70% ... WCT donated R1,4 million to Somkhanda
>
> (CEO, WCT, 2018)

ECT still requires substantial financial support. Hence, they entered into a ten-year co-management agreement with WCT to assist in the capacitation of ECT trustees, mostly through the Joint Management Board. Horwich and Lyon (2007) indicate that the role of an NGO within a community conservation project includes creating an empowered community group to carry on the social sustainability of the project. NGOs are to assist in preparing community-based organisations to manage key aspects of the project through various skills transfer initiatives, including capacity building. WCT indicated that they intend to leave SGR once the ten-year management agreement lapses – hence their investment to capacitate ECT to manage the **R**eserve independently. SGR has a shadow reserve manager, identified by the ECT, whom the WCT reserve manager mentors. Small local businesses were also trained to maintain the trails and provide other services for the management of the **R**eserve.

According to WCT, community beneficiation from SGR includes the direct employment of 100 people (of whom 60 are permanent staff), investment into SGR through the introduction of game to develop the Reserve as an asset, and investments into SGR for it to grow and employ more people. Other initiatives include homestays in the communities surrounding SGR, community hubs, youth development projects, and the training of small local businesses. Community conservation has been dubbed by many as the future of conservation. Therefore, capacity building initiatives for community-based organisations focused on conservation are an investment towards the sustainability of community conservation projects and improving the livelihoods of local communities. Despite the aforementioned, the respondents, including iNkosi, still find substantial economic benefits elusive. Hence the need for institutional support as discussed below.

## Institutional support and capacity for robust institutional emergence at Somkhanda Game Reserve

The success of SGR can be attributed to the collective efforts and support from various institutions carrying similar mandates related to nature conservation. According to a Memorandum of Agreement (initially signed 23 August 2013 and later extended) between ECT and WCT, WCT has the primary responsibility for all management, funding, and commercial operations at SGR. African Insight and Soul Destinations also operate at SGR, generating rental income for the Reserve through the capturing and selling of game. However, the long-term sustainability of SGR rests on ECT and the traditional authority being able to exercise governance roles harmoniously. This section reflects on institutional support and evaluates SGR on the likelihood of robust institutional emergence as a process reflected in the Theory U model.

The WWF for Nature in South Africa was instrumental in supporting SGR to become the first COPA to benefit from its Black Rhino Range Expansion Programme. The Wildlife ACT Fund provided support through biodiversity monitoring, particularly for priority species in the Reserve. Ezemvelo KZN Wildlife provided support through its Biodiversity Stewardship programme, which led to the declaration of SGR as a protected area and the donation of game to support the community-owned initiative. The Department of Environmental Affairs provided much-needed support through initial funding for infrastructure development and natural resource management.

The establishment of SGR by a community trust comprising land reform beneficiaries was essentially a social learning process for all stakeholders involved. According to the Theory U framework, all the stakeholders involved underwent a learning process by going through all the stages of Theory U, namely seeing, sensing, presencing, crystallising and prototyping, performing, and embodying (Scharmer, 2007). ECT and its beneficiaries realised the chaos their institution was in, and they insightfully sensed their future destination in the present, which is presencing at the bifurcation point (see point 2 in Figure 4.1). Therefore, they have acted from the state of awareness in the now ("sensing and actualising emerging futures"). The ECT learning exchange between the ECT and the Makuleke Communal Property Association (CPA) reaffirms ECT's calibration and prototype process to prepare leaders and operationalise the institution. SGR, being the first COPA in KwaZulu-Natal, was indeed an emerging future, and its involvement in the Black Rhino Range Expansion Programme was also the result of transition and growth for SGR through partnerships with institutions such as WCT and WWF. New leadership has emerged, and iNkosi has taken over the leadership role, minimising tension and discontent amongst the land reform beneficiaries, ordinary community members, and former labour tenants.

As demonstrated by Figure 4.2 on the Theory U pattern of change diagram, ECT has been resilient when faced with disturbances that may have destabilised the Trust. The Trust is now on the path of emergence since the harmonisation of roles between the ECT and the traditional authority. Information gleaned from the study participants indicated that the discord between ECT and the traditional authority underpinned most of the leadership and governance challenges at SGR, and it appears that the appointment of iNkosi Gumbi as the chairman of ECT on the current term of trustees was a strategic move to quell the longstanding conflict between the two institutions. However, agencies and structures have an interactive relationship whereby the one can influence and constrain the other. The appointment of iNkosi Gumbi as the chairman of the ECT may be a short-term solution for the jurisdictional challenge between the two institutions as it remains to be seen whether the tension between the ECT and the traditional authority will not arise again once iNkosi Gumbi's term as the chairman of the Trust lapses. A long-term solution would be the formalisation of the role of iNkosi Gumbi on the Trust through the amendment of the Trust Deed to recognise iNkosi Gumbi as an ex officio member of the ECT.

## Conclusion

SGR is a flagship COPA that distinctively has had its landowning community trust formally designated as the management authority. However, the success of protected area management at SGR is inextricably linked to the ongoing institutional and management support provided by WCT. Governance at SGR is complicated by the multiple land tenure systems around SGR, including the traditional authority, land restitution beneficiaries, and former labour tenants who all claim to have a vested interest in and rights to SGR. The ongoing legal challenge by the former labour tenants to be included on the ECT beneficiary list will affect the leadership and governance of SGR, hence the need for strong, adaptive, and decisive leadership from the ECT. The power and authority wrangling between the ECT and the traditional authority have caused frustration and infuriation from the land reform beneficiaries and former labour tenants.

There are also varying views on the economic benefits derived from SGR, hence the elusiveness of what is regarded as substantial economic benefits for rural communities and land reform beneficiaries from reserves. Nevertheless, it appears that there is a need for capacity building for the land reform beneficiaries regarding their land rights and available recourses for holding unaccountable trustees accountable. A harmonious relationship needs to be fostered between the ECT and the traditional authority due to an overlap in constituencies and for the sake of good governance in SGR. The inclusion of the former labour tenants on the ECT beneficiary list would be an act of social justice, but it is a matter for the courts to decide. Theory U encapsulated the varying levels of perception and change of the ECT, which has gone through a lengthy process of learning and adapting since the inception of SGR. It can be confidently stated that the ECT has achieved significant social and institutional empowerment from their role as the management authority for SGR by jointly managing the Reserve with WCT.

## Note

1 iNkosi Gumbi initially supported the notion of incorporating the former labour tenants on the ECT beneficiary list to ensure fair representation. However, he later (in 2018) indicated that labour tenants were not entitled to inclusion on the beneficiary list.

## References


Adams, W.M., & Hulme, D. (2001). If community conservation is the answer in Africa, what is the question. *Oryx, 35*(3): 193–200.

Barley, S.R., & Tolbert, P.S. (1997). Institutionalization and structuration: Studying the links between action and institution. Retrieved [16 June 2020] from Cornell University, ILR School site: http://digitalcommons.ilr.cornell.edu/articles/130/

Bennis, W. (2007). The challenges of leadership in the modern world. Introduction to the special issue. *American Psychological Association, 62*(1):2–5.

Bond, I., & Frost, P.G.H. (2005). *CAMPFIRE and the payment for environmental services.* Bogor, Indonesia: Center for Development Research (ZEF), University of Bonn, Germany and Center for International Forestry Research (CIFOR).

Borrini-Feyerabend, G., & Hill, R. (2015). Governance for the conservation of nature. In G.L. Workboys, M. Lock, A. Kothari, S. Feary, and I. Pulsford (Eds.), *Protected area governance and management* (pp. 169–206). Canberra: ANU Press.

Cameron, G. (2013). *Authentic African leadership.* Johannesburg, South Africa: Real African Publishers.

Case, P., Evans, L.S., Fabinyi, M., Cohen, P.J., Hicks, C.C., Prideaux, M., & Mills, D.J. (2015). Rethinking environmental leadership: The social construction of leaders and leadership in discourses of ecological crisis, development and conservation. *Leadership,* 11(4): 396-423. DOI: 10.1177/1742715015577887.

Cundill, G., Thondhlana, G., Sisitka, L., Shackleton, S., & Blore, M. (2013). Land claims and the pursuit of co-management on four protected areas in South Africa. *Land Use Policy, 35,* 171–178.

Dibella, A.J. (2007). Critical perceptions of organisational change. *Journal of Change Management*, 7(3–4): 231–242.

Horwich, R.H., & Lyon, J. (2007). Community conservation: Practitioners' answer to critics. *Oryx*, *41*(3): 376–385.

Jones, B.T.B. (2004). *CBNRM, poverty reduction and sustainable livelihoods: Developing criteria for evaluating the contribution of CBNRM to poverty reduction and alleviation in Southern Africa.* Centre for Applied Social Sciences University of Zimbabwe and Programme for Land and Agrarian Studies School of Government, University of the Western Cape. Cape Town, South Africa.

Jones, G.R., & George, J.M. (2011). *Contemporary management.* New York. McGraw-Hill/Irwin.

Kauzya, J.M. (1998). *Local governance capacity building for full range participation: Concepts, frameworks, and experiences in African countries.* In 4th Global forum on reinventing government, Marraketch, Morocco (pp. 10-13).

Kepe, T. (2004). Land restitution and biodiversity conservation in South Africa: The case of Mkambati, Eastern Cape Province. *Canadian Journal of African Studies, 38*, 688–704.

Knieter, D. (2014). *Decolonizing conservation? Co-management of natural resources in Bushbuckridge Nature Reserve (BBR NR), South Africa.* University of Missouri-Columbia. Missouri, Columbia.

Kolzow, D.R. (2014). *Leading from within: Building organizational leadership capacity.*

Maxwell, J.C. (2013). *How successful people lead.* New York: Center Street.

Merriam, S.B. (2002). Introduction to qualitative research. In *Qualitative research in practice: Examples for discussion and analysis* (Vol. 1, pp. 1–17)

Mthimkhulu, O., & Nel, A. (upcoming). Communally-owned protected areas in KwaZulu-Natal: The contested juxtaposition of land reform and capitalism. University of KwaZulu-Natal.Unpublished Dissertation. Pietermaritzburg, South Africa.

Musavengane, R. (2019). Land reform and the promotion of collaborative community-based ecotourism at Somkhanda Game Reserve, South Africa. In M. Mkono (Ed.), *Positive tourism in Africa. Contemporary geographies of leisure, tourism and mobility* (pp. 23–35). London: Routledge.

Musavengane, R., & Kloppers, R. (2020). Social capital: An investment towards community resilience in the collaborative natural resources management of community-based tourism schemes. *Tourism management perspectives, 34*, 100654.

Musavengane, R., & Simatele, D.M. (2016). Community-based natural resource management: The role of social capital in collaborative environmental management of tribal resources in KwaZulu-Natal, South Africa. *Development Southern Africa, 33*(6):806–821. DOI: 10.1080/0376835X.2016.1231054.

Musavengane, R., Tantoh, H.B., & Simatele, D. (2019). A comparative analysis of collaborative environmental management of natural resources in Sub-Saharan Africa: A study of Cameroon and South Africa. *Journal of Asian and African Studies, 54*(4): 512–532. DOI: 10.1177/0021909618825276.

Naughton-Treves, L., & Sanderson, S. (1995 August). Property, politics and wildlife conservation. *World Development, 23*(8): 1265–1275.

Neuman, W.L. (2000). *Social research methods.* Boston, MA: Allyn & Bacon.

Nyambe, N. (2005). *Organizational culture and its understanding basic assumptions as a determinant of response to change.* Pietermaritzburg: Centre for Environment, Agriculture and Development, University of KwaZulu-Natal. Unpublished.

Olivier, I. (2021). *Map of Somkhanda Game Reserve in northern KwaZulu-Natal, South Africa.* Unpublished. Skukuza, South Africa.

Reid, H., & Turner, S. (2013). The Richtersveld and Makuleke contractual parks in South Africa: Win–win for communities and conservation? In *Rights resources and rural development* (pp. 238–249). London: Routledge.

Scharmer, O. (2007). Theory U: Leading from the emerging future. A Social Technology of Freedom (working title). San Fransisco: Berret-Koehler publishers.

Scharmer, O. (2010). *The blind spot of institutional leadership: How to create deep innovation through moving from egosystem to ecosystem awareness*. Cambridge, MA: Massachusetts Institute of Technology Presencing Institute.

Schuller, R.H. (1983). *Tough times never last, but tough people do!*. New York.Thomas Nelson. Inc.

Sebola, M.P. (2014). Sustaining tourism in South African game farms: The benefits of ownership of restituted land by African communities. *Sustainable Tourism IV*, *187*(1), 15.

Senge, P., Scharmer, C.O., Jaworski, J., & Flowers, B.S. (2005). *Presence: Exploring profound change in people, organizations and society*. London: Nicholas Brealey.

Skelcher, B. (2003). Apartheid and the removal of black spots from lake Bhangazi in KwaZulu-Natal, South Africa. Sage. *Journal of Black Studies, 33*(6), 761. DOI: 10.1177/0021934703033006003.

Stake, R.E. (1995). *The art of case study research*. Thousand Oaks, CA: SAGE Publications.

Tekié, A. (2016). *A precarious success: Land reform and governance of the commons at the Amangcolosi Community Trust* (Doctoral dissertation).

Ungard, B. (2015). *Pattern of change, leadership in complex environments, kinship conservation fellows*. Unpublished. Bellingham, United States.

Whittington, R. (2010). Giddens, structuration theory and strategy as practice. In *Cambridge handbook of strategy as practice* (pp. 109–126). Cambridge, England: Cambridge University Press.

Williams, C. (2007). Research methods. Grand Canyon University. *Journal of Business & Economic Research*, 5(3) 65-72.

Yazan, B. (2015). Three approaches to case study methods in education: Yin, Merriam, and Stake. *The Qualitative Report, 20*(2): 134–152. Retrieved from http://www.nova.edu/ssss/QR/QR20/2/yazan1.pdf.

# Part 2

# Managing natural disasters and land reform tourism crises

# 5 Complex effects of natural disasters on protected areas

## the case of Cyclone Idai in Mozambique

*Pekka Virtanen, Luis Cristóvão, and José Mourinho*

### Introduction

The community conservation paradigm, which largely replaced the fortress conservation paradigm in Southern Africa after the 1980s, consists of two main principles. The first asserts that people in and around protected areas (PAs) must be allowed to participate in the management of conservation resources. The second derives from the observation that PAs can have serious negative effects on local residents, who must be compensated. Imposing costs without equivalent benefits tends to create hostility to conservation activities among those affected (Adams & Hulme, 2001). In Mozambique, the second principle, in particular, has been adopted to the national wildlife policy. The overall goal of the 1996 wildlife policy is "to conserve, utilize and develop forest and wildlife resources to gain social, ecological and economic benefits for present and future generations of Mozambicans" (Soto, 2011, 90). More specifically, creating a situation whereby the benefits that wildlife brings to local communities are sufficient to offset the costs they incur for living with wildlife has been defined as a focal objective in key policy documents, such as Mozambique's national elephant strategy (MIT, 2010). Adoption of the first principle has, on the other hand, been less enthusiastic.

With respect to the second principle, critical studies soon noted that, in most cases, economic benefits from PAs tend to go mostly to national and international actors, including both public authorities and the private sector, while the costs fall mainly on local communities (Wells 1992). In Mozambique, 16% of the revenue generated within PAs should legally go to neighbouring communities, but in practice, the revenue received by them is only a small part of this. In 2013, for example, only approximately 2% reached the communities (Rylance, 2017). At the same time, shrinking public funding has covered only a fraction of the conservation budget (UNDP, 2010), and the government's conservation strategy is based on giving a dominant role for the private sector and international donors (GoM, 2018).

An alternative source of sustainable funding has been sought from ecotourism, which is sometimes presented almost as a panacea (Krüger, 2005). The idea is that by maintaining attractive natural landscapes and a rich biodiversity,

DOI: 10.4324/9781003188902-7

local communities can earn money from ecotourism, which provides both an incentive for conservation and an economic alternative to destructive activities. Ideally, tourism earnings should be so high that community members actively support conservation activities in order to protect their source of income (Kiss, 2004; Silva & Khatiwada, 2014). Over the last two decades, community-based tourism has received significant coverage in ecotourism-oriented media. The term is, however, rather vague, and can refer to anything from ensuring that at least some community members participate in tourism-related activities, to ownership of ecotourism enterprises (Kiss, 2004). In this article, the term is used in a strong sense, which includes both main principles of the community conservation paradigm.

To be successful, the benefits from ecotourism should be substantial and widely distributed, while it should not threaten the local population's main sources of livelihood. In reality, however, many ecotourism projects produce only modest economic gains, which often benefit only a few members of the community (Kiss, 2004; Silva & Khatiwada, 2014). The hyped 'win-win' outcome requires that certain natural and manmade conditions considered favourable for upmarket ecotourism, the prime source of income for PAs, are fulfilled. These include adequate infrastructure, relatively easy access to and mobility within the PA, high probability of seeing charismatic wildlife, such as lions and elephants, and political stability, as well as a favourable legal and policy framework (Krüger, 2005; Silva & Khatiwada, 2014; Wells, 1992).

Many PAs are vulnerable to natural disasters and epidemics, which can reveal the fragility of local support to conservation (Lendelvo et al., 2020; Zhang et al., 2018). The frequency and severity of natural disasters have been projected to increase in the future because of climate change and other anthropogenic disturbances (Walters et al., 2015; Zhang et al., 2018). Disasters often cause widespread damage to the local population, such as human casualties, destruction of housing, social and transport infrastructure, loss of livelihoods, food shortages, epidemics, and an impaired security situation. Such effects tend to negatively affect the tourism industry, thereby increasing the economic plight of the population (Genç, 2018). Destruction of livelihoods, including the income from tourism due to a disaster, may prompt community members to pursue alternative livelihoods and labour migration, but they may also expand traditional activities, for example by clearing more forest to open fields. Therefore, even if a disaster does not seriously affect biodiversity, changed economic activities may do so (Zhang et al., 2018).

Natural disasters may, however, also foster feelings of solidarity and draw national and international attention to the affected region (Matos & Ndapassoa, 2020). In addition to emergency aid and basic reconstruction activities, a disaster may have more long-term effects in the form of increased national and international investment for new economic or conservation projects (Genç, 2018). This is especially likely in the case of an internationally renowned PA, which is likely to draw intensive media coverage to the disaster (Zhang et al., 2018). Aside from material consequences, disasters can also strengthen or undermine existing power relations at different levels (Arnall, 2014; Matos & Ndapassoa, 2020).

The focus of this chapter is on the impact of natural disasters on PAs that differ in relation to attractiveness for tourists and access to external funding. It is based on comparative analysis of the impact of Tropical Cyclone (TC) Idai in two contrasting PAs and their buffer zones (BZs) in Mozambique, the national parks (NPs) of Chimanimani (CNP) and Gorongosa (GNP). The former is a relatively little-known PA where local benefits derive mainly from a community eco-lodge, and other activities are supported by a set of externally funded microprojects. The latter is a world-famous wildlife park operated as a public-private joint venture, which enjoys generous external funding from international donors. TC Idai, which hit Mozambique in 2019, was one of the worst weather-related disasters in Africa. The storm affected nearly 3 million people and left over 1 000 people dead. The total economic loss was estimated to be at least 2 billion USD, which makes it the costliest tropical cyclone in the South-West Indian Ocean basin (Yu et al., 2019).

The study is based on interviews with 55 individuals (including 3 government representatives) conducted in March 2021 in four communities of the CNP BZ. This data set was complemented with earlier interviews done in May 2018 (both sites) and May 2019 (CNP), relevant public documents, and research literature. Due to previous studies and training activities the researchers were already familiar with the study sites, in particular with CNP, the primary case.

## Context of the comparative study: The national parks of Gorongosa and Chimanimani

In Mozambique the management of PAs is based on a national 10-year strategic plan, and its implementation is coordinated by a central body. Individual PAs can be managed by the state alone, as in the case of CNP, or together with a private operator, as in the case of GNP. Other alternatives include management by communities or by NGOs (ANAC, 2015). One of the plan's strategic objectives is community development. The aim is to organise populations living inside and adjacent to PAs to support implementation of the strategy and the PA management plan in such activities as conservation and sustainable use of natural resources. This includes resettlement of scattered populations affected by the activities of the PAs to reduce human-wildlife conflict. Organising also refers to creating community management committees and formal associations, which can receive the 16% share of PA revenue and act as contractual parties in relation to private sector operators (Ibid).

The PA of Gorongosa was created in the colonial period, initially as a hunting reserve in 1921, but upgraded to NP status in 1960 (Table 5.1). Due to abundance of charismatic wildlife and easy access it became one of the best-known sites for upmarket safari tourism in Southern Africa (Morley and Convery, 2014). Its geographical boundaries were expanded gradually from

*Table 5.1* Gorongosa and Chimanimani in brief

| | | *GNP* | *CNP* |
|---|---|---|---|
| Established | Earlier status | Hunting reserve 1921 | Forest reserve (3) 1953<br>National reserve 2003 |
| | Current status | NP 1960 | NP 2020 |
| Land area | PA | 4 067 $km^2$ | 634 $km^2$ |
| | BZ | 5 333 $km^2$ | 1 723 $km^2$ |
| Landscape type | Elevation | c. 15 – 1 863 m | c. 200 – 2 436 m |
| | Eco-region | Situated in the Rift Valley, the park consists of savanna, woodlands, grasslands, and rainforests at Mount Gorongosa. | Tropical mountain biome consisting of a forest-grassland mosaic. It is part of the Afromontane centre of endemism. |
| Population inside BZ (2017 est.) | | 177 000 | 37 000 |
| Number of visitors/year | | 4 219* | 67** |

*average/year, 2011–2020; **average/year, 2017–2020

the initial 1 000 $km^2$ to 5 300 $km^2$ in 1960 (Walker, 2015). The expansion, together with the increasingly strict level of conservation led to the eviction of several thousand local African inhabitants – albeit not all – from the PA. This caused strong opposition from the target communities, and in the context of the incipient struggle for national independence the authorities decided to reduce the PA to 3 770 $km^2$. More densely inhabited lands were therefore excised from the park in order to ensure the separation of people from nature following the then-dominant conservation paradigm (Walker, 2015).

In Chimanimani, the initiative for a PA in the border zone came from Rhodesia (now Zimbabwe), where a NP was created along the national border to protect the unique mountain biome in 1949 (Ghiurghi et al., 2010). On the Mozambican side, three forest reserves were created at the foot of the Chimanimani massif in the 1950s, but the restrictions placed on the local inhabitants were relatively loose, and – different from the Rhodesian NP – no evictions took place. In the early 1970s, there was a plan to create a large PA covering the Mozambican side of the mountains adjacent to the Rhodesian NP, which would benefit from Rhodesian tourists arriving through a newly opened border post and road connection to Beira, a popular beach resort. However, Mozambican independence in 1975 and subsequent international boycott of the minority rule regime in Rhodesia made the plan obsolete and it was shelved for 20 years (Virtanen, 2020).

The wildlife in both Gorongosa and Chimanimani suffered heavily during the civil war (1976–1992), which started soon after independence. The rebel movement Renamo established important military bases in both areas, which became major scenes of military operations. The opposition has enjoyed strong support in these areas even after the peace agreement in 1992 and the first democratic elections two years later, and part of the population has continued to be hostile toward any projects initiated by Frelimo, which has maintained its position as the ruling party. The political situation complicated the efforts started in the late 1990s to rehabilitate GNP and to create a new PA in Chimanimani (Morley and Convery, 2014; Virtanen, 2005).

The new community conservation paradigm was promoted by international donors, such as the World Bank and the African Development Bank, through broad nationwide projects in which support to individual conservation areas was incorporated. Despite the participatory ethos, most of the resources went to strengthening government authorities with largely unsustainable results. Though the numbers of both wildlife and visiting tourists started to grow in GNP, according to a senior staff member the facilities were in decay by 2006 (interview, May 2018). In Chimanimani, the situation was even worse: in 2000 a cyclone largely destroyed the simple improvised infrastructure built by then, and in the mid-2000's artisanal gold miners, numbering approximately 10 000 at the peak phase, invaded the PA. From 2005 to 2008 the average number of tourists entering the recently declared reserve was approximately 80 per year, which was not sufficient for maintaining even the few rustic services, such as campsites and tourist guides (Virtanen, 2020).

In Gorongosa, the gradual return of wildlife combined with favourable conditions for upmarket safari tourism was reflected in increasing income from tourism. This evoked the interest of a wealthy American philanthropist, who set up the Gorongosa Restoration Project (a US-based foundation) to support rehabilitation of the park and in 2008 the project signed a 20-year contract for joint management of GNP. The large financial commitment by the foundation has enticed a number of other international donors and public institutions to join, and in 2018 the contract was extended for another 25 years (Gorongosa Project, 2018; Walker, 2015). Although the park enjoys relatively high income from upmarket safari tourism, it constitutes only approximately 3% of the total income. The substantial sums the project uses annually on tourism infrastructure and community development – in addition to basic operations, conservation, and research – come from external sources (Gorongosa Project, 2017).

Since 2006, Chimanimani has benefited from two subsequent nationwide projects to support trans-frontier conservation areas, funded again mainly by the World Bank. As the community participation and tourism promotion activities of the earlier project had largely failed, the new projects have placed considerable effort on these areas. The rugged landscape is not suitable for traditional safari tourism, and the existing potential for adventure or cultural tourism has failed to attract significant numbers of visitors (Virtanen, 2020). There is only one small lodge in the BZ of CNP,[1] operated since 2010 as a joint venture between a local community association and MICAIA, a UK-based foundation (Kingman, 2010). Initially, the venture benefited from the World

Bank funding, but has since struggled on its own. The only other self-sustained economic activity is a cooperative beekeeping project (Virtanen, 2020).

Although the development strategies of the two NPs appear quite similar – largely due to donor influence – except for differences in scale, they are actually dissimilar with respect to the first element of the community conservation paradigm, namely that people in and around PAs should be allowed to participate in the management of conservation resources. In GNP the conservation objectives are decisive, and – as affirmed by senior staff members – the objective is to remove people from the PA. While this is not pursued by force, the communities living inside are not entitled to the benefits offered to those living in the BZ (interviews, May 2018). They do not have any say in the park's management, and the community land delimitation exercise[2] – intended to recognise rights to natural resources – was not extended to the PA (Dondeyne et al., 2012). Even the social and economic benefits for the BZ populations are mainly decided top-down, either drawn from the government's sectoral plans or devised to address specific conservation issues defined by the experts (interviews, May 2018). Particularly in the early years, the project showed little respect for traditional values of the people, which caused serious friction (Jacobs, 2010). Even today its continuing effort to expand protection (and related use restrictions) in different forms to an ever-widening area is a source of fear and resistance to many community members (Walker, 2015).

In Chimanimani, a similar land delimitation exercise was extended into the PA, which strengthened the communities' sense of ownership. Moreover, the new plan finalised in 2010 adjusted the boundaries of the PA to exclude two major settlements, and there are no plans to expand it (Dondeyne et al., 2012). Although most of the community development activities and development of conservation infrastructure depend on donor funding, both the community eco-lodge and the honey cooperative are joint enterprises with formal structures for community participation (Virtanen, 2020). Discussions with community members indicated, however, that active participation is limited to a rather small group within the community (interviews, May 2019).

## The cause of disaster: Tropical Cyclone Idai

Cyclones are not exceptional in the southern Indian Ocean: on average, Mozambique experiences cyclones 1–2 times per year (Matyas & Silva, 2013). Usually, cyclones in the Mozambique Channel move southeast into the open ocean, but atypically Idai penetrated deep inland. According to statistics, the frequency of cyclone landfalls over Southeastern Africa has not increased since the 1940s (Fitchett & Grab, 2014). However, the warming of sea surface temperature and the increase in upper ocean heat caused by climate change is likely to intensify cyclones and increase their duration (Vidya et al., 2021). In 2019, TC Kenneth – the strongest ever to make landfall in Mozambique – caused havoc in the north of the country only one month after Idai (Mawren et al., 2020), and in 2021 tropical storm Chalane crossed deep into the continent following closely the track of Idai, albeit with considerably less damage (IOM, 2021).

TC Idai originated from a tropical depression and made its first landfall in Quelimane on the coast of Mozambique on 4 March 2019 (Figure 5.1). It returned back into the Mozambique Channel where it remained for the next six days and developed into a TC before it made a second landfall near the city of Beira on 14 March (Yu et al., 2019). The cyclone brought strong winds (180–220 km/h) and heavy rain (more than 200 mm in 24 hours) across the provinces of Sofala and Manica, causing rivers to overflow and bringing a large storm surge in the coastal city of Beira and surrounding areas. It is estimated that more than 1.5 million people were affected, over 1 600 injured, and more than 600 died in Mozambique (GoM, 2019). Six months after the disaster, an estimated one million people still experienced food shortages and nearly 100 000 remained displaced (Matos & Ndapassoa, 2020).

TC Idai caused severe damage in the PAs and related BZs situated on its path, including Gorongosa and Chimanimani (GoM, 2019). In Sofala Province, the worst impact of the cyclone fell on those living in areas prone to flooding, such as the Gorongosa District where government sources reported almost 15 000 ha of cultivated land affected and over 2 100 dwellings damaged (INGC, 2019). Many of those affected were living in the southwestern BZ of GNP. Even though the park's extensive areas of intact vegetation and soils absorbed large amounts of water, flooding destroyed houses, fields, and harvests particularly in the communities downstream of the Pungwe and Urema rivers. Many households were cut off from land access and help for weeks (Gorongosa Project, 2020). Inside the PA, extensive stretches of road and five small bridges worth 150 000 USD were destroyed, and two cars and an excavator (valued

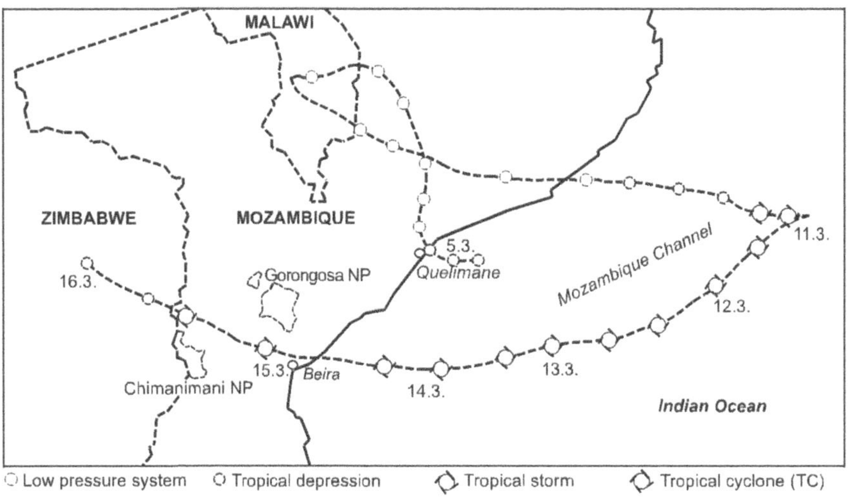


*Figure 5.1* The track of Tropical Cyclone Idai Source: Based on OCHA, 2019.

at 140 000 USD) were lost. Infrastructure damage to the hotel amounted to 600 000 USD, and foregone revenues were estimated at 270 000 USD (GoM, 2019). The park is normally closed to visitors during the rainy season (mid-December to the end of March), but in 2019 it was also closed for April as the damage caused by Idai was repaired (Gorongosa Project, 2020).

GNP staff had a crucial role not only in rehabilitating the park infrastructure, but in food distribution and medical support to assist the neighbouring communities even before international response got into motion. Park rangers waded through flooded land to reach those trapped on points of higher ground bringing emergency rations and assistance until helicopters, canoes, and vehicles could be mobilised (Gorongosa Project, 2020). During the first month, they distributed 97 tons of food they had purchased at the local market (Meldrum, 2019). They also set up an emergency response unit to coordinate the relief effort, hired two helicopters, and collaborated with a team of African Parks who also provided their helicopter and technical team to support the ground action (Gorongosa Project, 2020).

In the following months, the park worked with the World Food Programme (WFP) distributing more than 500 tons of food provided by the latter to approximately 80 000 people. They received substantial support for the relief effort from concerned individuals, business, and organisations, including 400 000 USD from a web-based fundraising effort (Gorongosa Project, 2020), and a USAID grant to provide seeds to 10 000 households. The park also collaborated with WFP on a recovery project in which residents helped rebuild health posts, schools, and roads in return for food (Meldrum, 2019), and was directly involved in planning and coordination of the post-flood assistance programme with national and international authorities (Gorongosa Project, 2020).

A natural disaster like TC Idai is likely to have a direct impact on the number of visitors to PAs that were affected by it. However, despite the shortened season, the annual number of visitors to GNP remained stable as the park authorities had sufficient resources to fix the relatively light or replaceable damages quickly. Actually, the period of insecurity due to the resurgence of armed conflict between Renamo and the government (2013–2016), which was particularly acute in Gorongosa (Regalia, 2017), had a more drastic impact (Table 5.2). In 2020 the park was closed due to a new natural disaster, the COVID-19 pandemic (Gorongosa Project, 2020). In Chimanimani, the number of visitors has not increased beyond the annual average of 80 reached in the early years (Virtanen, 2020), remaining economically insignificant.

*Table 5.2* Annual number of visitors to GNP and CNP

| *Year* | *2011* | *2012* | *2013* | *2014* | *2015* | *2016* | *2017* | *2018* | *2019* | *2020* |
|---|---|---|---|---|---|---|---|---|---|---|
| **GNP** | 7 000 | 6 311 | 1 244 | 1 247 | 2 597 | 1 992 | 5 700 | 5 446 | 6 432 | closed |
| **CNP** | n.a. | n.a. | n.a. | n.a. | n.a. | n.a. | 56 | 103 | 78 | 30 |

In the Sussundenga District, where CNP is located, approximately 13 500 households and over 40% of the cultivated area were affected by Idai (CISP, 2019). In Dombe, which covers part of the CNP BZ and was one of the most affected areas, local authorities reported several destroyed bridges and drifts, collapse of roads in some places, destruction of irrigation systems and other water infrastructure, damage to classrooms, and loss of forest resources. In addition to the government, the interviewed local authorities named 20 NGOs or international organisations that provided some form of emergency aid. Together they provided food and water, tents and other temporary dwellings, building materials, clothes, hygiene products, seeds and other agricultural inputs, household items, and school supplies (interviews, March 2021).

In Chimanimani, the damage caused by the cyclone to PA infrastructure was more serious than in GNP. Due to the mountainous terrain, flood waters burst riverbanks and swept away bridges, flooded houses, and devastated wide areas of fields and forest. Key elements of the recently built transport infrastructure worth USD 1600 000, including roads, two bridges, and one drift were damaged, along with some management and tourism infrastructure worth USD 29 000. In the joint venture lodge situated in the BZ, solar panels worth USD 6 000 were damaged, but foregone accommodation revenue amounted only to USD 1 000. Over 300 beehives distributed by the honey project were destroyed, while flooding of crop areas severely reduced food production. Loss of forest resources also impacted negatively on immediate and long-term availability of timber, fuelwood, and medicine for local communities (GoM, 2019).

In a rapid survey conducted in March 2021 in four traditional communities inside the BZ (Mpunga, Mukawaia, Goto-Goto, and Matsia), 52 individuals (54% female) from different households were interviewed. The average age of the interviewees was 42 years, ranging from 18 to 71 years. Agriculture was the main livelihood for most of the households, but approximately 20% had additional sources of income, such as small-scale commerce or temporary work. Only 15% had a permanent salaried job, which is typical for the study region. Maize is the main subsistence crop, and also an important source of cash income – along with sesame and bananas. Goats and chicken are relatively common, whereas only a few households own cattle.

Ten of the survey's 14 questions addressed the damage caused by TC Idai and subsequent emergency aid. All interviewees reported some damage, most often loss of crops and soil fertility (75% of respondents), damage to dwellings (67%), fruit trees (58%), and beehives (52%), or loss of small stock (goats and chicken, 33%). Similar – albeit somewhat higher – figures were recorded by another survey of 100 households who received emergency kits in the neighbouring community of Mucamba in 2019 (CISP, 2019). With regard to public infrastructure, 63% of our interviewees reported damage to roads and bridges, or schools (54%), whereas only five reported damage to irrigation systems or other water-related infrastructure. Almost 80% noted damage to cemeteries (fallen trees and flooding), but only seven mentioned damage to sacred forests or specific trees. Most respondents also mentioned damage to fish stocks in the rivers and loss of important tree resources (timber, wild fruits, and sources of medicine). The most significant long-term impacts were expected from loss of crops and soil fertility (42%), damage to dwellings (31%), loss of domestic animals (19%), and destruction of fruit trees (13%).

Almost all interviewees said they had received emergency aid from the government, although six respondents named the actual source as the WFP. The aid consisted of basic groceries, and in a few cases also maize seeds. In addition to the government, emergency aid was also received from institutions linked to the PA, either CNP management (21% of respondents), MICAIA (50%), or the World Bank project (21%). The aid consisted mainly of seeds (85%) and agricultural implements (67%), but a few respondents had also received beehives, school supplies, food, or hygiene products.

In terms of nature conservation, the main threat caused by the cyclone arises from deforestation to open up new agricultural fields mainly in the BZ, but in some cases inside the PA. Although 42% of the respondents said they continue cultivating the same fields, 27% planned to open new fields to compensate for the losses. Only 23% intended to resort to alternative livelihoods, such as commerce or temporary work outside. The strategies to cope with future risk of flooding were also conflicting. Whereas representatives of local government administration, following the objective to consolidate settlements, referred to plans to resettle those from the worst flooded areas (interviews, March 2021), some interviewees insisted on replanting in the fertile fields along the rivers, whereas others planned to intensify cultivation on the less flood-prone areas higher up on their current lands. Only one respondent intended to move to a safer area. Previous experience from flood resettlement projects has been controversial (see e.g. Arnall, 2014), and in the interviews we did prior to the disaster most respondents expressed strong reluctance to move from their current homesteads (interviews, May 2018). MICAIA, on the other hand, prepared a small project for replanting forests destroyed by TC Idai, but managed to get only USD 660 in donations (MICAIA Foundation, no date).

## Discussion and conclusions

The financial resources available to a PA are the key factor in its ability to overcome the impact of major natural disasters, such as cyclones or epidemics. Without a large and long-term secured source, even a PA with access to abundant upmarket tourism revenue is vulnerable to such disasters. GNP is a prime example of such a fortunate situation: with a strong resource base it was able to rapidly fix the damages caused by TC Idai, and has been able to withstand the disturbance caused by regional insecurity and even alleviate the recent pandemic by providing health equipment and training (Rego, 2020). CNP is, on the other hand, in a much more vulnerable position. It continues to be dependent on fixed-term external project funding for the conservation and development activities, and due to its natural conditions and geographical location it has not been able to attract large numbers of tourists. Whereas its long-term sources of income, the eco-lodge and the honey cooperative, are based on active community participation, they continue to struggle with financial sustainability (Virtanen, 2020). Tourism is a challenging entry-level business for rural communities with little previous experience (Kiss, 2004), and both activities are particularly vulnerable to natural disasters.

As noted above, aside from material consequences, disaster relief can also change existing power relations (Matos & Ndapassoa, 2020). Due to its strong resource base and international connections, GNP was able to take a leading role in provision of emergency aid and the subsequent reconstruction process. This is likely to have improved its stature among the local population, who already benefit from various development projects. While the Chimanimani area benefited from relief provided by the government and numerous NGOs, inside the BZ it was MICAIA that gained most credits – albeit on a more limited scale than the Gorongosa Project. The low level of sustainability of the activities that support conservation in CNP compels the population to depend on consumptive use of forest-based resources. In the post-disaster context, many households have pursued recovery by felling timber for rebuilding and opening new fields in the forest, whereas seeking non-consumptive sources of income has been less common.

Investment for post-disaster reconstruction by the government (funded largely by international donors) has increased significantly in both areas. This has helped to restore transport connections to PAs, as well as created some job and business opportunities for local households. Some of the post-disaster rehabilitation initiatives in Chimanimani, such as MICAIA's reforestation project and the resettlement proposal aired by district authorities, could facilitate ecological restoration directly or indirectly. Especially the latter is likely to be contested and can lead to long-lasting land conflicts in the resettlement sites (Arnall, 2014). As the local population often does not differentiate between different government authorities, unpopular initiatives, such as possible forced relocation, are likely to undermine the gains achieved by CNP administration through its participative approach.

## Notes

1 The lodge is actually situated in one of three forest reserves inside the BZ. However, this category does not exist in the new conservation legislation (Ghiurghi et al., 2010), and in fact all three reserves have suffered extensive transformation to agricultural land (Müller et al., 2005).

2 Delimitation of community lands, a category of communal tenure established in the 1997 Land Law, is a process defined in a Technical Annex of the 1998 Land Law Regulations.

## References

Adams, W., & Hulme, D. (2001). Conservation & community. In D. Hulme & M. Murphree (Eds.), *African wildlife & livelihoods: The promise and performance of community conservation* (pp. 9–23). Oxford: James Currey.

Administração Nacional das Áreas de Conservação (ANAC). (2015). *Strategic plan for the national administration of conservation areas, 2015–2024*. Maputo: ANAC.

Arnall, A. (2014). A climate of control: Flooding, displacement and planned resettlement in the Lower Zambezi River valley, Mozambique. *The Geographical Journal, 180*(2), 141–150. doi: 10.1111/geoj.12036

Comitato Internazionale per lo Sviluppo dei Popoli (CISP). (2019). *Distribution of agricultural kits & assessment following IDAI cyclone*. Manica Province: Mozambico. https://www.humanitarianresponse.info/en/operations/mozambique/document/distribution-agricultural-kits-assessment-following-idai-cyclone. [Accessed on 6 January 2021].

Dondeyne, S., Kaarhus, R., & Allison, G. (2012). Nature conservation, rural development and ecotourism in central Mozambique: Which space do local communities get? In I. Convery, G. Corsane & P. Davis (Eds.), *Making sense of place: Multidisciplinary perspectives* (pp. 291–301). Woodbridge: Boydell Press.

Fitchett, J., & Grab, S. (2014). A 66-year tropical cyclone record for south-east Africa:temporal trends in a global context. *International Journal of Climatology, 34*(13), 3604–3615. doi: 10.1002/joc.3932

Genç, R. (2018). Catastrophe of environment: The impact of natural disaster on tourism industry. *Journal of Tourism & Adventure, 1*(1), 86–94. doi: 10.3126/jota.v1i1.22753

Ghiurghi, A., Dondeyne, S., & Bannerman, J. (2010). *Chimanimani National Reserve management plan, Vol. I-II*. Rome: Agriconsulting.

Gorongosa Project. (2017–2020). *Gorongosa National Park highlights, annual reports 2017–2020*. Beira: Gorongosa Project.

Government of Mozambique (GoM). (2018). *Nature-based tourism 2018*. Maputo: GoM.

Government of Mozambique (GoM). (2019). *Mozambique Cyclone Idai: Post disaster needs assessment*. Maputo: Post-Cyclone Idai Cabinet for Reconstruction.

Instituto Nacional de Gestão de Calamidades (INGC). (2019). Sofala Province: Gorongosa District Profile, 19/04/2019. https://reliefweb.int/sites/reliefweb.int/files/resources/MOZ_MRA_Gorongosa_Profile_19042019.pdf. [Accessed on 6 January 2021].

International Organization for Migration (IOM) Mozambique. (2021). Flash report: Tropical storm Chalane, 3 January 2021. https://fscluster.org/sites/default/files/documents/iom_mozambique_flash_report_-_tropical_storm_chalane_sofala_and_manica_provinces_-_jan_2021.pdf. [Accessed on 6 January 2021].

Jacobs, C. (2010). Navigating through a landscape of powers or getting lost on Mount Gorongosa. *The Journal of Legal Pluralism an Unofficial Law, 42*, 81–108. doi:10.1080/07329113.2010.10756643

Kingman, A. (2010). Joint venture ecotourism business in Mozambique, In L. Cotula & R. Leonard (Eds.), *Alternatives to land acquisitions: Agricultural investment and collaborative business models* (pp. 41–51). London: IIED.

Kiss, A. (2004). Is community-based ecotourism a good use of biodiversity conservation funds? *Trends in Ecology and Evolution, 19*(5), 232–237. doi: 10.1016/j.tree.2004.03.010

Krüger, O. (2005). The role of ecotourism in conservation: panacea or Pandora's box? *Biodiversity and Conservation, 14*, 579–600. doi: 10.1007/s10531-004-3917-4

Lendelvo, S., Pinto, M., & Sullivan, S. (2020). A perfect storm? The impact of COVID-19 on community-based conservation in Namibia. *Namibian Journal of Environment, 4*, 1–15.

Matos, P., & Ndapassoa, A. (2020). Cyclone Idai and humanitarian aid challenges in Mozambique. *Veredas do Direito, 17*, 161–181. doi: 10.18623/rvd.v17i38.1819

Matyas, C., & Silva, J. (2013). Extreme weather and economic well-being in rural Mozambique. *Natural Hazards, 66*, 31–49. doi: 10.1007/s11069-011-0064-6

Mawren, D., Hermes, J., & Reason, C. (2020). Exceptional Tropical Cyclone Kenneth in the Far Northern Mozambique Channel and Ocean Eddy Influences. *Geophysical Research Letters, 47*, e2020GL088715. doi: 10.1029/2020GL088715

Meldrum, A. (2019). Thousands in Mozambique rebuild after devastating cyclones. Associated Press, 26 August 2019. https://abcnews.go.com/International/wireStory/thousands-mozambique-rebuild-devastating-cyclones-65190730. [Accessed on 6 January 2021].

MICAIA Foundation. (n.d.). Help 5 communities restore forests in Mozambique. https://www.globalgiving.org/projects/help-restore-forests-in-mozambique. [Accessed on 16 March 2021].

Ministry of Tourism (MIT). (2010). *Strategy and action plan for the conservation and management of elephants in Mozambique, 2010–2015.* Maputo: National Directorate of Conservation Areas.

Morley, R., & Convery, I. (2014). Restoring Gorongosa: Some personal reflections. In I. Convery, G. Corsane, & P. Davis (Eds.), *Displaced heritage: Responses to disaster, trauma and loss* (pp. 129–141). Woodbridge: Boydell Press.

Müller, T., Sitoe, A., & Mabunda, R. (2005). Assessment of the forest reserve network in Mozambique. https://cf.tfcg.org.pubs/FRNetwork_M2Q.pdf. [Accessed on 18 December 2020].

Office for the Coordination of Humanitarian Affairs (OCHA). (2019). Cyclone Idai snapshot (as of 26 March 2019). https://reliefweb.int/sites/reliefweb.int/files/resources/SA_Cyclone_and_Flooding_Snapshot_26032019.pdf. [Accessed on 18 December 2020].

Regalia, S. (2017). *The resurgence of conflict in Mozambique: Ghosts from the past and brakes to peaceful democracy.* Paris: IFRI.

Rego, G. (2020). How Gorongosa National Park battles Covid-19 and not only. https://plataformamedia.com/en/2020/09/10/how-gorongosa-national-park-battles-covid-19-and-not-only/. [Accessed on 14 June 2021].

Rylance, A. (2017). Estimating tourism's contribution to conservation area financing in Mozambique. *Tourism and Hospitality Research, 17*(1), 24–33. doi:10.1177/1467358415613119

Silva, J., & Khatiwada, L. (2014). Transforming conservation into cash? Nature tourism in southern Africa. *Africa Today, 61*(1), 17–45. doi: 10.1353/at.2014.0033

Soto, B. (2011). Protected areas in Mozambique. In H. Suich, & B. Child (Eds.), *Evolution and innovation in wildlife conservation* (pp. 85–100). London: Earthscan.

United Nations Development Programme (UNDP). (2010). *Sustainable financing of the protected area system in Mozambique.* UNDP Project Document.

Vidya, P., Ravichandran, M., Murtugudde, R., Subeesh, M., Sourav Chatterjee, S., Neetu, S., & Nuncio, M. (2021). Increased cyclone destruction potential in the Southern Indian Ocean. *Environmental Research Letters, 16*(1), 1–21, 014027. doi: 10.1088/1748-9326/abceed

Virtanen, P. (2005). Community-based natural resource management in Mozambique: A critical review of the concept's applicability at local level. *Sustainable Development, 13*(1), 1–12. doi:10.1002/sd.240

Virtanen, P. (2020). Making conservation sustainable under unfavourable conditions: the case of Chimanimani National Reserve, Mozambique. *Development in Practice, 30*(3), 320–331. doi: 10.1080/09614524.2019.1682521

Walker, M. (2015). Producing Gorongosa: Space and environmental policies of degradation in Mozambique. *Conservation and Society, 13*(2), 129–140. doi: 10.4103/0972-4923.164192

Walters, G., Mair, J., & Ritchie, B. (2015). Understanding the tourist's response to natural disasters: The case of the 2011 Queensland floods. *Journal of Vacation Marketing, 21*(1), 101–113. doi:10.1177/1356766714528933

Wells, M. (1992). Biodiversity conservation, affluence and poverty: Mismatched costs and benefits and efforts to remedy them. *Ambio, 21*(3), 237–243.

Yu, P., Johannessen, J., Yan, X-H., Geng, X., Zhong, X., & Zhu, L. (2019). A study of the intensity of tropical cyclone Idai using dual-polarization Sentinel-1 data. *Remote Sensing, 11*(23), 2837. doi: 10.3390/rs11232837

Zhang, J., Connor, T., Yang, H., Ouyang, Z., Li, S., & Liu, J. (2018). Complex effects of natural disasters on protected areas through altering telecouplings. *Ecology and Society, 23*(3), 17. doi: 10.5751/ES-10238-230317

# 6 The challenges and prospects of community-based tourism after Zimbabwe's land reform programme in the Midlands Province

*Zibanai Zhou and Dzingai Kennedy Nyahunzvi*

## Introduction

Access to land has always been a highly contested issue in Africa in general and Zimbabwe in particular (Chavunduka & Bromley, 2010; Masiiwa, 2004; Quan et al., 2004). While land reforms have largely been pushed into the limelight due to pressure caused by indigenous people worldwide, land reform programmes largely came to the national and international agenda in a major way in the post–World War II period (Sharma & Jha, 2016; De Villiers, 2003). Land reform programmes were established against the backdrop of a global campaign against poverty and as a response to the historically skewed distribution of land (Kodir, 2018; UN, 2015; Quan et al., 2004). De Villiers (2003) conceded that land is one of the most difficult domestic policy issues in many jurisdictions. In addition, Quan et al. (2004) and Degeorges and Reilly (2007) posit that people in Africa are now increasingly competing to get access to arable land, hence land conflicts are becoming more common.

A thorough review of the Zimbabwean literature showed that tourism and land reform debates revolve around property rights issues; change of land use conflict; and destination perception issues associated with violent land reform programmes and restitution (Moyo, 2000; Besley & Burgess, 2000; Marongwe, 2002; De Villiers, 2003). In addition, lawsuits, land reform benefits, successes and failures, productivity, community livelihood, and empowerment have dominated land reform discourses (Chavunduka & Bromley, 2010; Wolmer et al., 2004; Scoones et al., 2010; Cliffe et al., 2011; Matanda, 2012). However, there has not been much scholarly focus on community-based tourism (CBT) projects, particularly in Zimbabwe's Midlands province.

Tourism is driving economies globally (UNWTO, 2019; Adeola et al., 2018; WTTC, 2018). The sector's prowess in generating employment, stimulating infrastructural development, and promoting poverty alleviation among a host of other favourable socioeconomic spin-offs in different communities has resulted in many countries putting tourism at the forefront of their policy agenda (Zhou, 2019; 2020; Kim et al., 2016; Christie et al.,

DOI: 10.4324/9781003188902-8

2014; Sharpley, 2014). While tourism's efficacy as a catalyst to communities' socioeconomic transformation is glorified by global institutions, the industry's role in poverty alleviation remains a contentious issue (Dzvimbo et al., 2018; Gandiwa et al., 2013).

Zimbabwe's economy is anchored in agriculture and supported by mining and tourism (Zhou, 2018). Tourism contributes an estimated 12 per cent of the country's gross domestic product (GDP) (MOTHI, 2017; ZTA, 2018). Zimbabwe's tourism industry experienced sustained growth since 1980, but was interrupted by several challenges in the 1990s. One of the challenges to beset the sector was the 2000 Fast Track Land Reform Programme (hereinafter, 2000 FTLRP), sanctioned by the Government of Zimbabwe (GoZ), supposedly undertaken to give land back to the Black people. While Mkono (2012) and Manwa (2007) noted the lacklustre performance of Zimbabwe's mainstream tourism industry at the national level – partly attributed to the 2000 FTLRP – the land reform-linked challenges at a micro level, specifically tourism subsectors like CBT, have rarely been empirically examined. This chapter therefore seeks to examine the 2000 FTLRP-induced challenges and prospects for CBT in the Midlands province after the 2000 FTLRP.

The Midlands province has many defunct CBT projects. The present chapter is significant given Matondi's (2012, p. 12) observation that "many debates about Zimbabwe's land reform were happening at the national and international level yet the impact of that land reform was being felt more intensely at the local level"; hence, the choice of the Midlands province as a case study. In addition, Abel et al. (2013, p. i) bemoaned a "... lack of inter-governmental policy coordination as different [Zimbabwean] government institutions promulgate policies and regulations without considerations of their impacts on other sectors hence impacting negatively on the tourism sector". In support, Mandizadza et al. (2014) acknowledge there is still sparse attention on CBT as policy debates on land reform tend to either downplay or outright ignore the impact of land reform on rural tourism enterprises. Most studies around tourism dynamics after the 2000 FTLRP, such as those by Wolmer et al. (2004) and Scoones et al. (2010), seem to be largely national in outlook, with broad findings that make limited reference to specific CBT enterprises. In light of this, there is a need for site-specific studies that examine the intersection of land reform programmes and CBT.

The dynamics of land reform in Zimbabwe on the agrarian space prior to 2000 and its general implications on the country's agro-driven economy have been extensively examined (Sadomba, 2011; Cliffe, 2000; Moyo, 1995b). However, these studies had their foci predominantly on productivity and food security, not the tourism sector. The intersection of land reform and CBT has rarely been examined at a micro level in the Zimbabwean tourism discourse, with studies such as Wolmer et al. (2004), Manwa (2007), Mkono (2010), and Mkono (2012) mentioning land reform in passing. The current chapter is situated in the property rights, rule of law, and land use conflict strands of the land reform discourses. It seeks to contribute to these broad strands of land reform scholarly debates in the context of Zimbabwe's Midlands province, where such issues have not received attention after the 2000 FTLRP at the CBT subsector level. Therefore, the chapter may inform policymakers about system-wide tourism challenges induced by land reform. It may also provide government departments with fresh insights on strategies that can be implemented to reduce conflict in two different sectors of the economy over the use of land resources. Finally, land administrators and policymakers may be better equipped to enact land reform programmes appropriate for their contexts.

By unravelling the challenges and prospects of CBT in land-reformed spaces, the chapter seeks to update the works of Dinda (2016), Mandizadza et al. (2014), Nyahunzvi (2014), and Cliffe (2000). In addition, despite Borras et al. (2021), Hall (2013), and Akram-Lodhi and Kay (2010) acknowledging a growing stream of research focusing on land reform in the economic sphere of agriculture, land reform-induced challenges related to CBT largely remain invisible to scholarly scrutiny.

The tourism industry in Zimbabwe is framed as a low-hanging fruit capable of accelerating economic development. This was confirmed by a Ministry of Climate, Environment, and Tourism and Hospitality Industry (MOTHI) (2017) study, which established there is an increasing consensus among government arms and policymakers on the importance of tourism as a strategic sector in the national economy. A case in point is the Ministry of Finance and Economic Development, which cited tourism as a strategic sector, vital in achieving the country's Vision 2030 economic development agenda. Vision 2030 seeks to help the country attain an upper middle-income status by 2030 by leveraging agriculture, mining, and tourism. Consequently, the MOTHI (2017) set an ambitious target of welcoming five million tourists, who would generate 5 billion USD in the next five years, emphasising the significance and policymakers' recognition of the tourism sector in Zimbabwe's economic growth trajectory. Given that Zimbabwe's economy is agro-based, the 2000 FTLRP becomes even more significant in the country's economic landscape as it intersects with the tourism industry.

Tourism is one of the most sensitive sectors that can be easily affected by land reform (Honggang et al., 2017). Land reform directly impacts tourism's sensitive property rights issues, the rule of law, and the subdivision of land meant for wildlife sanctuaries (Quan et al., 2004). Subdividing land for commercial enterprising and agriculture can also cause previous landowners to resort to the legal system for protection. This may lead to divesture in the sector and increase poaching, as the tourism and agriculture arenas compete for the same finite land resource.

Therefore, understanding the land reform-induced challenges affecting CBT neatly fits into the current GoZ's narrative of attaining an upper middle-income economy by 2030. To this end, the chapter's objectives are to establish land reform–related challenges confronting CBT in the Midlands province. The future prospects of CBT in land-reformed communities are also determined, and a set of recommendations to inform land reform and tourism development policymakers is provided. The next section presents more details on the 2000 FTLRP and elaborates on the CBT concept as practised in Zimbabwe.

## Fast track land reform programme (2000 FTLRP) in Zimbabwe

Zimbabwe instituted radical land reform in 2000, backed by veterans of the liberation struggle. Zikhali (2010) posits that Zimbabwe inherited a racially skewed agricultural land ownership pattern at independence in 1980. Moreover, Rukuni et al. (2006) argue that the land issue in Zimbabwe dates to the colonial era and consequent social imbalances, particularly the Land Apportionment Act of 1930, that contributed to the outbreak of the war of liberation.

After independence, resettled land could only be acquired on a willing-buyer willing-seller basis, with the government paying the full market price for the land and competing for it with other buyers on the open market (Rukuni et al., 2006; Mutepfa et al., 1998). Through an amendment to section 16A of the Zimbabwean constitution, enabling it to recognise the colonial dispossession of land from Zimbabweans, the government gained ownership of land through the compulsory acquisition of agricultural land for resettlement (Chimbisa et al., 2010).

The 2000 FTLRP entailed the acquisition and subdivision of mainly large-scale White-owned commercial farms and their subsequent redistribution to supposedly Black subsistence farmers – mostly veterans of the armed liberation struggle of the 1960s and 70s (Moyo, 1995a; Marongwe, 2002). However, land audit results suggest the ruling ZANU (PF) elites benefited more from the land reform programme at the expense of ordinary people. Sadomba (2011) observed that structurally, the landmark 2000 FTLRP caused a seismic shift in the Zimbabwean tourism landscape, with adverse effects across many economic sectors. The effects on tourism included constrained capacity utilisation, a drop in tourist arrivals and revenue, the issuance of travel advisories, and bad publicity (Mkono, 2012).

There seems to be scholarly convergence that land reform is a complicated affair, confronted by the competing needs of satisfying diverse expectations on land use options by different actors (Kamuti, 2018; Musavengane & Simatele, 2016). In the context of Zimbabwe, the land reform issue is deeply rooted in the displacement of local native people from their ancestral land during colonisation. However, while it appears imperative for emergent economies to undertake land reform, an emerging stream of literature – for example, Manwa (2007), Degeorges and Reilly (2007) – seems to caution that land reform could pose permanent harm to thriving economic sectors if it is implemented without due regard for the tenets of law, justice, and equity.

Zimbabwe's land reform was not well received by the international community but rather seen as a fundamental breach of human rights. Compared to

Zimbabwe, most Southern Africa Development Community (SADC) countries took a gradual land reform path. For instance, the Namibian government is abiding by the willing-buyer willing-seller approach (Rukuni et al., 2006). Furthermore, South Africa's land reform is based on three main pillars, namely the restoration of rights to ancestral land, acquisition of land, and securing tenure to land (De Villiers, 2003). Further afield, China's land reform recalibrated the use of land, improved the governance of the land, and reduced the government's dependence on revenue from land sales. China's land policy illustrated that tenure security, property rights, and market mechanism are important prerequisites before undertaking a land reform programme. Finally, land reform in India was anchored on equity and premised on four main principles: abolishing intermediaries, tenancy regulation, a ceiling on land holdings, and commoditisation of disparate land holdings (Besley & Burgess, 2000). It has been suggested that a poorly thought-out land reform plan could damage a country's international image, and may cause food insecurity (Moyo, 1995a; Selby, 2006; Cliffe et al., 2011). Additional lessons learnt from other countries which have implemented land reform policies are that a lack of resources for compensation, limited capacity in implementing agencies, institutional constraints, and an increase in land prices can harm the implementation of land reform programmes (Van Vlier, 2017; Quizon, 2012; Larsi et al., 2004). Therefore, it is critical that all key stakeholders are involved to ensure land reform is not pursued merely on the basis of political ideology and expediency, as the economic and social costs will outstrip the perceived benefits of radical land acquisition (De Villiers, 2003).

Zimbabwe's land reform programme had wide ramifications for CBT. As a concept, CBT is expansive and embraces a range of tourism products such as local culture and folklore, gastronomy, and traditional handcrafts (Gohori & van der Merwe, 2020). Lucchetti and Font (2013) view CBT as tourism that involves community participation and aims to generate benefits for local communities in the developing world by allowing tourists to visit communities and learn about their culture and the local environment. Therefore, CBT can be construed as involving grassroots empowerment as it seeks to develop the industry in harmony with the needs and aspirations of host communities (Mtapuri & Giampiccoli, 2016; Godwin et al., 2014; Synman, 2012; Kontogeorgopoulos, 2005; Jones, 2005). The nature of CBT is that it takes place in communities where economic opportunities are somewhat limited; these communities are often prime targets for land reform (Gohori & van de Merwe, 2020; MOTHI, 2017).

One major feature of tourism development in Zimbabwe has been its inclination towards small-scale, non-consumptive CBT, which can promote regional development and poverty reduction (Gohori & van der Merwe, 2020). Saarinen (2010) observed that CBT is the most pursued strategy used to ensure the active participation of local communities in the broad area of tourism. The CBT concept entails a scenario where local people have substantial control and are involved in its development and management, and a major portion of the benefits remain with the community. Like in any other developing country, the GoZ recognises the importance of CBT, as shown by their national tourism policy. It aims to empower host communities in managing their own tourism projects and maximise the benefits (Gohori & van der Merwe, 2020; Scheyvens & Monsen, 2008). Salazar (2012) and Robinson and Wiltshier (2011) argue that communities where the impacts of tourism are most felt should get the most benefits; hence, CBT aims to create a more sustainable tourism industry focusing on the host communities in terms of planning and maintaining tourism activities.

## Study context

Located at the heart of Zimbabwe, the Midlands province is one of the largest provinces in Zimbabwe, and its economic activity is mainly mining and cattle ranching. It is also the mineral hub of the country, with 18 mined minerals. The province is considered generally dry, and CBT is spread throughout the region. The Midlands province is a significant study area because it has several defunct CBT operators (MOTHI, 2017). The Midlands province is predominantly rural, with very limited economic activities. Such contexts provide an appropriate setting in which CBT has maximum socioeconomic impact and significance (Gohori & van der Merwe, 2020). The region's total population of 1.6 million people, according to the 2012 census, is made up of Tonga, Ndebele, Karanga, Venda, and Sotho speaking communities.

## Methods

A qualitative research approach involving document analysis was employed to examine the challenges and prospects of CBT in land-reformed contexts due to its unobtrusive and relatively inexpensive nature. Qualitative research methods are deemed to provide a better understanding of certain phenomena under consideration than traditional quantitative methods (Bloomberg & Volpe, 2008). Specifically, data were gleaned from the government's provincial documents, Zimbabwe Tourism Authority (ZTA) publications, the Zimbabwe Business Council for Tourism (ZBCT) periodicals, and research articles on Zimbabwe's land reform programme. Interviews were also conducted with officials from the provincial land offices, Ministry of Land and Resettlement, ZTA, CBT operators, and staff from CBT in order to understand the challenges they were facing as a result of the 2000 FTLRP. The identified documents were examined and interpreted to gain an understanding of the possible CBT challenges created by land reform.

Face-to-face interviews, coupled with personal observations and informal conversations with CBT operators whose land was expropriated, were used. The questions posed in the interviews sought to establish the CBT challenges induced by the 2000 FTLRP, the number of CBT operators affected, prospects for CBT post land reform, communities' lost livelihood, land use conflict induced by the 2000 FTLRP, compensation issues, and land rights violations, among others. In accordance with Mullan et al.'s (2011) work, the face-to-face interviews were conducted directly without interference from local officials, thus ensuring the completeness and accuracy of the data. Semi-structured face-to-face interviews were used on the strength of their ability to yield a better understanding of participants' thinking than overly structured interviews (Mullan et al., 2011). The interviews were then augmented by non-participant observations and informal conversations.

The sample size encompassed government officials, traditional leaders, the ZTA local regional office and community residents. Overall, 25 interviews were conducted. Field notes were taken each day, and these notes were subsequently analysed for key themes (Bernard, 2017). The raw data underwent thematic analysis, a systematic technique of identifying, analysing, and constructing patterns of data and classifying them into themes (Clarke & Braun, 2017).

The CBT communities were selected with the help of the local provincial land resource bureaus, then the CBT proprietors were selected through snowball sampling (Tracy, 2013). CBT and land reform stakeholders were identified from a database of functional CBT operators in the Midlands province, obtained from the ZTA.

## Findings

The land reform-induced challenges for CBT projects were themed: withdrawal of CBT funding, disruption and demise of CBT activities, exposing the CBT sector to rent-seeking actors, looting of CBT infrastructure, and undermining CBT community peace.

### *a) Withdrawal of CBT funding*

Results showed that foreign investors and donors were hesitant to support CBT ventures following the disruptions and uncertainty created by the 2000 FTLRP. For example, one CBT operator had its funding withdrawn after disruptions and looting of property surged during the 2000 FTLRP. Field evidence further showed that a number of traditional donors had withdrawn their support, citing uncertainty surrounding the future of CBT as their reason. As one participant said:

> Within a year into the land reform programme, Midlands province CBTs lost donor support from 5 key donors. This was a sad development because these CBT enterprises were substantially improving communities' livelihoods. Diplomatic efforts by the regulatory authority lobbying for the donors to reconsider their decisions did not bear any fruit.
>
> (National tourism regulatory body, Participant 20, Male, 47, 20 March 2021 interview).

Another representative of the Campfire Association of Zimbabwe expressed similar sentiments. She confirmed that most of their members lost about 90 per cent of budgetary support since land reform was initiated. This finding seems to suggest that the national re-engagement drive spearheaded by the Ministry of Foreign Affairs and International Trade, together with the ZTA, appears not to have made significant progress in unlocking much-needed funding for CBT ventures. According to Participant 5, a female local community resident, some CBT operators withdrew their support:

> Out of frustration, the owners of Sebakwe and Cheetah ne Shamwari parks pulled out and secured land in neighbouring Zambia. They have since relocated to Zambia, leaving behind former employees without income.
>
> (Participant 5, Female, 67, 20 March 2021 interviews).

Of serious concern was the fact that CBT operators operated on a joint venture basis with local communities. By the time CBT proprietors left, local communities had not yet reached a stage where they had the capacity, resources, and technical know-how to run the projects. Community capacity building and a deliberate skills transfer programme would have been the ideal route to ensure the future sustainability of such projects in the absence of the benefactors. Given that land reform was spontaneous, it seems there was no well-thought-out strategy to harness and transfer technical know-how to community residents, which could have ensured the long-term sustainability of CBT ventures.

***b) Disruption and demise of CBT activities***

The majority of participants (95%) were of the view that land reform induced a series of endless disputes and lawsuits. This gave the impression that the land reform process would never be finalised, thereby severely curtailing CBT operations. Facing incessant disruptions, CBT proprietors turned to the legal system for protection. (Participant 18, March 2021, personal interview), a local male resident, said:

> There are several court cases in which the former owner of this land is determined to return. No business is taking place here until the court cases have been finalised. We are told the owner even went to as far as filing a court appeal with some international court. Investment has since dried up.

Given the slow pace of the justice delivery system in Zimbabwe, it takes an inordinate amount of time before court judgements are pronounced, hence there is no closure. The publicity associated with such court cases is further damaging the reputation of Zimbabwe's CBT sector. Overall, the publicity of land reform cases and the alleged compromised judiciary system impacted the international community's perception and confidence in Zimbabwe's sincerity in her re-engagement drive and desire to coexist within the global community of nations. They have also dented the country's commitment to upholding the rule of law. This finding seems to support Wolmer et al.'s (2004) view that Zimbabwe's 2000 FTLRP gained global notoriety and controversy.

Interviews further revealed that land reform caused not only abrupt termination of leases but also the revoking of operating permits. Participant 16 (personal interview, 2021), a former CBT proprietor who was now in the trucking industry, said:

> My lease still has some 15 more years running yet I got a letter of termination and was forcibly evicted from the premises.

The above finding resonates with Smith's (2003) assertion that tenure security influences greater productivity as land tenure becomes more secure and individualised. The participants reported continuous threats and incessant disruption to CBT activities by ruling party activists. Indeed, some participants indicated that areas surrounding CBT operations in the Midlands province were at one time declared 'no-go' areas under the de facto control of youths affiliated with the ruling party. Residents added that the eviction of former owners made tourists stop visiting the park. As attested to by Participant 12 (personal interviews, 2021), security officer at one of the CBT ventures:

> Visitors for CBT are no longer coming given the violence and threats made to owners. So there is no more cash flow and other CBT nationally have since stopped operating.

A visit to the local police station also confirmed a spike in intermittent conflicts around CBT operators within the resettled areas. In addition, the number of violent and assault cases reported seemed to be increasing. One participant, a retired civil servant, made the telling observation that:

> The brutal truth is that CBT is dead. Land reform authored its demise.

These sentiments align with Mkono's (2012) view that the adverse impact of conflict on land reform seems to be far-reaching and often results in a reduction in tourist arrivals. This phenomenon is either caused by negative travel advisories, by tourists' concerns about safety and risk, or by. Furthermore, the above seems to give credence to Degeorges and Reilly's (2007) claim that land reform sent the economy into a tailspin. In the final analysis, and based on field evidence, it can be concluded that land reform placed severe strain on the tourism sector, as similarly observed by Manwa (2007).

### *c) Exposing the CBT sector to rent-seeking actors*

Most participants reported that the land reform saw rampant abuse of one's race and political affiliation. These elements were used to extract money from CBT proprietors whose operations were affected by the land reform programme. The participants claimed there was manipulation and extortion through demands for 'protection fees' or 'mediation fees' by some ruling party activists. To quote Participant 11 (personal interviews, March 2021), a representative of the civic society leadership:

> The other nearby CBT project was taken over by a well-known ruling party activist and the situation at the CBT is not pleasing. All workers were fired, all the donor funds were looted and monies directed to funding lavish parties and weddings.

It is also worth noting that personal observations confirmed the sorry state of Sebakwe and Cheetah neShamwari CBT sanctuary parks, with all operations having stopped.

### *d) Looting of CBT infrastructure*

Several participants observed that the land reform programme resulted in the rampant looting of infrastructure, like perimeter fences, poles, razor wire, running down facilities, poaching wild animals, firewood, and fish harvesting. Personal observations confirmed the looting in and around the five CBT sites. The finding supports Scheyvens and Monsen's (2008) stance that if people are ignorant or have little knowledge regarding the direct potential benefits likely to flow from a tourism project, they lack attachment, resulting in vandalism and wanton destruction of millions of financial resources sunk in such investments. Participant 02 (personal interviews, 2021), a former park supervisor, said:

> People are looting anything they could lay their hands on. At this rate, 2–3 years down the line you would not find a single wild animal in this sanctuary. The previous owner of this sanctuary reported many times to the police, however, the officer in charge reportedly told him that the issue was political and could be best handled by the political leadership in the area.

Another participant, Participant 10 (personal interview, March 2021), also explained:

> Most boreholes have been vandalised, a transformer and the solar system were stolen. Land reform caused the community to miss out the many positive benefits which it used to get from the sanctuary.

Still another community resident, Participant 05 (personal interview, 2021), said:

> People from resettled communities just needed game meat and firewood. There is a thriving fish market in Kwekwe, where illegally harvested fish

> from the water reservoir is sold to artisanal gold panners. This is investment that has gone to waste out of our own making. This venture used to bring in foreign currency.

From the above sentiments, it is evident that the land reform-induced eviction of CBT proprietors saw the rapid deterioration of most CBT businesses.

### *e) Undermining CBT community peace*

According to participants, land reform seems to have seriously undermined the atmosphere of goodwill and coexistence within CBT neighbourhoods by stoking antagonism and civil strife, thus creating hostility between CBT proprietors and the newly resettled farmers. This was evident at Gokwe's Mapfungautsi forest and mountain range, Cheetah ne Shamwari park, Sebakwe recreational park, and the areas surrounding Naletale ruins. In these areas, there was outright antagonism between local community residents and former owners.

In support, Participant 14 (personal interview, 2021), a representative of the local community's traditional leadership, said:

> There is tension within the community. There was a time when some youths used to have day and night vigils threatening the CBT owners to cede the control of the project or leave. That is when we intervened as the local community leadership; sadly we could not salvage the situation as it turned political.

Similar views were also expressed by the representatives from the Ministry of Lands and Resettlement and the community's neighbourhood watch committee. The above finding is supported by Kodir and Mushoffa (2017) and Quizon (2012), who warned that in some instances, land acquisitions make the poorer sections of society more vulnerable, exacerbates instability and inequalities, and creates conflict among stakeholders. These claims seem to suggest that the intersection of tourism and land reform in the context of Zimbabwe's Midlands province weakens the long-held perspective that tourism unifies people from different social classes and cultures, as asserted by Musavengane and Leonard (2019). Interview narratives showed that instead of fostering harmony and social cohesion, land reform compounded mistrust between government and private sector capital.

## Conclusion and recommendations

In conclusion, this chapter has discussed various challenges for CBT caused by land reform in the Midlands province, putting the future prospects of CBT in serious jeopardy. These challenges have practical implications for policymakers and investors.

Going forward, local community residents should ideally be at the centre of tourism development, and government should therefore consider their views before embarking on developmental projects like land reform, which may end up disrupting communities' source of livelihood (Nunkoo & Ramkisson, 2011). The success of any form of tourism hinges on local community residents' buy-in and coexistence with investors in various subsectors of the tourism industry. This is critical for future long-range planning and policy consideration. It is therefore imperative that governments in emergent economies where poverty and social polarisation are significant reflect on possible challenges spawned by land reform on a sensitive tourism subsector like CBT.

Within the Southern Africa region, Zimbabwe's land reform programme could be an eye-opener. This should be understood in the context of the works of Degeorges and Reilly (2007), who warned that if South Africa's and Namibia's land reforms take similar paths, it would not augur well for their economies. Countries contemplating land reform programmes need to be pragmatic, especially in the context of the evolving trend and growing calls for the redistribution of land to Blacks. A case in point is Julius Malema's Economic Freedom Fighters Party (EFF), causing tremors in South Africa's economy given its stance and increasing calls to take over land without compensation. In the future, international best practices should guide the land reform programmes to avoid haphazard, spontaneous, and populist land reform. A well-thought-out approach, anchored on the sustainability of a programme that minimises system shocks to other sectors of the economy, is preferred.

In the context of Zimbabwe's Midlands province, it is evident that government should be much more concerned about empowerment outcomes instead of being fixated on the number of people receiving land. While there is a CBT revitalisation programme at the national level, the snag is that the country's pariah image persists, and donors are not forthcoming. This, in a way, suggests the 'limited prospects' of CBT under the new dispensation.

Instead of having a radical land reform, CBT could be spared and owners encouraged to undertake significant poverty alleviation programmes in immediate localities. This could be achieved, for example, through drilling boreholes and building schools and clinics from profits. It is also possible to allocate a percentage of the CBT sector's proceeds to neighbouring communities.

CBT operators need to practise skills transfer and institute preferential procurement and employment practices. By making local communities suppliers and deliberately employing local people, CBT proprietors would create a win-win situation with local communities that improves relations and cements goodwill. Moreover, CBT lands cannot be subdivided into farms, as some have animals that require large tracts of land.

Instead of viewing tourism as disrupting and undermining agriculture, there are opportunities local communities can leverage through synergies with CBT proprietors. For example, locals can sell artefacts to tourists who visit CBT ventures, and can also seek employment at CBT ventures to earn an income. This could help change perceptions and mend relations in which CBT businesses were misconstrued as disrupting the agriculture agenda of the country. If the above is done, the problems of rampant looting, poaching, and deforestation in land-reformed communities could be reduced.

It is critical that outstanding CBT court cases are fast-tracked so finality can be reached on the land reform programme. At the same time, authorities should expedite the implementation of the land audit, which exposed that the political elites have multiple farms. Such multiple farms and those with limited production should be earmarked for a redistribution programme that allows the continued existence of CBT.

The final recommendation is that the re-engagement drive needs to be accompanied by adherence to rules of law and respecting property rights as a way of unlocking much-needed CBT funding. This could be leveraged upon by expediting the compensation of former owners as proposed by the Finance and Economic Development Ministry.

## References


Abel, S., Nyamadzawo, J., Nyaruwata, S. & Moyo, C. (2013). *Positioning the Zimbabwe tourism sector and growth: Issues and challenges.* Zimbabwe: USAID Strategic Economic Research and Analysis, Zimbabwe-SERA.

Adeola, O., Evans, O. & Hinson, R.E. (2018). Tourism and economic well-being in Africa. *MPRA, 93685*, 11, 37.

Akram-Lodhi, A.H. & Kay, C. (2010). Surveying the agrarian question (Part 1): Understanding foundations, exploring diversity. *The Journal of Peasant Studies, 37*(1), 177–202.

Bernard, H.R. (2017). *Research methods in anthropology. Quantitative and qualitative approaches.* Lanham, MD: Rowman and Littlefield.

Besley, T. & Burgess, R. (2000). Land reform, poverty reduction, and growth: Evidence from India. *Quarterly Journal of Economics, 115*(2), 389–430.

Bloomberg, L. D. & Volpe, M. (2008). *Completing your qualitative dissertation: A roadmap from beginning to end.* London: SAGE. doi: 10.4135/9781452226613.n3.

Borras, S.M., Hall, R., Scoones, I., White, B. & Wolford, W. (2021). Towards a better understanding of global land grabbing. An editorial introduction. *The Journal of Peasant Studies, 39*(2), 237–261.

Chavunduka, C. & Bromley, D.W. (2010). Beyond the crisis in Zimbabwe: Sorting out the land question. *Development Southern Africa, 27*(3), 363–379.

Chimbisa, P., Ruzive, A. & Mandipa, C.T. (2010). The 2000–2004 fast track land reform program and biodiversity issues in the Middle Save conservancy. *Journal for Sustainably Development in Africa, 12*, 6.

Christie, I., Fernandes, E., Messer, I. H. & Twining-Ward, L. (2014). *Tourism in Africa: Harnessing tourism for growth and improved livelihoods* (pp. 1–12). Washington, DC: The World Bank.

Clarke, V. & Braun, V. (2017). Thematic analysis. *The Journal of Positive Psychology, 12*(3), 297–298.

Cliffe, L. (2000). The politics of land reform in Zimbabwe. In Bowyer-Bower, T.A.S & Stoneman, C (Eds.), *Land reform in Zimbabwe: Constraints and prospects* (pp 47–57). Aldershot: Ashgate.

Cliffe, L., Alexander, J., Cousins, B. & Gaidzanwa, R. (2011). An overview of fast track land reform in Zimbabwe: Editorial introduction. *Journal of Peasant Studies, 38*(5), 907–938.

Degeorges, A. & Reilly, B. (2007). Politicisation of the land reform in Zimbabwe: Impacts on wildlife, food production and the economy. *International Journal of Environmental Studies 64*(5), 571–586.

De Villiers, B. (2003). *Land reform: Issues and challenges. A comparative overview of experiences in Zimbabwe, Namibia, South Africa and Australia.* Dunkeld, Johannesburg, South Africa: Konrad-Adenauer-Stiftung.

Dinda, S. (2016). Land acquisition and compensation policy for development activities. *Journal of Land and Rural Studies, 4*(1), 111–18.

Dzvimbo, M.A., Monga, N. & Magijani, F. (2018). The dilemma on reconceptualising natural resources in Campfire areas in Zimbabwe. *Advances in Social Sciences Research Journal, 5*(8), 522–533.

Gandiwa, E., Heitkonig, I.M.A., Lokhurst, A.M., Prins, H.H.T., & Leeuwis, C. (2013). Campfire and human-wildlife conflicts in local communities bordering Gonarezhou national park, Zimbabwe. *Ecology and Society, 18*(94), 7. doi: 10.5751/ES-05817-180407.

Gohori, O. & Van der Merwe, P. (2020). Towards a tourism and community development framework. Am Africa perspective. *Sustainability, 12*, 5305. doi: 10.3390/su12135305.

Goodwin, G., Santilli, R. & Armstrong, R. (2014). Community-based tourism in the developing world. In Goodwin, H. & Font, X. (Eds.), *Progress in responsible tourism 3(1)* (pp. 31–56). Oxford, UK: Goodfellow.

Hall, D. (2013). Primitive accumulation, accumulation by dispossession and the global land grab. *Third World Quarterly, 34*(9), 1582–1604.

Honggang, X., Zhenying, X. & Huang, X. (2017). Land policies, tourism projects and tourism development in Guangdong. *Journal of China Tourism Research, 13*(2), 161–177. doi: 10.1080/19388160.20171350612.

Jones, S. (2005). Community-based tourism: The significance of social capital. *Annals of Tourism Research, 32*, 303–324.

Kamuti, T. (2018). Intricacies of game farming and outstanding land restitution claims in the Gongolo area of Kwa-Zulu-Natal, South Africa. In Brandt, F. & Mkodzongi, G. (Eds.), *Land reform revisited: Democracy, state making and agrarian transition in post-apartheid South Africa.* Boston, MA. Brill.

Kim, N., Song, H. & Pyun, J.H. (2016). The relationship among tourism, poverty and economic development in developing countries: A panel regression analysis. *Tourism Economics, 22*(6), 1174–90.

Kodir, A. (2018). Tourism and development: Land acquisition, achievement of investment and cultural change (case study of tourism industry development in Batu city, Indonesia). *GeoJournal of Tourism and Geosites, 21*(1), 253–265.

Kodir, A. & Mushoffa, I. (2017). Islam, agrarian struggle and natural resources: The exertion of Front Nahdliyin for sovereignty of natural resource struggle towards socio-ecological crisis in Indonesia, Karsa. *Journal of Social and Islamic Culture, 25*(1), 57–89.

Kontogeorgopoulos, N. (2005). Community-based eco-tourism in Phuket and A Phangnga, Thailand. Partial victories and bitter sweet remedies. *Journal of Sustainable Tourism, 1391*, 4–23.

Larsi, W.O., Antwi, A. & Olomonaye, P. (2004). Compulsory land acquisition in Ghana-Policy and praxis. *Land Use Policy, 21*, 115–127.

Lucchetti, V.G. & Font, X. (2013). *Community-based tourism: Critical success factors.* Available online: https://pdfs.semanticscholar.org/dzad/be19582abbe79179f726bdbb61f54b571eb .pdf. Accessed 30 March 2021.

Mandizadza, E.J.R., Bhatasara, S. & Nyamwanza, O. (2014). Land reform programme and rural tourism in Zimbabwe. In Mararike, C.G. (Ed.), *Land: An empowerment asset for Africa. The human factor perspective*. UZ Publications.

Manwa, H. (2007). Is Zimbabwe ready to venture in cultural tourism market? *Development Southern Africa, 24*(3), 465–474. Routledge: Taylor and Francis.

Marongwe, N. (2002). *Conflicts over land and other natural resources in Zimbabwe*. Harare, Zimbabwe: ZERO Regional Environmental Organisation.

Masiiwa, M. (2004). *Post-independence land reform in Zimbabwe: Controversies and impact on the economy*. UZ, Harare: Friedrich Stiftung and Institute of Development Studies.

Matanda, P.B. (2012). *Zimbabwe's fast track land reform*. Sweden: Nordic Africa Institute.

Matondi, O.B. (2012). *Zimbabwe's fast track land reform*. New York: Ruzivo Trust, The Nordic Africa Institute, Zed Books Limited.

Mkono, M. (2010). The future of tourism in Zimbabwe: Towards sustainability. *Tourism Analysis, 15*(3), 387–391.

Mkono, M. (2012). Zimbabwe's tourism woes in the last decade: Hindsight lessons for Africa tourism planners and managers. *Tourism Planning and Development, 9*(2), 205–210.

MOTHI Report (2017). *Community based tourism master plan. Targeting poverty alleviation in the Republic of Zimbabwe*, Final Report. JICA.

Moyo, S. (1995a). *The land question in Zimbabwe*. Harare, Zimbabwe. SAPES Books.

Moyo, S. (2000). The interaction of market and compulsory land acquisition processes with social cohesion in Zimbabwe's land reform. Paper read at the South African Regional Institute for Policy Studies' Annual Colloquium, 24–27 September 2000, Harare.

Mtapuri, O. & Giampiccoli, A. (2016). Towards a comprehensive model of CBT development. *South Africa Geography Journal, 98*, 154–168.

Mullan, K., Grosjean, P. & Kontoleon, A. (2011). Land tenure arrangements and rural-urban migration in China. *World Development, 39*, 123–133.

Musavengane, R. & Leonard, L. (2019). When race and social equity matters in nature conservation in post-apartheid South Africa. *Conservation and Society, 17*(2), 135–146.

Musavengane, R. & Simatele, M.D. (2016). Community-based natural resource management: The role of social capital in collaborative management of tribal resources in Kwa-Zulu-Natal, South Africa. *Development Southern Africa, 33*(6), 806–821. doi: 10.1080/0376835x.2016.1231054.

Mutepfa, F., Marongwe, E., Guveya, E. & Lue Mbizvo, C. (eds.). (1998). *Enhancing land reforms in southern Africa: Case studies on land reform strategies and community-based natural resources management*. Harare, ZERO: IUCN.

Nunkoo, R. & Ramkisson, H. (2011). Developing a community support model for tourism. *Annals of Tourism Research, 3*, 964–988.

Nyahunzvi, D.K. (2014). The resurgence in resource nationalisation and private protected areas: Through the lens of Save Valley Conservancy's indigenisation. *Journal of Nature Conservation, 22*(1), 42–49.

Quan, J., Sui, F.T. & Camilla, T. (2004). Land in Africa. Market asset or secure livelihood? In Proceedings and Summary of Conclusions from the Land in Africa Conference, London, November 8–9.

Quizon, A. (2012). The rush for Asia's farmland: Its impact on land rights and security of the rural poor. *LOK NITI, 18*(1), 7–18.

Robinson, P. & Wiltsher, P. (2011). Community-based tourism. In Robinson, P.P., Heitman, S. & Dieke, D.P. (Eds.), *Research themes for tourism* (pp. 87–99). Oxfordshire, UK: CABI.

Rukuni, M., Tawonezvi, P.C., Eicher, C., Munyuki-Hungwe, M. & Matondi, P. (Eds.) (2006). *Zimbabwe's agricultural revolution revisited*. Harare: University of Zimbabwe Publications.

Saarinen, J. (2010). Local tourism awareness: Community views in Katitura and King Nehale conservancy, Namibia. *Development Southern Africa, 27*(5), 713–724.

Sadomba, W.Z. (2011). *War veterans in Zimbabwe's revolution: Challenging neo-colonial and settler and international capital*. London, Harare: James Currey and Weaver Press.

Salazar, N.B. (2012). Community-based cultural tourism: Issues, threats and opportunities. *Journal of Sustainable Tourism, 20*, 9–22.

Scheyvens, R. & Monsen, J.H. (2008). Tourism and poverty reduction: Issues for small islands. *Tourism Geography, 10*(1), 22–41.

Scoones, I., Marongwe, N., Mavedzenge, B. & Murimbarimba, F. (2010). *Zimbabwe's land reform: Myths and realities*. London, UK: James Currey.

Selby, A. (2006). *Commercial farmers and the state: Interest group policies and land reform in Zimbabwe*. DPhil thesis, Oxford, UK: Oxford University Press.

Sharma, R. & Jha, P.K. (2016). *Land reform experiences. Some lessons from across South Asia*. A research document prepared for the World Forum for Access to Land, 2016. FAO.

Sharpley, R. (2014). Host perceptions of tourism: A review of the research. *Tourism Management, 42*(2), 37–49.

Smith, R.E. (2003). Land tenure reforms in Africa: A shift to the defensive. *Progress in Development Studies, 3*, 210–222.

Synman, S.L. (2012). The role of tourism employment in poverty reduction and community perception of conservation and tourism in southern Africa. *Journal of Sustainable Tourism, 20*, 395–416.

Tracy, S.J. (2013). *Qualitative research methods: Collecting evidence, crafting analysis, communicating impact*. Hoboken, NJ: Wiley.

UN (2015). United Nations. In *Transforming our world: The 2030 Agenda for sustainable development*. New York: UN.

United Nations World Tourism Organisation (UNWTO) (2019). *International tourism highlights* (2019 ed., pp. 2–3). Madrid: UNWTO. doi: 10.18111/9789284421152.

Van Vlier, L. (2017). *Comparative property law*. Cheltenham, UK: Edward Elgar.

Wolmer, W., Chaumba, J. & Scoones, I. (2004). Wildlife management and land reform in southeastern Zimbabwe: A compatible pairing or a contradiction in terms? *Geoforum, 35*(1), 87–98.

World Travel and Tourism Council (WTTC) (2018). *Travel and tourism economic impact: World*. London, UK: WTTC.

Zhou, Z. (2018). The tourism sector: A bright light in Zimbabwe's depressed economic environment. *African Journal of Hospitality, Tourism and Leisure*, 7(1), 1–19.

Zhou, Z. (2019). Trans-frontier parks as vehicles for Tourism Development and Poverty Alleviation: Lessons from Southern Africa. *International Journal of Hospitality and Tourism Systems, 12*(2), 67–81.

Zhou, Z. (2020). Critical shifts in the global tourism industry: Perspectives from Africa. *Geojournal*. doi: 10.1007/s10708-02-10297-y.

Zikhali, P. (2010). Fast Track Land Reform Programme, tenure security and investments in soil conservation: Micro evidence from Mazowe district in Zimbabwe. *Natural Resources Forum, 34*(1), 124–139.

ZTA. (2018). *"Zimbabwe Tourism Authority Annual Report"*. Harare, Zimbabwe.

# 7 A review of post-restitution land rights agreement conflicts and their resolution at & Beyond Phinda Private Game Reserve in KwaZulu-Natal, South Africa

*Jones Mudimu Muzirambi, Simon Naylor, and Kevin Mearns*

## Introduction

Participation in wildlife-based community tourism within and around protected areas is viewed as a tool for sustainable biodiversity conservation and community livelihoods enhancement (Stone & Nyaupane, 2017). For effective community-based conservation and tourism to be possible, it is necessary to resolve serious problems which negatively affect sustainability, for example, exclusion from decision-making, a breakdown in communication between management and community, power relations, marginalisation and poverty, and poor governance (Jusoh, 2012; Fisher et al., 2019; Ngubane & Diab, 2005; Sahide et al., 2018).

&Beyond (and Africa Foundation, a social development partner) has attempted to overcome some of the social disparities through successful implementation of projects involving local communities in the areas of health, education, skills development, small business development, and natural resources conservation education, among others. However, the study by Muzirambi (2017) identified a number of governance problems affecting &Beyond Phinda Private Game Reserve and the Makhasa and Mnqobokazi communities, such as exclusion of the communities from active participation in decision-making and management of conservation and tourism, power dynamics, failure of the devolution of power to lower levels, and inadequate communication. For the purpose of this chapter, the names &Beyond Phinda Private Game Reserve, &Beyond Phinda, and Phinda will be used interchangeably to refer to the game reserve.

The study reported in this chapter reviews some of the findings and recommendations by Muzirambi (2017) to establish the extent to which Phinda and local communities were able to resolve some of the governance problems raised. It provides a platform allowing stakeholders at the game reserve to reach agreement on identifying existing and potential threats to conservation and ways to overcome them. Hence, the Bending the Curve model proposed by

DOI: 10.4324/9781003188902-9

Muzirambi (2017) has been applied. This model is based on using problems as a springboard and transforming them into robust strengths and solutions for sustainable natural resources management.

The purpose of the study was to review achievements in and obstacles to community participation in conservation, tourism, and social development at Phinda, and to identify persistent problems which might need further exploration and resolution. It also sought to consolidate successful strategies to improve stakeholder relations which might make a positive contribution to sustainable wildlife conservation and tourism development.

This chapter is organised as follows: the first part of the data presentation deals with the perceptions of the Makhasa and Mnqobokazi communities concerning persisting obstacles to genuine participation in the management and decision-making processes as regards conservation, tourism, and community development, and progress made in responding to them. By way of triangulation, the perceptions of the game reserve management and Africa Foundation (a social development partner of &Beyond) are also discussed in order to clarify issues raised by the community participants. Finally, an analysis is conducted of the converging and diverging views to establish progress made in resolving the conflict and removing persistent stumbling blocks.

## Literature review

There is general consensus in community-based natural resource management literature that community livelihoods improvement can help biodiversity conservation goals, and vice versa (Coria & Calfucura, 2011; Horisch et al., 2014; Nyaupane & Poudel, 2011; Pegas & Castley, 2014; Stone & Nyaupane, 2017). However, in South Africa, substantial evidence from literature shows that land rights restitution agreements did not create a favourable environment for active community participation in wildlife conservation and tourism management (Bosch, 2003; Hottola, 2009; Naguran, 2002; Ngubane & Diab, 2005; Nustad & Sundnes, 2011). Moreover, a growing number of conflicts associated with protected area governance and land reform communities have been extensively documented (Kamuti, 2018; Musavengane & Simatele, 2016; Musavengane & Leonard, 2019). According to Africa Foundation (2021), rural communities in South Africa continue to be underserved and neglected to a certain extent. Musavengane and Leonard (2019) observe that there is correlation between the continued exclusion of Black South Africans from accessing the land and their lack of interest in conservation.

In this regard, Nyaupane and Poudel (2011) explain that relationships between community livelihoods, tourism, and conservation are dynamic and complex, and that more research is required if a complete understanding of the context of these relationships is to be arrived at. The findings of the studies by Musavengane and Kloppers (2020) at the Somkhanda Game Reserve in KwaZulu-Natal, and Asriyani and Verheijen (2020) in Ruing Flores, Indonesia, on the causes of governance problems bear out those of Muzirambi (2017) at

&Beyond Phinda. Conservation efforts often clash with local diversity and interests, including the livelihoods of local communities at the conservation sites (Asriyani & Verheijen, 2020). Power dynamics are apparent in community-based conservation and tourism ventures, and if they are not properly managed, they may pose a threat to the sustainability of these efforts (Jamal & Getz, 1995; Mariki et al., 2015; Wright, 2017).

The private sector is often dominant in terms of tourism ownership and finances (Waligo et al., 2013), and is principally profit-driven, as it seeks a maximum return on investment. Murphy (1985) argues that tourism nevertheless relies on the goodwill and cooperation of local people, because they are critical stakeholders. Authors such as Bello et al. (2016), Byrd (2003), Woodroffe & Redpath (2015), and Zou et al. (2014) emphasise that the host community needs to be actively involved in planning and development, and not merely the recipient of tourism plans.

Sustainable community development (and tourism) can be realised only if there is effective participation by all key stakeholders (Musavengane, 2019). Central to collaborative management of community-based natural resources are the issues of power, participation, funding, devolution, resilience, and community capital (Child, 2019; Muzirambi et al., 2020; Musavengane & Kloppers, 2020). Colbry et al. (2014) describe cooperative efforts or collaboration as an ongoing interpersonal interaction not characterised by significant power imbalances, engaged in with the express purpose of achieving common goals. Collaboration helps avoid conflicts. It is characterised by a joint decision-making approach, where power is shared and stakeholders have a collective responsibility for their actions and subsequent outcomes (Bello et al., 2016). This means that conservation and tourism authorities should be prepared to devolve some of their decision-making powers to other stakeholders, the local communities in particular. Devolution of power empowers the local communities through concession of some of the decision-making authority and responsibility to the grassroots (Muzirambi et al., 2020).

Colbry et al. (2014) state that collaborative theory encourages the motivation and active participation of stakeholders in the management of and access to their natural resources (Sitorus, 2011). A healthy community reinforces connections and relationships (social capital), respect for and inclusion of cultures (cultural capitals), access to different levels of power (political capital), sustainable use and care of communal natural resources (natural capital), sustainable harnessing of natural resources to meet economic needs (financial capital), developments or investments in local skills and knowledge (human capital), and infrastructure (built capital) (Emery et al., 2007). The review of the achievements of and areas for improvement of community-based conservation and tourism at &Beyond Phinda as undertaken during the course of the study by means of the Bending the Curve model takes into account the ideas of the community capitals framework so as to effectively analyse the complex factors affecting the stakeholders.

The Bending the Curve model was proposed as one way of viewing and overcoming some of the obstacles in question. Figure 7.1 illustrates the

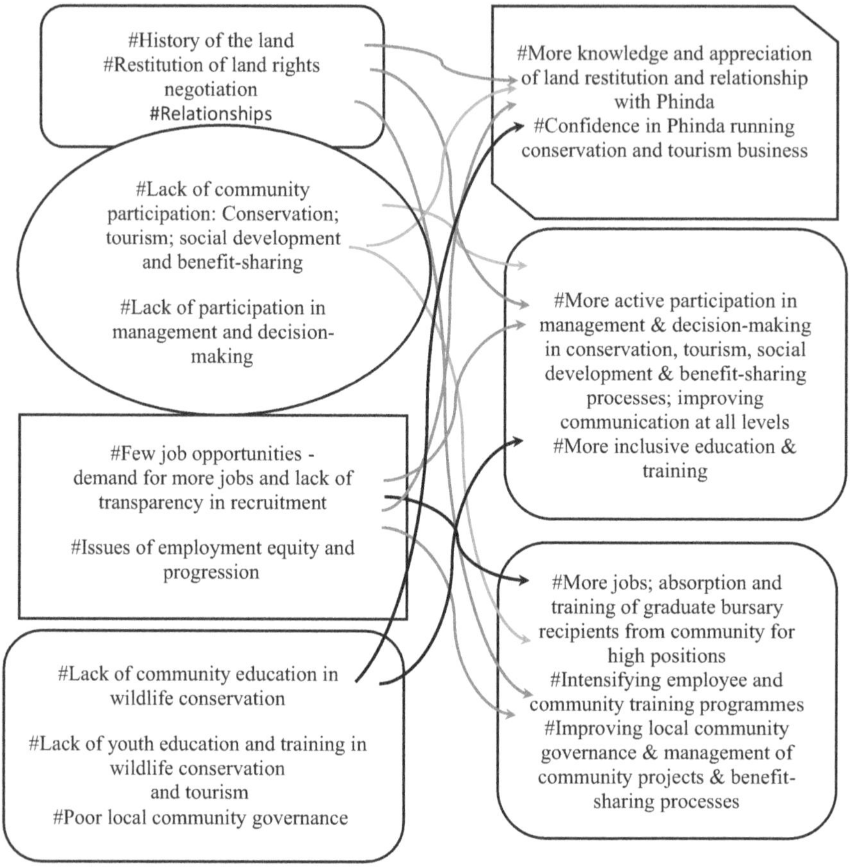


*Figure 7.1* Application of the Bending the Curve model in the context of perceptions relating to participation in conservation and ecotourism as a means to enhance collaboration and communication (Muzirambi, 2017)

application of the Bending the Curve model, which is based on the notion of identifying problems and threats and transforming them into solutions and opportunities which would contribute to sustainable conservation and communities (Muzirambi, 2017).

The research project reported on in this chapter investigated the achievements and areas still requiring attention in respect of land ownership following restitution agreements, and community participation in conservation and tourism management and decision-making at &Beyond Phinda Private Game Reserve. Through the application of the Bending the Curve model, the study assessed the progress made by Phinda and its stakeholders in overcoming some of the obstacles identified in the previous projects. The strength of the model lies in its emphasis on converting negative factors into constructive and progressive attributes for sustainable development.

## Case study research design, data collection, and analysis

The study area for the project was &Beyond Phinda Private Game Reserve, together with the Makhasa and Mnqobokazi communities of the Umkhanyakude District of KwaZulu-Natal, South Africa. Due to the nature and purpose of the study, a qualitative approach was adopted, as this would support an understanding and processing of behavioural changes and power dynamics within the target community. An extensive documentary analysis was conducted to establish the extent to which &Beyond Phinda and the local community stakeholders had been able to deal with some of the governance issues raised in the study by Muzirambi (2017), and also to establish and understand the current state of affairs. Documents, in the form mainly of reports from &Beyond and Africa Foundation, were analysed. Participatory approaches such as researcher immersion in the community and group interviews were adopted to elicit the attitudes and perceptions of the stakeholders regarding the successes and failures with regard to the identified governance issues subsequent to 2016, when Muzirambi (2017) undertook his fieldwork.

Participants from Phinda Private Game Reserve and Africa Foundation management were interviewed individually. Fourteen participants from the Makhasa and Mnqobokazi communities were interviewed, both individually and as a group. The participants included four trustees (three of whom had been in the executive since the signing of the agreement), two iziNdunas, and eight community members.

Purposive sampling was applied to ensure that important stakeholders were given a chance to express their views and to take advantage of the wealth of knowledge and experience held by the identified target participants. Semi-structured individual and group interviews were held during the data collection phases of the project to deal with pertinent issues affecting community stakeholders and employees of &Beyond Phinda. Participant consent was obtained, and confidentiality assured prior to the interview dates.

Both group and individual interview guides were pre-tested and improved prior to actual implementation. The application of combined approaches to data collection and analysis made the cross-checking and triangulation of the findings possible. Aspects of both narrative summary and grounded theory were used in the presentation and analysis of data, as it was felt that they would be effective in the assessment and the explanation of the dynamics of social relationships at &Beyond Phinda Private Game Reserve.

## Findings

This section starts with the presentation of community perceptions on the progress made in overcoming shortcomings in community participation in management and decision-making processes at different levels since 2016. Views and opinions expressed by the community participants were then tested by exploring the perspectives of the management of Phinda Private Game Reserve and Africa Foundation. Finally, a comparative analysis of the diverse views was undertaken to establish the progress made in the resolution of some of the potential points of conflict, and also to identify persistent areas of disagreement.

### *Community perceptions*

Livelihoods drive conservation rather than being compatible with it, and they have the potential to halt external threats to biodiversity (Coria & Calfucura, 2011). Once local communities are involved and benefit directly from conservation, they are much more likely to support and embrace conservation goals and participate in conservation management (Sitorus, 2011). Since communities are vital stakeholders, their perceptions matter.

Participants from the community believed themselves to have acquired sufficient knowledge, experiences, and skills to interrogate the restitution of land rights agreement signed in 2007. The interviewees, especially the trustees, felt strongly that it was high time that Phinda and Africa Foundation started to regard them as partners instead of recipient charity cases. A participant made the following statement:

> *"Phinda was like angels to us, we accepted everything they brought to us but now time has changed"*

Another participant stated:

> *"They behave like our bosses – They dictate things to us"*

The community interviewees expressed the view that Phinda should continue engaging with the community before taking actions which concern them. They urged Phinda to treat them as equal partners:

> *"We want Phinda to treat us as equal partners"*
>
> *"If only Phinda can do away with the bossy attitude and come to the table with the community leaders to discuss things in a fair and respectful way, we could be the best partners"*

The community participants stated that their participation in decision-making processes was minimal and expressed the wish for Phinda to involve the community leaders more meaningfully before finalising their decisions, especially on matters affecting them. Some interviewees felt that nothing had changed since 2016, or that the relationship with Phinda had in fact worsened and cited an impending court case against the community in which Phinda was the complainant. Some Trust members explained that one of the points agreed to in the land restitution negotiations was that the community would receive an equalisation share, but that at the time of data collection, this had not happened.

The community interviewees cited poor communication between Phinda and the community, the tribal (traditional) council in particular. Participants argued that both Phinda and Africa Foundation did not consult when making important decisions. In the words of one of the interviewees:

> *"We never share ideas with them, they come to tell us what to do"*

Other views were:

> *"Africa Foundation does projects without informing the community"*
> *"Phinda does not accept our concerns"*

The majority of the participants expressed the wish that Phinda would iron out their differences with the community leaders and have shared goals and a common understanding of the needs of the community and the capacity of the game reserve to fulfil these.

Some community members felt it important to also highlight positive aspects in their relationship with Phinda and Africa Foundation, however. Everyone in the group interview appreciated the fact that Phinda had honoured the rent payments as stipulated in the agreements. It was also apparent that since 2016, Phinda had increased employment opportunities for the local youth from the five communities. However, some interviewees pointed out that although there had been an increase in the employment of local residents, employment equity remained a problem, as the perception persisted that Phinda continued to reserve top decision-making positions for Whites. One interviewee even remarked that:

> *"Apartheid still exists within Phinda"*

According to the community participants, at the signing of the agreement Phinda promised to educate and train the community youth for involvement in conservation and tourism management, but that this promise had not fulfilled:

> *"Phinda does not want to train our children for higher positions at the game reserve"*
> *"No one has ever been sent for any training, which means we will never run the game reserve"*

The participants identified skills transfer as one of the significant points of disagreement between the community and Phinda, feeling that the undertaking as regards capacity-building and skills development and transfer had been only partially fulfilled. The interviewees made the observation that the Stars-in-Training programme, a collaboration effort between the Trusts and Phinda, focused on the training of community members for lower-ranking jobs only, such as positions as table staff, bar keepers, butlers, housekeeping staff, and chefs.

> *"The White people are being trained for higher positions by the Blacks of lower positions"*

As an example, the interviewees cited the example of an employee who had been working for Phinda for more than 20 years, and stated that despite his capabilities, he nevertheless remained a tracker. The interviewees argued that had he been White, he would have been trained and would have been a ranger by that time.

The participants stated that according to the agreement, Phinda was supposed to build a lodge for the Makhasa community, but had not yet done so. The community then renovated the Makhasa Lodge, which had belonged to and been abandoned by a private owner. The interviewees alleged that Phinda refused to assist with the renovation. The community participants stated that communication between Phinda and the community, through the Trust, was at an all-time low due to disagreement relating to the fence bordering the Makhasa Lodge; the interviewees claimed that Phinda had previously agreed to take down the fence to allow for game drives for the Makhasa Lodge guests. However, after the previous owner had withdrawn from the partnership with the community, Phinda refused to take down the fence. According to the participants, Phinda came up with a counter-proposal: a comprehensive business plan for the Makhasa Community Tent Lodge that entailed the demolition of Makhasa Lodge structures and construction of a tent lodge in its place. The community categorically rejected the demolition of the lodge and insisted on the taking down of the fence. At the time of data collection, the negotiations concerning the new Makhasa Community Lodge were at a stalemate. In the words of some participants:

> *"As long as they have not pulled the fence down, we will not talk with them"*
>
> *"Phinda has taken our community leaders to court, talks can only resume when the game reserve withdraw the charges"*
>
> "Drop the case, drop the fence and we will listen to you"

There was a general perception among participants that Phinda did not want to help the community run their own lodge. This is suggestive of a breakdown in communication between Phinda and the local community, a speedy resolution to which will be of benefit to sustainable conservation and tourism.

In the previous study (Muzirambi, 2017), the participants made no distinction between Phinda and Africa Foundation, with the close relationship and partnership between the two organisations being evident from the responses of the community participants. As a result of the communication breakdown between Phinda and the community, community participants in the study dissociated Phinda from the Africa Foundation–run projects. They suggested that Phinda was not contributing to community development and was taking advantage of Africa Foundation.

> *"Africa Foundation runs the projects"*
>
> *"It is time for the community to defend Africa Foundation from being exploited by Phinda"*
>
> *"Bursaries come from Africa Foundation"*
>
> *"Phinda even failed to help the community during the Covid-19 pandemic, even with food parcels as other organisations did"*

### *&Beyond Phinda Game Reserve Management*

Positive outcomes of the signing of the restitution of land rights agreements included the fact that communities benefitted financially and also that the whole process was peaceful compared with similar processes elsewhere, such as the Mbangweni-Ndumo (Naguran, 2002) and St Lucia (Nustad & Sundnes, 2011) cases. The management participant also noted that since then, community Trusts had evolved to become much more knowledgeable, skilled, and organised as a result of training and development programmes put in place by the game reserve. However, the interviewee had reservations as to whether the money received was properly invested. There had been a deterioration in the relationship between Phinda and the traditional council, as evidenced by a response from the participant:

> *"The divide between community Trusts and traditional council has created communication challenges as Phinda mostly deals with the Trustees but rarely with the traditional councils"*

The management was pursuing ways to close the communication gap between the game reserve and the traditional council.

With regard to capacity-building concerning the new roles of the community as partners, the participant indicated that considerable skills development and transfer had been carried out involving the trustees. However, little had been done for the beneficiaries and community at large due to lack of capacity. The management participant remarked that efforts had been made in the form of skills transfer projects relating to small business development, but that these had not taken off because of poor coordination by the community Trusts, which then translated into poor response from community members.

According to the management participant, Phinda had developed a proposal for the Makhasa and Mnqobokazi communities in terms of which the game reserve would build lodges for the community, outside its boundaries and using its resources, help the communities in the management of these lodges, and also market them as &Beyond packages. The interviewee justified the proposal as one way to close the gap between Phinda and the community. The management also shed some light on their discussions with the Trusts on the issues of shareholding and equity. The interviewee stated that the disadvantages of shareholding and equity, especially in a turbulent economic environment such as that created by the COVID-19 pandemic, had been explained to the trustees. According to the interviewee, the trustees had some difficulties in understanding financial management and reporting, and that this had led to misconceptions about both Phinda as a business and the business potential of the community.

The issue of integrating the graduate bursary beneficiaries from the local communities into management training programmes at Phinda surfaced in the study conducted by Muzirambi (2017). The management participants indicated that while there was no programme as yet being offered, there were plans to integrate graduate bursary beneficiaries into management internship programmes. The interviewee conceded that there was a need to pay more attention to middle management training for the local youth. However, the major obstacle was funding, and the company was exploring ways of raising funds for these programmes.

Phinda has created a community conservation internship programme, a six-month course tailor-made for the local community members. According to Phinda documents, in partnership with Africa Foundation, Phinda aims to use their resources and experiences to make relevant training courses accessible to enthusiastic naturalists and conservationists from surrounding communities. The goal is thus to equip local people with the tools and experience required to pursue careers in wildlife conservation management and tourism while also developing and cultivating the future custodians of wildlife and wild areas (Phinda Conservation Training Programme, 2019). The interviewee clarified that the programme was not limited to graduates but was open to anyone who qualifies. At the time of data collection, there were five interns from the local communities. The game reserve is funding the community conservation internship programme at a cost of R 110 000.00 per learner per year. The main difficulty highlighted by the participant was accommodation for the students.

The game reserve management interviewee agreed with the community participants in identifying skills transfer as a major stumbling block in relations between Phinda and the community. However, the management participant noted that extensive skills development and transfer had taken place over the years and that there was a need for the Trusts and Phinda to come up with a common understanding of community expectations relating to skills transfer and development and the capacity and potential of Phinda to fulfil these.

### *"Otherwise, despite whatever effort, it will not be enough"*

Stars-in-Training had been devised as a way to resolve the shortage of skills within the local communities so that the youth are able to compete on a better footing when it comes to employment. The participant explained that when vacancies arose, preference was given to Stars-in-Training graduates. The Stars-in-Training Impact Analysis (2020) shows that 28 students from the 5 communities have been trained each year. Table 7.1 illustrates the number of students trained from 2016 to 2020 and the areas in which they had received training.

The participant emphasised that a larger number of local residents had been employed in the previous four to five years than before, especially in the lodges. The question of employment equity had been resolved at this level, as there were no more complaints from the Trusts and communities concerning employment of outsiders. However, the restriction of locals to lower levels of employment remained a bone of contention. The interviewee reiterated the need for Phinda, the Trusts, and community leadership to iron out the issues of skills transfer and establish a way forward.

The management participant agreed that there was a need to improve communication with the traditional council. Although the iNkosi was informed about the activities of Phinda, the Trust, and Africa Foundation, there was a need to establish an effective mechanism to ensure the flow of information between the traditional council, the community, Phinda, and Africa Foundation. The interviewee advocated for the revamping of the communication channels which existed before the Trusts were put in place and integrating them with the current methods.

Responding to the growing community perception that Phinda was not ploughing back into the community and was hiding behind Africa Foundation, the management interviewee made the observation that Africa Foundation would not exist without Phinda. The respondent explained that Phinda and the local Africa Foundation management always coordinated their efforts and worked together in social development projects implemented by the latter. The interviewee added that the local managers already envisaged the drafting of a plan for social development projects owned by both organisations and also intended to improve the communication strategies, especially with the local communities.

*Table 7.1* Number of Stars-in-Training students trained from 2016 to 2020

| *Area of training* | *2016* | *2017* | *2018* | *2019* | *2020* | *Total* |
|---|---|---|---|---|---|---|
| **Barman** | 5 | 3 | 4 | 3 | 2 | **17** |
| **Housekeeping** | 8 | 6 | 5 | 4 | 5 | **28** |
| **Chefs** | 5 | 8 | 8 | 2 | 4 | **27** |
| **Butlers** | 2 | 2 | 5 | 0 | 3 | **12** |
| **Waiters** | 4 | 5 | 2 | 0 | 0 | **11** |
| **Bayete Tented Lodge** | 4 | 4 | 4 | 2 | 2 | **16** |
| **Total** | **28** | **28** | **28** | **11** | **16** | **111** |

### *Africa Foundation Management*

The management participant explained that the organisation raised funds for projects identified by the communities. According to this interviewee, the community participated in decision-making processes, as evidenced by the steps followed by Africa Foundation for project implementation; these include project identification by the community, profiling of proposals, sharing the proposals with potential donors, fundraising, donor selection of projects profiled, and management by Africa Foundation of the implementation of the projects. The project committees appointed by the communities are involved throughout the process.

> *"It's not Africa Foundation who decide on what project to implement"*

The participant stressed that Africa Foundation works with traditional authorities and continues to educate the community concerning the process of project funding. The interviewee noted that in the previous two years, attention had been paid to educating communities on the process implemented by Africa Foundation to deal with issues of communication, transparency, and good governance raised by community participants in previous studies, such as that conducted by Muzirambi (2017). The Africa Foundation manager emphasised the importance of merging the vision of the community and the goals of Africa Foundation. The organisation facilitated the establishment of the development committees for the communities and their capacitation in all areas for effective implementation of community projects.

One of the salient issues raised by the community participants was their perceptions regarding the relationship between and roles of Phinda and Africa Foundation. The Africa Foundation manager explained that the organisation is a social development partner of Phinda, with the goal of project implementation, starting with fundraising conducted among &Beyond guests staying at Phinda lodges. This participant explained that during their welcoming events Phinda educates guests at their lodges about the situation of the surrounding communities. Africa Foundation approaches the guests at the lodges in order to fundraise for community projects. The interviewee reiterated that the core focus of both Africa Foundation and Phinda is conservation, and that the goal is to obtain the buy-in of communities to be custodians of wildlife and the surrounding wild areas. The Africa Foundation participant stated:

> *"Direct spin-off of benefits is job creation – more than 50% of staff working at Phinda lodges is from the five communities"*
>
> *"Africa Foundation is a link between communities and the game reserve and &Beyond"*

There were also benefits through community projects. The Africa Foundation manager emphasised that Africa Foundation worked with Phinda; Africa

Foundation would not exist in the absence of Phinda because then there would be no lodges, whose guests came thanks to &Beyond. The Africa Foundation manager clarified that the visitors came as guests and were then approached to make donations. Of all the Africa Foundation donors, almost 80% have come through &Beyond and Phinda. The participant emphasised that both he and his partner from Phinda would like the community to view Africa Foundation and Phinda as a single entity, rather than as two separate organisations.

## Discussion of the findings

The purpose of the study was to review achievements and areas for improvement relating to community participation in conservation, tourism, and social development at Phinda Private Game Reserve. The findings of this research indicate some development with regard to the issues identified in the previous studies. The signing of the restitution of land rights agreements brought with it the need to transform the role of the community from recipients of charity to business partners in conservation and tourism at Phinda. Muzirambi (2017) revealed that the community participants experienced uncertainty concerning the management of their new roles. It is apparent from the study reported on here that the community has acquired the knowledge, skills, and confidence to engage with their partners, Phinda and Africa Foundation, in a more meaningful way and also to interrogate some of the clauses of the signed agreements. The Trusts have become much more knowledgeable, skilled, and organised, as confirmed by both the game reserve management and the community participants. Rising to the challenge of adopting new roles has given rise to a more assertive cohort of community leaders who are capable of taking community-based conservation and tourism to a higher level, as proposed by the Bending the Curve model (Muzirambi, 2017).

There has not been much change in the perceptions of the community regarding their participation in decision-making processes. According to the participants in the study reported on in this chapter, participation in decision-making processes in conservation, tourism, and social development was still minimal and there was a strong call to overcome this shortcoming. A breakdown in communication persists as one of the greatest hurdles at all levels. For example, a communication gap was identified between Phinda and the Trusts on the one hand and the traditional council on the other. A solution was being discussed, which would involve the council appointing a representative to sit in during the Phinda–Trust meetings and report back to the traditional authority to facilitate the flow of information.

Since 2016, employment opportunities and employment equity have been partially achieved at Phinda. The issue of the employment of outsiders at the expense of the local residents as raised in the study by Muzirambi (2017) had been resolved. More local residents have been employed by Phinda, especially in the lodge section, over the four to five years preceding the study reported on in this chapter. Clearly a negative situation (unemployment of the locals) has been turned around so as to achieve employment equity in the form of the employment of local residents. The Bending the Curve model emphasises the transformation of problems into robust and positive solutions important for sustainable development. Community perceptions that Phinda reserves top decision-making positions for Whites and outsiders nevertheless persist.

Skills development and transfer issues raised in the previous studies were partially dealt with during the period 2016 to 2020. Success with regard to skills development at the lower levels was achieved, for example through the Stars-in-Training and the community conservation internship programme. Both Phinda management and community participants agreed on skills transfer as being the most important issue requiring urgent attention. Very little capacity-building effort appeared to have been put into developing deserving local residents to the point where they are equipped to occupy management positions. Phinda focused on skills training at the lower levels, and not on local community youth development for decision-making and managerial positions. There is still no programme for leadership training for the local residents. However, according to the Phinda management participant, there were plans to tailor-make training for the local graduates interested in conservation and tourism business. More skills development has been done for the trustees, but little has been done for the beneficiaries and the community. Inadequate communication strategies have been a stumbling block to the initiatives for small business management training for community members. Phinda needs to refocus on a capacity-building model in terms of which the local community members are considered genuine partners in development, as recommended by Musavengane and Kloppers (2020).

One of the points on which Phinda and the community had agreed was that the game reserve would build a community lodge, owned and run by the community, with its help. The community lodge has become a significant stumbling block in the relationship between Phinda and the community. The situation is exacerbated by the divergence between the perspectives of Phinda and the community, in that whereas the local residents advocated for retaining the renovated lodge and taking down the Phinda fence to facilitate game viewing by Makhasa Lodge guests, Phinda counter-proposed a community tent lodge business plan and the demolition of the renovated Makhasa Lodge. The stand-off between Phinda and the community is a result of deteriorating communication processes, leading to a total shutdown, which negatively affects both conservation and community livelihoods. The two parties need to find common ground as a matter of urgency.

Ripple effects of the breakdown in communication between Phinda and the community are manifesting in the local residents' attitudes towards the game reserve. In the previous study (Muzirambi, 2017) local residents made no distinction between Phinda and Africa Foundation with regard to social development, and projects were considered to be a result of the partnership between the two organisations. In the study reported on in this chapter, however, community participants saw Phinda as having no involvement in the projects implemented by Africa Foundation. The Africa Foundation participant nevertheless explained that the organisation is dependent on the conservation and tourism business of Phinda and that it raises funds through guests at the lodges, with roughly 80% of Africa Foundation donors coming through &Beyond and Phinda.

Figure 7.2 illustrates the role of the Bending the Curve model in a summary of the achievements and areas for improvement associated with community participation in conservation, tourism, and social development at Phinda since 2016.

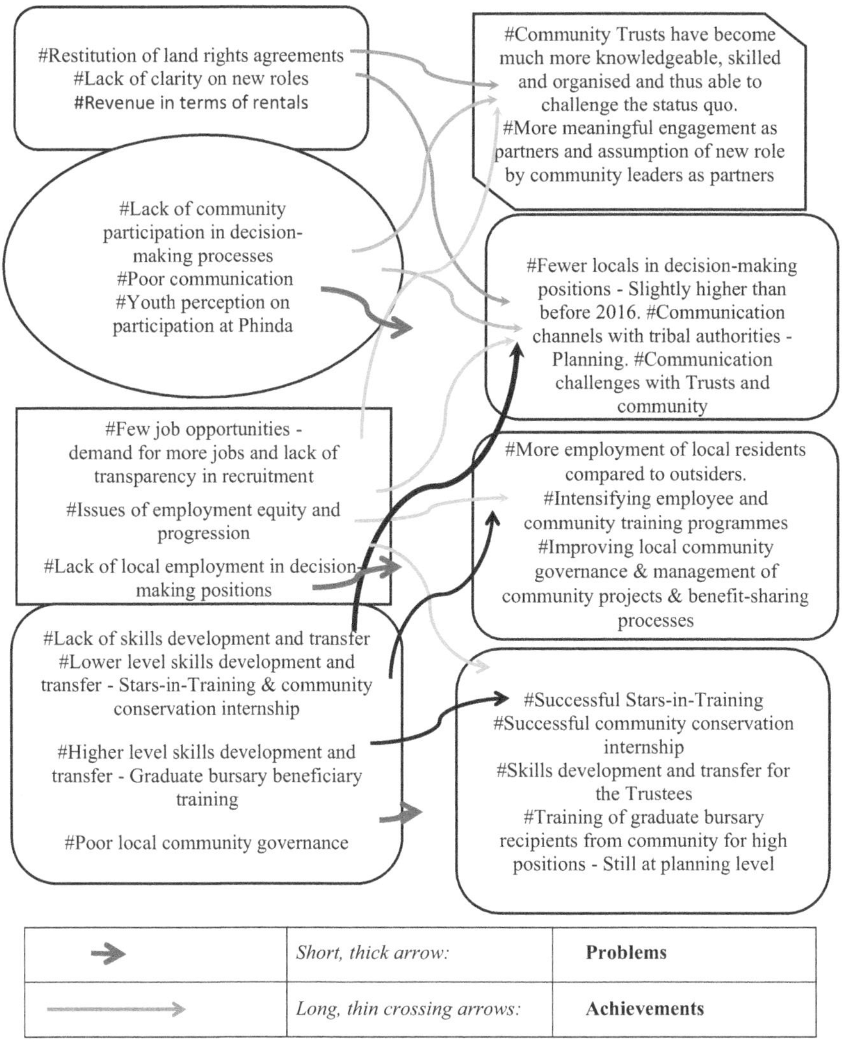


*Figure 7.2* Use of the Bending the Curve model (Muzirambi, 2017) to illustrate both achievements and problems relating to community-based conservation at Phinda from 2016 to 2020

According to the model as illustrated above, achievements in leadership development, improved employment opportunities for the locals, and skills development and transfer were recorded, while lack of participation in decision-making processes, poor communication, and skills transfer stood out as the most pertinent and persistent difficulties. To avoid conflicts, stakeholders must demonstrate the ability to align interests instead of competing for them (Burgoyne & Mearns, 2017).

## Conclusion

The purpose of the study was to review achievements and areas still requiring attention with regard to community participation in conservation, tourism, and social development at Phinda Private Game Reserve since 2016. Triangulation of respondents ensured both the reliability of the investigation and the validity of the findings. The application of the Bending the Curve model proved to be useful in assessing and reviewing how stakeholders of Phinda attempted to overcome some of the identified obstacles compromising sustainability of conservation, tourism, and social development. Leadership development, growth in the employment of the local residents, and skills development and transfer, to a certain extent, were some of the positive developments as illustrated by the Bending the Curve model. However, lack of active participation in decision-making, poor communication, and the lack of skills transfer for management and decision-making positions were identified as persistent difficulties.

This study provides a means for both researchers and practitioners to assess and review the stakeholder dynamics which would allow for informed decision-making processes aimed at resolving pertinent problems or consolidate the achievements gained. However, being a case study, this research is limited in scope, and this calls for further comparative studies of other cases in order to come up with a best practice database that would contribute to sustainable conservation and tourism.

## References

African Foundation. (2021). Home page. Available online: http://www.africafoundation.org.za

Asriyani, H. & Verheijen, B. (2020). Protecting the Mbau komodo in Ruing Flores: Local Adat, National Conservation and Ecotourism Development. *Forestry and Society*, 4(1), 20–34.

Bello, F.G., Lovelock, B. & Carr, N. (2016). Constraints of community participation in protected area-based tourism planning: The case study of Malawi. *Journal of Ecotourism*, 15, 1–21.

Bosch, D. (2003). Land conflict management in South Africa: Lessons learned from a land rights approach. In P. Groppo (Ed.), *FAO Land Reform: Land Resettlement and Cooperatives, 2003/2* (pp. 96–112). Rome, Italy: Rural Development Division of FAO.

Burgoyne, C. & Mearns, K.F. (2017). Managing stakeholder relations, natural resources and tourism: A case study from Ololosokwan, Tanzania. *Tourism and Hospitality Research*, 17(1), 68–78.

Byrd, E.T. (2003). An analysis of variables that influence stakeholder participation and support for sustainable tourism development in rural North Carolina. http://repository.lib.ncsu.edu/ir/bitstream/1840.16/5365/1/etd.pdf.

Child, B. (2019). *Sustainable governance of wildlife and community-based natural resource management: From economic principles to practical governance*. London: Routledge.

Colbry, S., Hurwitz, M. & Adair, R. (2014). Collaborative theory. *Journal of Leadership Education*, 13(4), 63–75.

Coria, J. & Calfucura, E. (2011). *Ecotourism and development of indigenous communities: The good, the bad and the ugly*. Working Papers in Economics, No. 489. University of Gottenburg School of Business, Economics and Law. ISSN 1403–2465.

Emery, M., Fernandez, E., Gutierrez-Montes, I. & Flora, C.B. (2007). Leadership as community capacity building: A study on the impact of leadership development training of community. *Community Development*, 38(4), 60–70.

Fisher, M.R., Dhiaulhaq, A. & Sahide, M.A.K. (2019). The politics, economics and ecologies of Indonesia's third generation of social forestry: An introduction to the special section. *Forestry and Society*, 3(1), 152–170.

Horisch, J., Freeman, R.E. & Schaltegger, S. (2014). Applying stakeholder theory in sustainability management: Links, similarities, dissimilarities and a conceptual framework. *Organisation and Environment*, 27(4), 328–346.

Hottola, P. (2009). Tourism development strategies: Lessons from Southern African experiences. In P. Hottola (Ed.) *Tourism strategies and local responses in Southern Africa* (pp. 181–202). Wallingford, UK: CAB International.

Jamal, T.B. & Getz, D. (1995). Collaboration theory and community tourism planning. *Annals of Tourism Research*, 22(1), 186–204.

Jusoh, H. (2012). Assessing natural capitals for sustainable ecotourism in Tasik chini Biosphere Reserve. *Advances in Natural and Applied Sciences*, 6(1), 1–9.

Kamuti, T. (2018). Intricacies of game farming and outstanding land restitution claims in Gongolo area of KwaZulu-Natal, South Africa. In F. Brandt & G. Mkodzongi (Eds). *Land reform revisited: Democracy, state making and agrarian transformation in post-apartheid South Africa* (pp 124–148). Boston: Brill.

Mariki, S.B., Svarstad, H. & Benjaminsen, T.A. (2015). Elephants over the cliff: Explaining wildlife killings in Tanzania. *Land Use Policy*, 44, 19–30.

Murphy, P.E. (1985). *Tourism: A community approach*. New York: Methuen.

Musavengane, R. (2019). Using systemic resilience thinking approach to enhance participatory collaborative management of natural resources in tribal communities: Towards inclusive land reform-led outdoor tourism. *Journal of Outdoor Recreation and Tourism*, 25, 45–56.

Musavengane, R. & Kloppers, R. (2020). Social capital: An investment towards community resilience in the collaborative natural resources management of community-based tourism schemes. *Tourism Management Perspectives*, 34, 1–15.

Musavengane, R. & Leonard, L. (2019). When race and social equity matters in nature conservation in post-apartheid South Africa. *Conservation and Society*,17(2), 135–146.

Musavengane, R. & Simatele, D.M. (2016). Community-based natural resource management: The role of social capital in collaborative environmental of tribal resources in KwaZulu-Natal, South Africa. *Development Southern Africa*, 33(6), 806–821.

Muzirambi, J.M. (2017). Perceptions of local community participation in wildlife and tourism management: Phinda Private Game Reserve, Umkhanyakude District, KwaZulu-Natal, South Africa. University of South Africa. http://hd.lhandle.net/10500/23274

Muzirambi, J.M., Musavengane, R. & Mearns, K. (2020). Revisiting devolution in community-based natural resources management in Zimbabwe: Towards inclusive governance approaches. In M.T. Stone, M. Lenao, & N. Moswete (Eds.), *Natural resources, tourism and community livelihoods in Southern Africa: Challenges of sustainable development* (pp. 143–158). London: Routledge.

Naguran, R. (2002). Property rights and protected areas: The case of Ndumo Game Reserve. In Conference on Property Rights and Environmental Degradation (pp. 27–30). Durban, South Africa: Beyer International Institute of Ecological Economics, 27–30 May 2002, Durban, South Africa.

Ngubane, J.S. & Diab, R.B. (2005). Engaging the local community in tourism development planning: A case study in Maputaland. *South African Geographical Journal*, 87(2), 115–122.

Nustad, K.G. & Sundnes, F. (2011). Conservation and land claims in St Lucia, South Africa. Unpublished Draft Paper for the Conference Nature Inc., June 2011 (22pp.).

Nyaupane, G.P. & Poudel, S. (2011). Linkages among biodiversity, livelihood, and tourism. *Annals of Tourism Research*, 38(4), 1344–1366.

Pegas, F. & Castley, G. (2014). Ecotourism as a conservation tool and its adoption by private protected areas in Brazil. *Journal of Sustainable Tourism*, 22(4), 604–625.

Phinda Conservation Training Programme. (2019). *Phinda private game reserve*. Hluhluwe: &Beyond.

Sahide, M.A.K., Fisher, M.R., Maryudi, A., Walundari, C., Kim, Y.S. & Giessen, L. (2018). Deadlock opportunism in contesting conservation areas in Indonesia. *Land Use Policy*, 77, 412–424.

Sitorus, T. (2011). Linking conservation of biodiversity and community livelihoods in Komodo National Park, Indonesia. In G. Baldacchino & D. Niles (Eds.), *Island futures: Conservation and development across the Asia-Pacific Region* (pp. 99–105). Tokyo: Springer.

Stars-in-Training Impact Analysis. (2020). *Phinda private game reserve*. Hluhluwe: Beyond.

Stone, M.T. & Nyaupane, G.P. (2017). Protected areas, wildlife-based community tourism and community livelihoods dynamics: Spiralling up and down of community capitals. *Journal of Sustainable Tourism*, 26(2), 307–324.

Waligo, V.M., Clarke, J. & Hawkins, R. (2013). Implementing sustainable tourism: A multi-stakeholder involvement management framework. *Tourism Management*, 36, 342–353.

Woodroffe, R. & Redpath, S.M. (2015). When the hunters become the hunted. *Science*, 348(6241), 1312–1314.

Wright, V.C. (2017). Turbulent Terrains: The contradictions and politics of decentralised conservation. *Conservation and Society*, 15, 157–167.

Zou, T., Huang, S. & Ding, P. (2014). Toward a community-driven development model for rural tourism: The Chinese experience. *International Journal of Tourism*, 16(3), 261–271.

# 8 Environmental Operational Research for sustainable tourism and conflict management in community-based natural resources management

*Regis Musavengane*

## Introduction

Despite the frequent exclusion of the rural population in processes that have a direct influence on their lives, it has been observed that there is an urgent need to promote strong, genuine, and grassroots-based community participation in environmental management decision-making (Tantoh & McKay, 2020; Siakwah et al., 2020; Su et al., 2021; Gohori & Van der Merwe, 2021). It is argued that community participation is at the heart of Environmental Operational Research (EOR) and Environmental Governance (EG) because it facilitates and promotes a sense of ownership in regard to decision-making and social development issues of society (Midgley & Reynolds, 2004; Child & Jones, 2006; Muzirambi et al., 2020). Therefore, the quest for more effective EOR and EG approaches in collaborative natural resource management (NRM) has led to the development of new frameworks for the analysis and understanding of socio-ecological systems, deliberative processes, and participatory approaches (Yang & Wu, 2009; Ostrom, 2010; Musavengane, 2019). Social learning is regarded as key to good EG and EOR by most researchers in both urban and rural contexts where there is a shared understanding and diverse interests (Chambers, 1988, 1994; Rodela et al. 2012; Ison et al., 2013; Midgley et al., 2013). Nevertheless, despite being the subject of increased research effort, both participatory modelling and social learning are yet to be established in EOR as well-understood, 'contemporary' governance mechanisms in tribal communities that have claimed their land.

It is important to note that participatory approaches have evolved over decades to establish tailor-made solutions for environmental wicked problems (Siakwah & Musavengane, 2021). For example, Participatory Rural Appraisal improved from top-down to bottom-up, from centralisation to localisation and from the blueprint to social learning (Chambers, 1994; Musavengane & Simatele, 2016). These changes led to the formation and growth of different social learning modes that emphasise a more in-depth inquiry where local people are actively involved in the decision-making process (Chambers, 1994).

DOI: 10.4324/9781003188902-10

Nevertheless, social learning (including its methods) remains widely contested as both a concept and a set of practices (Armitage et al., 2008; Reed et al., 2010; Ison et al., 2013). Chambers (1994: 953) points out that social learning as a participatory model leaves us with the question regarding "how much potential these approaches and methods have for making participation more practical and the rhetoric more real". This study attempts to answer this question through a systemic-resilience thinking approach in tribal communities of Sub-Saharan Africa.

Using systemic and resilience thinking as conceptual and environmental operational frameworks, this chapter reviews the current epistemological orientation of eco-social research in participatory community-based NRM (CBNRM) to inform future EOR. The attempt is to suggest other ways of knowing and thinking about CBNRM and to formulate alternative methodological considerations for developing EOR systems. An attempt is made to develop strategies for the use and management of sustainable natural resources in Sub-Saharan rural areas and other developing countries using the case of Zondi and Gumbi tribal communities in the KwaZulu-Natal (KZN) province of South Africa.

According to the Stockholm Resilience Centre (2014: 3),

> Resilience is the capacity of a system, be it an individual, a forest, a city or an economy, to deal with change and continue to develop. It is about the capacity to use shocks and disturbances like a financial crisis or climate change to spur renewal and innovative thinking. Resilience thinking embraces learning, diversity, and above all the belief that humans and nature are strongly coupled to the point that they should be conceived as one social-ecological system.

As with systemic thinking, resilience is a technique for gaining situation-wide insights into complex situations and problems. It combines both analytical and synthetical thinking in resolving collaborative conservation challenges (Midgley & Reynolds, 2004).

We can describe systemic-resilience thinking as *an analytic and synthetic approach with an ability to capacitate a system to adapt to changes, disturbances, and shocks through learning processes without negatively affecting its continual development.* Systemic-resilience thinking is anchored on the seven principles of resilience developed by the Stockholm Resilience Centre (2013). These principles are (i) to maintain diversity and redundancy, (ii) to manage connectivity, (iii) to manage slow variables and feedbacks, (iv) to foster complex adaptive systems thinking, (v) to encourage learning, (vi) to broaden participation, and (vii) to promote polycentric governance systems.

It is vital to note that EOR is yet to be fully employed in managing natural resources in tribal communities created through land reform processes in developing nations. Operational Research (OR) in general has been used considerably in developed nations in regard to the reciprocal relationships between supply chain and environmental management (Kleindorfer et al., 2005). There is, therefore, a need to focus on the role of EOR in the sustainable use of community natural resources through stakeholder participation. In view of this suggestion, the chapter will inform on EOR practice, specifically in land reform communities in developing nations. The following section discusses the significance of EOR in NRM. This is followed by a description of the methodology that was adopted. Thereafter, the results showing a systemic resilience EOR model are presented.

## Significance of Environmental Operational Research in natural resource management

Midgley and Reynolds (2004) posit that the general success of OR requires both environmental and community development practitioners to look beyond their areas and to collaborate with others in attaining a common goal. The authors emphasise that divergence of interests (should this occur) will not threaten EOR because the main goal of Community OR (COR) is for researchers to learn from each other (Midgley & Reynolds, 2004). This view is supported by White and Lee (2009), who write that an expansive scope is required for OR to deal with both environmental and social operational elements adequately. Hence, there is a need to address the environmental wicked problems in the broader intergenerational context, especially in tribal contexts. In the context of this study, wicked problems refer to the continuous conflict between community members and traditional leaders and conservation organisations on the use of community resources.

In their seminal study on COR, Midgley and Reynolds (2004) note that multidimensional and complex environmental issues and the associated political ramifications require the collective efforts of both COR and EOR practitioners. Furthermore, there is consensus among social scientists that generally the economy is on an unsustainable trajectory due to the overuse of both natural and non-renewable resources, which has a negative ecological footprint (Meadows et al., 1992; Rjoub et al., 2021). Therefore, EOR places significant emphasis on citizen participation in environmental management to attain sustainable community development (codified in Agenda 21) (Midgley & Reynolds, 2004).

At the centre of successful CBNRM in tribal areas is sustainable development and sustainable livelihoods (Musavengane & Matikiti, 2015). This assertion is supported by international policies such as Agenda 21, which declares a commitment to poverty eradication and reduction of disparities in living standards. Although sustainable development is anchored on the common three operational pillars – social, environmental, and economic – in general, most of the ORs tend to place more attention on the environment (White & Lee, 2009). For example, Bloemhof-Ruward et al. (1995) provided a consolidated analysis on the reciprocal links between the supply and environmental chains. To reduce negative environmental feedbacks, their study suggests the adoption of different OR methodologies and interventions. Although extensive research has been carried out on the dimension of the environment in OR, no single study exists on EOR in tribal communities that were established through land reform processes.

In our view, EOR has the potential to foster the dynamic and systemic applied practice of sustainable CBNRM in tribal areas where uncertainty is high due to diverse anticipations and values. Midgley and Reynolds (2004) reinforce this in their study, where they argue that both sustainable development and OR share three fundamental characteristics. Firstly, they both have 'wide boundaries' – referring to multiple and conflicting values and different clientele. Secondly, both schools foster 'interdisciplinarity' in problem-solving. Thirdly, the two schools are concerned with the 'design' and 'implementation' of planning approaches. The study of Midgley and Reynolds (2004) found that in both schools, three generic issues seem to recur – 'complexity and uncertainty' due to unpredictability of social and natural dilemmas in the communities; 'political effects', particularly on those who are not involved in planning processes; and 'multiple and conflicting values' of the stakeholders involved in the planning. We regard their study as comprehensive in EOR when addressing complex enviro-social situations such as those in tribal areas pursuing sustainable community development.

## Methodological consideration

The methodological positionality of this chapter is interpretive, and its operational framework base is qualitative research. The study used systemic-resilience thinking and a socio-ecological learning approach to analyse the participatory relationship and effects in managing community natural resources in Sub-Saharan Africa. The focus was on the Umvoti and uPhongolo tribal communities of KZN, South Africa, respectively, the Zondi and Gumbi communities (see Figure 8.1). Because this research is mainly qualitative, it is vital to first clarify the philosophical underpinnings of this EOR study.

Ritchie et al. (2013) point out that in qualitative research, there is no single, accepted way of obtaining data. Therefore, the way the researcher conducts the study depends upon a range of factors. Firstly, the researcher's *ontology*, which includes beliefs about the social nature of the environment that may influence the way that the researcher will conduct the research process. Secondly, *epistemology*, which entails the nature of knowledge and how it can be acquired, may also influence the gathering of data on the role of EOR in collaborative EG in Zondi and Gumbi rural communities in KZN.

Ontologically, we saw reality as something that exists independently from those who observe it but is only accessible through the perceptions and interpretations of individuals. Thus, the author acknowledges the critical importance of participants' interpretations of the issues of governance in collaborative EG. The Author also believes that the varying vantage points will yield different types of understanding of social capital and EOR in the Gumbi and Zondi

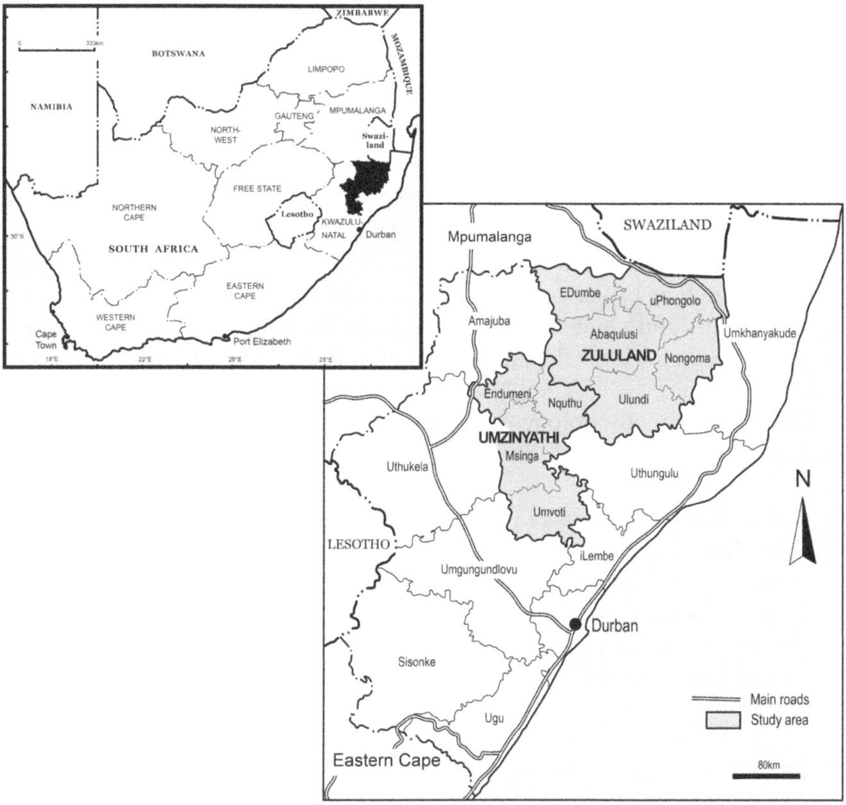


*Figure 8.1* Location of study sites: Umzinyathi (Umvoti: Zondi community) and Zululand (uPhongolo: Gumbi community)

communities. The author's position is that external reality is itself diverse and multifaceted, and the current research aims to capture that reality in all its complexity and depth to enhance this EOR.

Primary data were collected between December 2014 and February 2015 from the Gumbi community, which is located in uPhongolo Local Municipality in the Zululand District Municipality in the northern part of KZN in South Africa. Data was also obtained from the Zondi community, which is located in the Umvoti Local Municipality in the Umzinyathi District that is situated north of Greytown in KwaZulu-Natal (See Figure 8.1). The two sites are tribal areas and own a common pool of natural resources and game reserves. The Gumbi and the Zondi community own the Somkhanda Game Reserve (Somkhanda Game Reserve) and the Ngome Game Reserve (Ngome Game Reserve), respectively. The communities thus provide a good scenario for EOR in terms of comprehending the interactions of social capital in NRM and ecological conservation.

The Gumbi and Zondi communities consist of approximately 312 and 415 households, respectively. The first households in both locations were purposely selected and then specific intervals were applied to select the actual households (systematic random sampling). In the case of Gumbi, every 10th household was selected and in Zondi, it was every 18th household that was selected for inclusion in the study. A total of 44 households participated in the study (30 in Zondi and 14 in Gumbi). For the interviews, purposive and snowball sampling techniques were employed in approaching individual persons working or involved in the game reserve project and other related community projects. Furthermore, the snowball technique was applied to identify and engage with key actors such as project coordinators (2) and managers (4), and local community leaders and chiefs (2). Data collection tools included semi-structured interviews and checklists that were used during the focus group meetings and field observations.

The study's methodology borrows from the three main principles of Midgley and Reynolds's Critical Systems Thinking:

- *Improvement* – in terms of power relations within the local communities
- *Boundary critique* – in the context of our study, this involves constant questioning of methodological approaches used in CBNRM and exploration of values and boundary judgements
- *Methodological pluralism* – implies learning from past methodologies and drawing on appropriate methods to suit the situation (Midgley & Reynolds, 2004)

Combined, these principles were used to develop a systemic-resilience model that enhances community participation and informs future EOR. The conceptual model focused on the formulation of alternative solutions for collaborative NRM through systematic and resilience thinking and the development of causal flows to gain a clear understanding of the environmental operational processes and systems that underlie participatory NRM in co-managed game reserves in KZN. Content analysis was used for data analysis.

## Results and discussion

The methodological underpinnings have been outlined. This section presents the research findings and provides a discussion on EOR and systemic-resilience thinking.

### *Environmental Operational Research in community-based natural resource management in KwaZulu–Natal*

There is evidence to suggest that most of the tribal communities in KwaZulu–Natal and in South Africa generally comprise households that were previously marginalised and displaced from their land during the apartheid era (Ngubane

& Brooks, 2013). It is believed that the displacement of local people from their traditional land marked the beginning of the intervention of external actors in the South African development process (Spierenburg & Brooks, 2014). Kamuti (2014) observed that most communities that successfully claimed their land in KZN pursue community-based ecotourism (CBET) to improve their livelihoods. The current status of the CBET efforts in the Zondi and Gumbi communities can be attributed to either formation processes or collaborative structures and communication processes.

The Gumbi people who were forcibly removed from their land in the 1960s were restored their land under the Land Reform Process in 2005. According to Nathi Gumbi, the founder and beneficiary of the Somkhanda Game Reserve, after successfully claiming the land, the community partnered with Wildlands Conservation Trust (henceforth referred to as Wildlands) after failing to manage it on their own for the first five years. The Emvokweni Community Trust (ECT) contracted Wildlands to manage and transfer skills to local community members. The ECT is a legally constituted board that is responsible for operations of the Somkhanda Game Reserve. Board members comprise the owners of the game reserve, and members are voted in by land beneficiaries. The ECT also leased the tourism section to African Insight to oversee all tourism operations. Each entity is operating on a five-year lease. The established collaboratives necessitate skills development projects that ensure the transfer of skills from conservation groups to local people. The reserve is the first community-owned private wildlife reserve to be created from land reform processes in South Africa. According to Wildlands, the game reserve spans 16 418.82 hectares of land, with settlement and grazing area constituting 5 209.40 hectares and 11 508.72 hectares still pending land claim.

### *Formation processes of Somkhanda and Ngome game reserves*

Participants were first asked to explain the formation processes of the community game reserves. In response to this question, seven of the total eight experts who participated in the focus group discussions indicated that the Ngome Game Reserve was established to pursue conservation efforts by involving the local people. One individual stated that the Ngome Game Reserve was to establish a consultation process involving all interested groups through the Ngome Community Land Trust in order to capture the aspirations of all stakeholders. Further interviews with the households revealed that such a process was never implemented. None of the participants reported any involvement in the formation of the Ngome Game Reserve. Thus, the majority (96 %) of the focus group participants linked the violence against the game reserve to the exclusion of community members in decision-making. The current state of the Ngome Game Reserve necessitates community members and government and conservation organisations to respond to the balance between resource use and NRM. An elderly female participant in her late 70s of the Zondi community lamented the exclusion of local people in managing and using their resources:

> The Chief and his friends forcefully removed us from our homes to pave way for the game reserve. We were informed that we had to move as the place was supposed to be turned into a game reserve … We were never consulted by the community leaders or Trust, and we don't even know what a Community Trust is and how it came into being. To them [conservationists], we are like enemies and undesirable species inhibiting the progress of conservation … they don't even care about us. They fenced the game reserve to stop our livestock from grazing in the reserve; the initial fence they erected was further moved closer to our new houses without any consultation. That's why we dismantled it, and we don't want to hear anything about this game reserve! Now there is a rumour that they want to reopen the reserve. I believe it's true as there are unusual cars coming into the reserve. They must leave us alone and our livestock must feed freely on our land.
>
> (Focus group members [a] in Gumbi and Zondi Communities in Kwa-Zulu Natal, personal communication, March 2014–July 2015)

Similarly, another set of questions to measure fairness within the community were asked. When participants were asked whether there was fairness in resource use and ownership, the majority (93%) commented that there was a lack of clear structure for resource allocation. The evidence provided thus suggests that there was a deficiency in transparency within the Zondi community. All household participants reported that there was a lack of openness, and there were no discussions with stakeholders in the management of the game reserve. A common agreement among community members is that only the elite are considered in decision-making. This scenario, therefore, raises the question regarding the selection of participants in making community decisions. Chambers (1995) regards this situation of consulting only the elite in society as upper-to-upper bias, thus bypassing the poor. The causal flow diagram (Figure 8.2) demonstrates that aggressive management style and exclusion of people in decision–making contribute to lack of community participation in CBNRM schemes.

Spierenburg and Brooks (2014) comment that most reclaimed farms in KZN are closely juxtaposed with former 'native reserves', creating an intricate hodgepodge of agrarian and tenure arrangements. Comments such as this suggest that Zondi community members equate apartheid reserves to current game reserves, thus causing them not to participate in CBNRM. Apartheid reserves were meant to quarantine or separate people from their land and the associated resources. This is the reason why one of the interviewees, Nathi Gumbi, a founder and beneficiary of Somkhanda Game Reserve, emphasised the importance of public consultation:

> When we successfully claimed the land, the first thing I did was to do community consultations to educate people on the true or current meaning

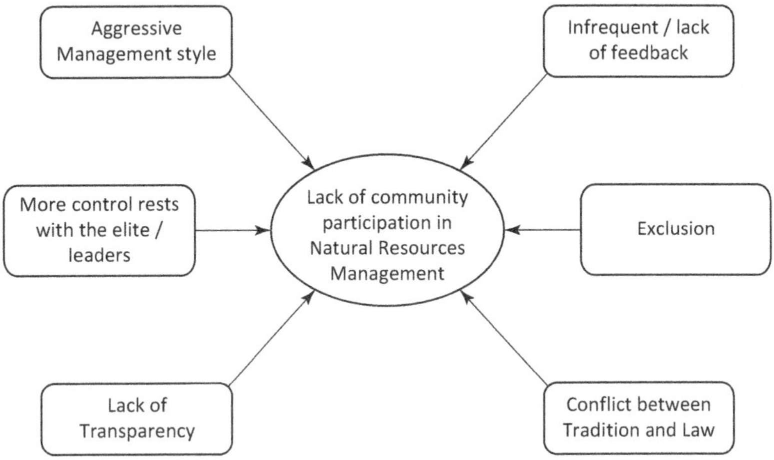


*Figure 8.2* Causal flow diagram: Causes of lack of participation in community natural resource management

> of reserve as they still had a mind of apartheid reserves. I was blamed by people, even my closest relatives, who didn't understand what a reserve is. I had to explain to them that the game reserve belongs to them and is meant to benefit them.
>
> (Focus group members [b] in Gumbi and Zondi Communities in Kwa-Zulu Natal, personal communication, March 2014–July 2015)

However, the question here is whether the founder was using participation as a 'cosmetic label' to make the game reserve proposal favourable to people (in real terms, a top-down approach) or was it an empowering process that enabled local people to do their analysis (Chambers, 1995). The latter is the 'we' approach, whereby participants would feel that they were involved in the conservation project. In a follow-up question on whether the act was done in utmost good faith, the founder of the Somkhanda Game Reserve highlighted,

> Before we started operating the reserve, we had a workshop with conservation experts, in particular Wildlands, on how to conduct consultations. I called the traditional leaders for the workshop and recorded all minutes. We then went to the grassroots with the business plan and some things were changed upon agreeing. Other people were scattered all over South Africa due to work commitments, and they are the ones who feel left out. We aimed to empower our own people.
>
> (Focus group members [c] in Gumbi and Zondi Communities in Kwa-Zulu Natal, personal communication, March 2014–July 2015)

The participants' accounts of the events surrounding the Gumbi Game Reserve indicated that during the inception stage, there was more involvement of community members and the founders, and ECT members were more visible and provided feedback on time (high bonding social capital). During the interviews, 91% of participants reported that they were consulted during the formation stages of the Gumbi Game Reserve, and the majority (90%) cited the existence of harmonious relationships within the community. Regardless of these findings, the important question to answer is whether the relationships and communication processes are being maintained (see Section 3.5.2).

*Collaborative structures and communication processes*

The Gumbi tribe is the majority populace in the Gumbi community and the peoples' lives are rooted within their culture. From the focus group discussions that were held, it was clear that the research participants' way of life and perceptions are heavily embedded and shaped by traditional norms and values. More than half of the participants (60%) reported that they have strong ties with traditional leaders. In conjunction with this, 87% of the participants indicated that they work closely with family members in conserving local resources. Thus, the loyalty of the people to the traditional system of governance and their culture seems to form the basis of their everyday lives. This is reflected in the inclusion of the chief in the decision-making and operations of the community game reserve that was established as a CBNRM scheme. When asked whether they were happy with the decision, 98% of the Gumbi participants reported that they were happy with the involvement of the late chief in decision-making because he was faithful and resembled the cultural emblem.

Despite the loyalty of the Gumbi community towards their traditional leaders, there is a general feeling among the research participants that the current decay in traditional systems of governance is rapidly resulting in high levels of corruption and unfair distribution of the benefits arising from their natural resources. Only 30% of the participants reported fairness regarding the rules in the community, and 46% cited the presence of fairness in resource allocation. For example, a former member of the ECT in Gumbi stated:

> The passing away of our old chief has brought new dynamics in the power structure. The new chief wants to have the overall voice in the decision–making of the Somkhanda Game Reserve. We now have a lot of tensions between the Trust members and the traditional authorities, and this is having a multiplier effect on the extent to which local people can participate in managing the Somkhanda Game Reserve. The current traditional authorities have sour working relationships with the existing Emvokweni Community Trust and the community at large.
>
> (Focus group members [d] in Gumbi and Zondi Communities in Kwa-Zulu Natal, personal communication, March 2014–July 2015)

Moreover, the challenge of collaborative structures is whether the communication processes will be continually maintained throughout the project lifetime (Musavengane, 2019). When asked about the flow of information and communication, 33% of participants highlighted that they have open dialogue and 55% indicated that they share information with traditional leaders. However, only a minority of participants (5%) reported that they receive feedback from the current ECT. This contradicts the initial findings that show that 91% of participants were involved in decision-making during the formation stage of the Somkhanda Game Reserve. In addition, 90% of participants indicated the presence of harmonious relationships among community members. An elderly Gumbi man who was born in 1936 lamented:

> After the formation of Somkhanda Game Reserve, we never had meetings with the Trust [Emvokweni Community Trust]. We just know that there is a Trust, but we don't know what it is and who is in it. No one provides us with information or reports on the use of financial benefits for the community except seeing our children getting work there. I am so angry with Ngome Game Reserve about that; we should be allowed to participate in decision–making.
>
> (Focus group members [e] in Gumbi and Zondi Communities in Kwa-Zulu Natal, personal communication, March 2014–July 2015)

As reflected in Figure 8.2, lack of feedback and transparency in addition to the exclusion of other stakeholders in decision-making are contributory factors for the lack of community participation in CBNRM. Based on these findings, it is important to highlight the operations of community land trusts in the Ngome Game Reserve and the Somkhanda Game Reserve. One of the major challenges facing the management of the Ngome Game Reserve is embedded in the governance structures. For example, one key informant reported that much of the decision-making process sits within the traditional realms of power, with the local chief being the absolute authority. This development, however, is contrary to the South African legislation that governs Communal Property Associations, which indicates that traditional rulers are not to be wholly involved in the management of these associations (Oomen, 2005). Thus, the heavy involvement of traditional structures in the management of natural resources in the Ngome Game Reserve has tended to create tensions among community members who oftentimes feel disenfranchised from accessing or having a voice in the resources. It is evident in the Ngome Game Reserve that power relationships are at the centre of the disenfranchisement of local people's participation. Hence, there is an urgent need to devolve the power structure and shift the locus of resource management to the people. There is a need to develop a strategy that will strengthen local people's participation in the management of their resources, failure of which will result in any intervention measures being inadequate.

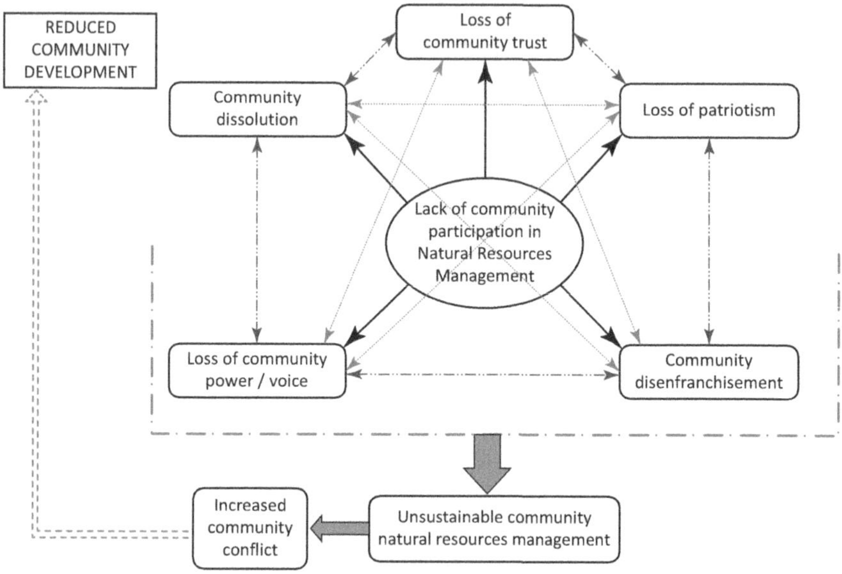


*Figure 8.3* Causal flow diagram: Consequences of lack of participation in community natural resource management in KwaZulu-Natal

In Figure 8.3, it is clear that unless there is devolvement of power, the lack of effective participation in CBNRM schemes will continue to cause loss of community trust, loss of patriotism, community dissolution, loss of community power, and community disenfranchisement.

All of the above-mentioned issues will eventually lead to unsustainable community NRM, resulting in reduced community development, as has occurred in the Zondi community.

### *Towards 'systemic-resilience thinking' and the participatory modelling approach in Environmental Operational Research*

To develop more participatory and sustainable forms of community NRM, particularly in the rural areas of Sub-Saharan Africa, there is a need to rethink contemporary approaches that have influenced current management policies and practices in EOR. Most analytical and operational conservation frameworks seek to examine the ordinary management of community natural resources. It is, therefore, vital to adopt and develop methodologies that examine the embedded complexity in managing natural resources in tribal communities that have successfully claimed their land from previous oppressors. Thus, systemic-resilience thinking is used in developing an integrated participatory model for managing communal natural resources in turbulent areas such as those of the Gumbi and Zondi communities. In this chapter, emphasis is placed on the vertical structure models, in particular, the power to influence. Community power dynamics influence the participation of stakeholders and can have positive or negative effects on the natural resources and other social capital elements.

In a social-ecological system such as the one in the Gumbi and Zondi communities, components such as cultural beliefs and institutions provide different options for responding to change with uncertainty. To maintain diversity and redundancy, which is one of the principles of resilience (SRC, 2013), the Gumbi and Zondi communities need to build diversity and redundancy into the governance system by incorporating diverse sources of knowledge. An implication of this is the possibility that it will motivate community members and further facilitate the development of new operational systems and processes that benefit all stakeholders. The maintenance of diversity and redundancy enhances three of the six asset factors – collaborative conditions, collaborative work relationships, and group-life balance.

The findings of this study reveal that there are weak communication relationships among community members and the community trusts and traditional leaders in both communities. One of the issues that emerged from these findings is that conflict prevails in such environments. There is a strong possibility that this can be resolved by applying systemic-resilience techniques. According to the Stockholm Resilience Centre (2013), systemic-resilience techniques place emphasis on engaging various participants, establishing suitable social context for the sharing of knowledge, and enabling people to network and create communities of practice.

The importance of fostering complex adaptive systems thinking through rich collaborative work relationships (4th principle of resilience) was noted. Healthy co-relationships can lead to constructive debate regarding EOR, specifically in conservation and community development. This can be achieved by adopting a systems framework that helps people to interact and by expecting and accounting for change and uncertainly in fragile communities with a patchy history. Similarly, Cooper Flint-Taylor and Pearn (2013) and Musavengane and Woyo (2022) note that ignoring complex adaptive systems thinking can negatively lead to weak communication channels and can cause leaders to claim recognition for achievements at the expense of the community. As reflected in the interviews with the participants from the Zondi community, there was no involvement of ordinary community members, and all recognition was claimed by the leaders.

Furthermore, positive co-relationships help in promoting polycentric governance (5$^{th}$ principle of resilience). Negative pressures that emanate from weak relationships strain communication channels, as reported in both Gumbi and Zondi communities. Alternatively, positive polycentric governance leads to strong social relationships and enhances social capital. Positive polycentric governance can be achieved by balancing redundancy and observing the involvement of all concerned institutions such as legal, conservation, and tribal authorities (SCR, 2013). In addition, it is important to negotiate trade-offs

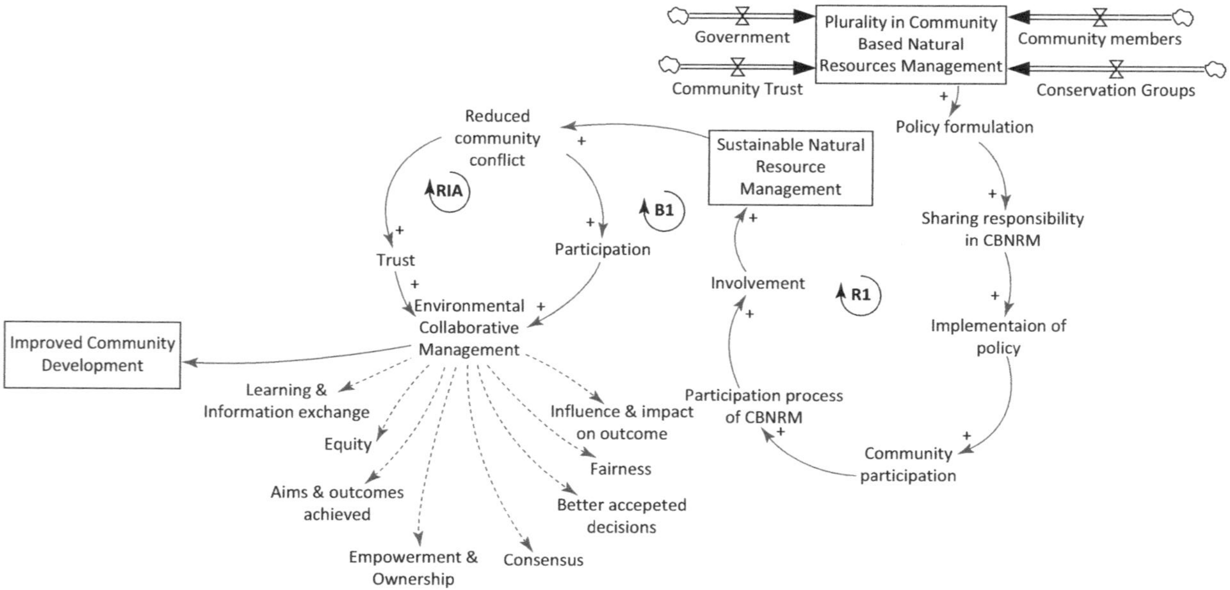


*Figure 8.4* Sustainable community development for EOR through participatory natural resource management

between users of resources. This avoids what is known as 'scale shopping' whereby dissatisfied people take their concerns to their preferred political party (SCR, 2013).

Figure 8.4 shows that through EOR, sustainable community development can be achieved through the effective participation of all stakeholders. It can, therefore, be asserted that the strength of the collaborative effort in managing the natural resources determines the outcome of the community development goals. Based on the findings of this study, community members, community trust, conservation groups, non-governmental organisations, and traditional leadership should collectively participate in CBNRM processes in both the Ngome Game Reserve and the Somkhanda Game Reserve (see Figure 8.4). Thus, plurality in co-managing natural resources helps in effective policy formulation, which further enhances the implementation of policy and strengthens the participation processes of CBNRM (Chambers, 1994). As seen in Figure 8.4, '*R1*' emphasises that reinforcement of all six strategies (from policy formulation to involvement) is necessary for producing or formulating effective, efficient, and socially acceptable solutions and systems to improve the NRM in the Gumbi and Zondi communities. This is possible through a plurality of governance coordination and the development of adequate and significant environmental policies (see Figure 8.4) that are pro-poor, environmental, and sustainably developed. It is important to note that if such a framework were employed in the management of natural resources in the Gumbi and Zondi communities, it would promote efficient management systems of community natural resources (see Figure 8.4). Taken together, the findings of this study on EOR suggest a role for sustainable NRM in positively increasing both trust and participation of all stakeholders and establishing effective and efficient collaborative groups. This combination of findings provides some support for the conceptual premise that collaborative environmental management will effectually result in learning and information exchange, fairness and equity, achievement of outcomes, and better decision-making (Musavengane, 2022).

## Conclusion

This study was undertaken to design an alternative EOR methodological framework for co-managing natural resources sustainably in complex tribal communities. The study examined the impact of systemic-resilience thinking in promoting participatory EOR in CBNRM. Using systemic-resilience thinking as conceptual and operational frameworks in EOR, this chapter reviewed the current epistemological orientation of eco-social research in participatory CBNRM. The chapter revealed that successful collaborative community-based projects involve vital social capital elements that include participation of all stakeholders, transparency, reciprocity, and effective communication. The findings of this study contribute to the existing body of knowledge on EOR in terms of devising an inclusive participatory methodological framework for managing common resources in tribal areas with a gloomy oppressive history.

This study reaffirms previous studies that suggest the need for urgent interventions to promote strong and genuine grassroots-based community participation in environmental management decision-making.

In EOR, it is a widely held view that stakeholder participation is fundamental for sustainable governance of community-based natural resources (Child & Jones, 2006; Midgley et al., 2013). Thus, to pass beyond the rhetoric of participation, experimentation with emerging participatory models is needed to bridge the gaps between the general participatory frameworks. The study used systemic-resilience thinking in modelling an integrated participatory model for managing communal resources in turbulent environments such as the Gumbi and Zondi communities. Looking at vertical structure models, in particular the power to influence, Chapter 4 revealed that community power dynamics influence stakeholder participation. The current study has contributed towards our understanding of the role in EOR of the participatory resilience-systemic model on the attainment of the seven resilience principles identified by the Stockholm Resilience Centre: maintain diversity and redundancy; maintain connectivity; manage slow variables and feedbacks, foster complex adaptive systems thinking; encourage learning; broaden participation; and promote polycentric governance. The findings of this study suggest that systemic-resilience participatory approaches to complex collaborative issues in NRM will facilitate social capital adaptation and encourage the support of institutions of local adaptation.

## References

Armitage, D., Marschke, M. & Plummer, R. (2008). Adaptive co-management and the paradox of learning. *Global Environmental Change*, 18(1): 86–98. https://doi.org/10.1016/j.gloenvcha.2007.07.002

Bloemhof-Ruwaard, J.M., Van Beek, P., Hordijk, L. & Van Wassenhove, L.N. (1995). Interactions between operational research and environmental management. *European Journal of Operational Research*, 85(2): 229–243. https://doi.org/10.1108/SCM-01-2014-0007

Chambers, R. (1988). *Rural development: Putting the last first*. Harlow, UK. Longman Group.

Chambers, R. (1994). The origins and practice of participatory rural appraisal. *World Development*, 22(7): 953–969. https://doi.org/10.1016/0305-750X(94)90141-4

Chambers, R. (1995). Paradigm shifts and the practice of participatory research and development. In: Nelson, N. (Ed.), *Power and participatory development* (pp. 19–30). London: Intermediate Technology Publication.

Child, B. & Jones, B. (2006). Practical tools for community conservation in Southern Africa. *Participatory Learning and Action*, 55: 6–12.

Cooper, C., Flint-Taylor, J. & Pearn, M. (2013). *Building Resilience for Success: A resource for managers and organisations*. London: Palgrave Macmillan.

Gohori, O. & Van der Merwe, P. (2021). Limitations to community participation in tourism from local people's perspectives: Manicaland Province, Zimbabwe. *Development Southern Africa*, 1–15. https://doi.org/10.1080/0376835X.2021.1913099

Ison, R., Blackmore, C. & Iaquinto, B.L. (2013). Towards systemic and adaptive governance: Exploring the revealing and concealing aspects of contemporary social-learning metaphors. *Ecological Economics*, 87: 34–42. https://doi.org/10.1016/j.ecolecon.2012.12.016

Kamuti, T. (2014). The fractured state in the governance of private game farming: The case of KwaZulu-Natal province, South Africa. *Journal of Contemporary African Studies*, 32(2): 190–206. https://doi.org/10.1080/02589001.2014.936678

Kleindorfer, P.R., Singhal, K. & van Wassenhove, L.N. (2005). Sustainable operations management. *Production and Operations Management*, 14(4): 482–492. https://doi.org/10.1111/j.1937-5956.2005.tb00235.x

Meadows, D.H., Meadows, D.L. & Randers, J. (1992). *Beyond the limits: Confronting global collapse, envisioning a sustainable future*. Post Mills, VT: Chelsea Green Publishing.

Midgley, G. & Reynolds, M. (2004). Community and environmental OR: Towards a new agenda. In: Midgley, G. & Ochoa-Arias, A. (Eds.), *Community operational research: OR and systems thinking for community development* (pp. 297–316). Boston, MA: Springer.

Midgley, G., Cavana, R.Y., Brocklesby, J., Foote, J.L., Wood, D.R.R. & Ahuriri-Driscoll, A. (2013). Towards a new framework for evaluating systemic problem structuring methods. *European Journal of Operational Research*, 229: 143–154. https://doi.org/10.1016/j.ejor.2013.01.047

Musavengane, R. (2019). Using the systemic-resilience thinking approach to enhance participatory collaborative management of natural resources in tribal communities: Toward inclusive land reform-led outdoor tourism. *Journal of Outdoor Recreation and Tourism*, 25: 45–56. https://doi.org/10.1016/j.jort.2018.12.002

Musavengane, R. (2022). Collaborative management. In: Buhalis, D. (Ed.), *Encyclopedia of tourism management and marketing* (pp 1–3). Cheltenham, UK: Edward Elgar Publishing. https://doi.org/10.4337/9781800377486.collaborative.management

Musavengane, R. & Matikiti, R. (2015). Does social capital really enhance community-based ecotourism? A review of the literature. *African Journal of Hospitality, Tourism and Leisure*, 4(1): 1–18.

Musavengane, R. & Simatele, D.M. (2016) Community-based natural resource management: The role of social capital in the collaborative environmental management of tribal resources in KwaZulu-Natal, South Africa. *Development Southern Africa*, 33(6): 806–821. https://doi.org/10.1080/0376835X.2016.1231054

Musavengane, R. & Woyo, E. (2022). Adaptive management. In: Buhalis, D. (Ed.), *Encyclopedia of tourism management and marketing* (pp. 1–3). Cheltenham, UK: Edward Elgar Publishing. https://doi.org/10.4337/9781800377486.adaptive.management

Muzirambi, J.M., Musavengane, R. & Mearns, K. (2020). Revisiting devolution in community-based natural resources management in Zimbabwe: Towards inclusive governance approaches. In: Stone, M.T., Lenao, M. & Moswete, N. (Eds.), *Natural resources, tourism and community livelihoods in Southern Africa: Challenges of sustainable development* (pp. 143–158). London: Routledge. E-Book ISBN: 9780429289422. https://doi.org/10.4324/9780429289422

Ngubane, M. & Brooks, S. (2013). Land beneficiaries as game farmers: Conservation, land reform and the invention of the 'community game farm' in. *Journal of Contemporary African Studies*, 31(3): 399–420. https://doi.org/10.1080/02589001.2013.811790

Oomen, B. (2005). *Chiefs in South Africa: Law, power and culture in the post-apartheid era*. Suffolk, UK: James Currey.

Ostrom, E. (2010). Beyond markets and states: Polycentric governance of complex economic systems. *American Economic Review*, 100(3): 641–672. https://doi.org/10.1257/aer.100.3.641

Reed, M.S., Evely, A.C., Cundill, G., Fazey, I., Glass, J., Laing, A., Newig, J., Parrish, B., Prell, C., Raymond, C. & Stringer, L.C. (2010). What is social learning? *Ecology and Society*, 15(4): r1. [online] URL: http://www.ecologyandsociety.org/vol15/iss4/resp1/

Ritchie, J., Lewis, J., Nicholls, C.M. & Ormston, R. (Eds.). (2013). *Qualitative research practice: A guide for social science students and researchers*. Thousand Oaks, CA: SAGE.

Rjoub, H., Ifediora, C.U., Odugbesan, J.A., Iloka, B.C., Xavier Rita, J., Dantas, R.M., Mata, M.N. & Martins, J.M. (2021). Implications of governance, natural resources, and security threats on economic development: Evidence from Sub-Saharan Africa. *International Journal of Environmental Research and Public Health*, 18(12): 6236. https://doi.org/10.3390/ijerph18126236

Rodela, R., Cundill, G. & Wals, A.E.J. (2012). An analysis of the methodological underpinnings of social learning research in natural resources management. *Ecological Economics*, 77: 16–26. https://doi.org/10.1016/j.ecolecon.2012.02.032

Siakwah, P. & Musavengane R. (2021). Re-imagining community-based tourism in rural Africa Through networks and management innovation. In: Ngoasong, M.Z., Adeola O., Kimbu A.N. & Hinson R.E. (Eds.), *New frontiers in hospitality and tourism management in Africa*. Tourism, Hospitality & Event Management. Switzerland: Springer, Cham. https://doi.org/10.1007/978-3-030-70171-0_14

Siakwah, P., Musavengane, R. & Leonard, L. (2020) Tourism governance and attainment of the sustainable development goals in Africa. *Tourism Planning & Development*, 17(4): 355–383. https://dx.doi.org/10.1080/21568316.2019.1600160.

Spierenburg, M. & Brooks, S. (2014). Private game farming and its social consequences in post-apartheid South Africa: Contestations over wildlife, property and agrarian futures. *Journal of Contemporary African Studies*, 32(2): 151–172. https://doi.org/10.1080/09637494.2014.937164

Stockholm Resilience Centre (SRC). (2013). *What is resilience? An introduction to social-ecological research*. Stockholm, Sweden: Stockholm University.

Su, F., Song, N., Shang, H., Wang, J. & Xue, B. (2021). Effects of social capital, risk perception and awareness on environmental protection behavior. *Ecosystem Health and Sustainability*, 7(1), 1-13. https://doi.org/10.1080/20964129.2021.1942996

Tantoh, H.B. & McKay, T.J.M. (2020). Rural self-empowerment: The case of small water supply management in Northwest, Cameroon. *GeoJournal*, 85: 159–171. https://doi.org/10.1007/s10708-018-9952-6

White, L. & Lee, G.J. (2009). Operational research and sustainable development: Tackling the social dimension. *European Journal of Operational Research*, 193: 683–692. https://doi.org/10.1016/j.ejor.2007.06.057

Yang, L. & Wu, J. (2009). Scholar-participated governance as an alternative solution to the problem of collective action in social–ecological systems. *Ecological Economics*, 68(8–9): 2412–2425. https://doi.org/10.1016/j.ecolecon.2009.03.021

Part 3

# Managing land use, access, and benefit-sharing conflicts

# 9 The state, community-based tourism, and wildlife user rights in tourism concessions in Botswana

*Joseph Mbaiwa and Emmanuel Mogende*

## Introduction

Community-based natural resource management (CBNRM) has been one of the leading themes of conservation in developing countries in the last 30 years (Mbaiwa, 2018). The programme, supported in Botswana by the Wildlife Conservation Policy of 1986 (revised in 2013) and the Tourism Policy of 1990, states that local communities in natural resource areas should benefit from the resources around them. A wide spectrum of global actors promotes CBNRM, including conservation NGOs, the World Bank, and the United Nations. By the mid-1990s the CBNRM approach had had a significant impact on conservation practice. It was presented as a 'win-win' scenario that could conserve wildlife, empower local communities, and bring economic development (Swatuk, 2005). CBNRM was largely promoted in Southern Africa in the late 1980s as a strategy to reverse the environmental injustice associated with fortress conservation (Mbaiwa, 2018), which is characterised by the physical, economic, and cultural displacement of indigenous populations, creating tense relations between the state and local communities in conservation areas (Brockington, 2002; Dowie, 2009).

CBNRM promotes reforms that decentralise resource rights from the central state to local communities, although this has been questioned (Dressler et al, 2010; Nelson, 2010; Hoon, 2014). The basic assumption of CBNRM is that communities will sustainably manage wildlife within their locality if they directly derive socioeconomic benefits from it (Murphree, 1993; Thakadu, 2005; Twyman, 2000, 2017). Therefore, CBNRM emphasises profit-making as an incentive to sustainably manage natural resources. This assumption is based on three conceptual foundations: a) economic, giving a resource such as wildlife a focused value that can be realised by the community or landowner; b) devolution, moving management decisions from government to the community or local land users to create positive conditions for sustainable wildlife management; and c) collective proprietorship, whereby a group of people are jointly given use rights over resources, which they then manage according to their own roles and strategies.

DOI: 10.4324/9781003188902-12

After several decades, CBNRM has yet to meaningfully devolve rights to communities, for several reasons including state ownership of wildlife resources, restrictions on wildlife user rights, elite capture of revenue, and inequitable distribution of benefits (Swatuk, 2005). In the last decade, the CBNRM programme has been re-centralised by the state, as we shall show later. In Botswana, decisions such as dispossession of land, revenue sharing between the state and CBT enterprises, the 2014 hunting moratorium that curtailed income for a majority of CBT ventures, and the tourism land bank provide a glimpse of how the state controls and governs the wildlife resources and the CBNRM programme and how it (re)structures state-citizen relations in CBT enterprises. The re-centralisation of CBNRM has further deepened the dominance of the foreign-owned and multinational companies in the tourism industry. We note that the struggle to access and control tourism concessions and wildlife resources by local communities participating in the CBNRM programme increases tension between government and local communities.

Kalabamu (2019) reveals that conflict over land resources occurred as a result of neoliberal policies and the emergence of an elite class in wildlife-based tourism. Neoliberalism draws on liberal economics, specifically that aggregate good is best acknowledged when people contend through the market. Some scholars refer to neoliberalisation as 'market environmentalism', which is a model of resource regulation that promises both economic and environmental ends via market means (Anderson & Leal, 2001). Neoliberalism accentuates three central principles: privatisation, marketisation, and deregulation/re-regulation (Castree, 2008). Botswana's tourism conforms to a business model that promotes profit-making and simultaneously protecting environmental assets through a High-Cost–Low-Volume (HCLV) strategy. Although it is often argued that the state's role has diminished under neoliberalism, it is still involved in creating and preserving a framework for capital accumulation and the protection of nature (Harvey, 2005). Wildlife-based tourism in Botswana is controlled by small foreign white elite, a traditional Tswana elite, and political, military, and business elites (Mbaiwa & Hambira, 2020). Tourism and land policies are shaped and enhanced by these groups, which mostly favour private interests over local communities.

In this chapter we consider how state control in CBNRM has created conflict between the state and its citizens and how this undermines the growth of community-based tourism (CBT) in Botswana. Our analysis is based on secondary published and unpublished data on CBNRM and wildlife-based tourism in Botswana.

## Data collection methods

The study on which this chapter is based was largely qualitative and used data from both primary and secondary sources. Secondary data was obtained from published and unpublished literature on wildlife-based tourism and the CBNRM programme, resource use conflicts, and wildlife conservation. This included policy documents and journal articles on safari hunting and tourism development and annual reports on wildlife-based tourism in Northern Botswana. Longitudinal data about the CBNRM programme and wildlife conservation in Botswana was also used, making it easy to track CBNRM development and conservation changes over the past decades. Primary data was derived from ongoing research in Northern Botswana dating back to 1998, including documents on land-use conflicts, tourism development, wildlife conservation, and related CBNRM issues, particularly livelihoods and wildlife conservation.

In thematic analysis, themes that emerge from data sources are pieced together to form a compressive picture of their collective experience (Braun and Clarke, 2006). This method was used to derive the themes of resource use conflicts, CBNRM, and wildlife conservation.

## Community-based tourism and tourism concessions in Botswana

Although the wildlife-based tourism industry was non-existent at independence, it has grown substantially to become the second-largest economic sector in Botswana after mining, contributing about 9.5% to the GDP (Mbaiwa, 2018). Botswana pursues HCLV, a greener model of tourism. This model was developed in and is concentrated in the northern conservation zone, which includes the unique fragile ecosystem of the Okavango Delta. This greener model aims to minimise the ecological footprint in Botswana's conservation areas by attracting fewer high-paying tourists from countries in the Global North. Botswana's conservation areas comprise protected and wildlife management areas (WMAs) covering 39% of Botswana's territory, with many located in Northern Botswana (Government of Botswana, 2013 ). Botswana's programme of CBNRM is the backbone of CBT activities such as photographic and safari hunting.

CBT takes place in tourism concessions, which are units of economic production and control leased by the government of Botswana to local communities and the private sector for profit-making, either for consumptive or non-consumptive use. The state has put this model in place to ensure capital accumulation and protection of environmental assets. Concessions place restrictions on land use: they forbid the creation of new settlements, cultivation, and keeping domestic animals (Government of Botswana, 1992). Concessions are leased out to either local communities under the CBNRM programme or private tourist safari operators by the relevant land authority. Where a concession is situated on communal land, that region's tribal land board becomes the appropriate land authority and use rights are provided for by the Tribal Land Act of 1968 (amended in 1993). However, with the increase in the financial value in photographic concessions in the Okavango Delta, the state is reluctant to give local communities full ownership of tourism concessions. With the advent of the land bank in 2014, the Botswana Tourism Organisation (BTO) controlled tourism land concessions to foreign investors and multinational tourism companies.

## Conflict over resource user rights in Botswana's tourism concessions

Struggles over access to and control of wildlife resources have been characterised by conflict and negotiation between the state and local communities and nonstate actors. Contestation over land and natural resources can be traced back to the colonial era when protected areas were first established. This was a critical aspect of the extension of state power, particularly in remote rural areas where it had been marginal (Neumann, 2004; Massé & Lunstrum, 2016). However, the recent struggle for control of land and management and user rights of tourism concessions is motivated by the state's desire to establish profitable models of capital accumulation and economic growth at the expense of local people's livelihoods. Ecotourism depends on protecting environmental assets from exploitation by local communities confined in these rural green spaces. The role of the state cannot be ignored, as it plays a crucial part in devising mechanisms for capital accumulation. Against this background we describe how this has played out in marginalising CBT enterprises and thus creating conflict between the state, the private sector, and local communities.

The Central Kalahari Game Reserve (CKGR) has been a site of struggles over land and resource rights for many years (Hitchcock, 2020 ; Sapignoli, 2015). CKGR was promulgated in 1961 with the intention to safeguard the cultural lifestyle of the Basarwa. However, this was not realised, as the Basarwa were dispossessed of their ancestral land by the postcolonial democratic government. Their relocation from the CKGR happened when Botswana had already adopted the CBNRM programme, which is meant to involve local communities in the management of wildlife resources. Central to the relocation was the government notion that Basarwa could not live in harmony with the animals in the reserve. Yet this contradicts government's strategy of CBNRM, which is designed to involve local communities in managing natural resources, thereby ensuring them direct benefits from these resources.

The forced removal of the Basarwa paved the way for alternative economic projects, namely diamond mining and ecotourism (Marobela, 2010; Vidal, 2014). For instance, in May 2007 it was reported that a mining company, Gem Diamonds, had purchased the mining licences for sites around Gope in the southeastern portion of the CKGR where in the 1980s De Beers had found kimberlite deposits indicating the presence of diamonds (Marobela, 2010; Hitchcock, 2020). Gem Diamonds paid a reported US$34 million for the licence (Marobela, 2010). Vidal (2014) points out that half of the reserve was allocated to Wilderness Safaris, a multinational tourism company dominating Botswana's booming ecotourism industry. As LaRocco (2018) points out, the CKGR became a potent symbol of the Basarwa's territorial claims to wildlife areas and is often a focal point in the deployment of historical memories when land ownership is contested.

Through the CBNRM policy of 2007, the state has continued to extend its authority over profit generated by CBT ventures. This policy emphasises the recentralisation of wildlife rents. For instance, a larger share (65%) of revenue generated by CBT enterprises is taken by the central government while 35% is retained by the community. The 65% share is then distributed nationally for conservation projects through the National Environmental Fund. The mismanagement of funds by CBT ventures became an opportunity for the government of Botswana to reassert control over wildlife, a resource that they never intended to give away to locals in the first place. The 65/35% clause undermines the relationship between the state and its citizens. In the eyes of the locals, the state of Botswana is not democratic and accountable when it comes to managing resources of high value such as wildlife, resulting in distrust between the state and local communities.

Maintaining central government control over wildlife resources in Botswana has enabled governing elites to promote their business interests over CBT ventures (Mbaiwa & Hambira, 2020). For example, in 2014, through a presidential directive the government of Botswana imposed a nationwide hunting ban in all controlled hunting areas except for private land. The decision was prompted in part by the decline of some wildlife species. Many commentators considered the move as promoting and further reinforcing the commercial interests of the ruling elite in the photographic tourism industry, which is highly politically connected (LaRocco, 2016; Mbaiwa & Hambira, 2020; Mogende & Ramutsindela, 2020). As Van de Walle (2001) points out, control over valuable resources is key to the construction of patronage networks and reinforcement of their privileged positions. For the most part, CBT enterprises were highly dependent on safari hunting for profit. The hunting ban deprived them of income, which they had mostly used to provide socioeconomic benefits to their members.

The tourism land bank initiated in 2014 became another tool to remove tourism concessions belonging to local communities, particularly prime concessions with abundant wildlife (Cassidy, 2020; Mogende & Ramutsindela, 2020). The land bank was initially developed to rehabilitate abandoned land that no private party would take on, perhaps because of unpaid taxes or contamination. In Botswana, the most aesthetically appealing and productive areas of tourist land countrywide are reserved for foreign direct investors through the land bank. Yet the tourism industry in the country is owned and controlled by multinational tourism companies. For this reason, tourism development in Northern Botswana has been described as enclave tourism (Mbaiwa, 2005, 2018; Mbaiwa & Hambira, 2020). CBT is, therefore, developing parallel to a better organised and advanced tourism sector which has skilled personnel with more experience in the tourism business. The multinational tourism companies can market themselves in developed countries, where most tourists visiting Northern Botswana come from; this means the rich tourism sector in Northern Botswana dwarfs any efforts to expand CBT.

Such dominance by multinational companies has led to much of the revenue generated from tourism being repatriated, with only a small share retained in the country (Mbaiwa, 2018). In Botswana, 55% of tourism revenue is spent outside Botswana and another 16% is spent as first-round linkages of receipts due to tourist-related imports. Only 29% is spent in Botswana on local goods, wages, taxes, and other activities (Mbaiwa, 2018). In addition, Glasson et al. (1995) note that the domination of the industry by foreign investors can reduce control over local resources and that a loss of local autonomy is certainly the most negative long-term effect of tourism. Local residents may also suffer a loss of sense of place, as their surroundings are transformed to accommodate the requirements of a foreign-dominated tourist industry.

Lucrative land deals are made through the land bank by private-sector individuals who are well connected to the political elites. For instance, there have been rumours that, through the land bank, the state wished to allocate a prime concession in the multi-billion-dollar asset the Moremi Game reserve to the British billionaire Richard Branson (Botswana Gazette, 2018). This decision has reignited the conflict between the Batawana royals and the state over the ownership of Moremi. The reserve was established in 1963 by the Batawana and in 1979 it was transferred to the central government (Bolaane, 2003; Mbaiwa, 2005). The Batawana royals have since waged a campaign to wrest control of the reserve from the government (Mmegi, 2016). There is a general consensus among communities in the Okavango Delta that the pristine environmental asset has been taken from them by government and given to foreign tour operators. We point out that the land bank facilitates what David Harvey (2005) refers to as accumulation by dispossession – "the enclosure of public assets by private interests for profit resulting in greater social inequity" (Bakker, 2005: 543).

Some local community concessions such as those owned by the Sankoyo and Khwai have been withdrawn from these communities without consultation. For instance, there has been a long battle between the state and Khwai Development Trust in relation to user and management rights over Tsaro Lodge, a prime safari lodge located in the southwest corner of WMA NG/19 on a plot abutting the northern boundary of the Moremi Game Reserve. This lodge, previously given to the community of Khwai in 2002, was subleased to the private sector by BTO through the land bank.

This case reveals that the state is reluctant to surrender management of valuable resources. The processes of the land bank have deepened the people's alienation from land and resources that surround Khwai, fuelling a source of bitterness in the community. It has also caused tension between communities and the private sector. Butler (1980), Prosser (1994) and Ceballos-Lascurain (1996) note that resentment, antagonism, and alienation often emerge between the host communities and foreign investors in tourism if efforts are not made to include local communities in the tourism business. Excluding hosts from certain tourist facilities will further increase resentment and may create conflict between the host population and the tourists. These developments contradict the principles of sustainable development and tourism, which presuppose equal access and opportunities for all user groups including local communities. Glasson et al. (1995) and Ceballos-Lascurain (1996) note that tourism should be sensitive to the needs and aspirations of the host population. It should provide for local participation in decision-making and the employment of local people in order to make it sustainable.

Although local communities participate in tourism in the absence of secure land tenure through CBNRM, they continue to face restrictions on the type of activities and development permitted, particularly in fragile areas of the Okavango Delta. For instance, as part of green branding, the regulations for the Okavango Delta Ramsar Site encourage concessionaires to build lodges that do not have adverse aesthetic, ecological, or physical impacts – that is, semi-permanent structures without mortar and brick. The limitations not only affect operations in the area, but more importantly make it difficult for people to build infrastructure on land they do not own and to attract the capital needed to develop tourism in Botswana. Local communities that are unable to operate prime concessions resort to joint venture partnerships (JVPs) with the private sector. JVPs encourage partnerships with the correct mix of financial strength, requisite experience, and strong empowerment credentials. Through such partnerships, it was believed that local communities would gain necessary managerial skills that will allow them to eventually run their own community tourism businesses efficiently. However, the JVP system is weak and there is no significant transfer of entrepreneurship and managerial skills between safari hunting companies and communities (Snyman, 2014; Mbaiwa, 2015). Instead of being at the forefront of the tourism business in their areas, the trust has been turned into a landlord with no evidence becoming the owner (Mbaiwa, 2015).

## COVID-19 and community-based tourism

COVID-19 has inadvertently impacted CBT in Botswana. The year 2020 was devastating, as COVID-19 posed serious challenges not only to the public health system but also the tourism economy across Southern Africa (Africa Outlook, 2020). Botswana's tourism industry is skewed towards the international market, mainly Europe, the US and Asian countries, so was extremely vulnerable to the effects of the disease. With the pandemic Botswana had to place a travel ban on tourists from these high-risk countries, leading to a temporary closure of tourism activities in the country. COVID-19 has also affected CBT, causing abrupt loss of employment and income. For instance, in 2019 the government reintroduced safari hunting but this was halted given the travel bans in 2020 (Hambira, 2020). Thousands of licences were made available to CBT enterprises and individual citizens. As a result, many CBT ventures entered into agreements with international professional hunters, mostly from the United States, Britain, and Italy. Since the hunting ban communities have not made any profit and development in their areas has been severely affected.

Those who had leased out photographic concessions did not receive full rental due to lack of business, as the private sector was also affected.

CBT ventures have been criticised for making poor investment choices and not diversifying their product, making them very vulnerable to economic shocks like COVID-19. We believe CBT should reinvest its money more wisely so that it can have a sustainable income stream even when its main source is no longer functional. In an effort to assist CBT, government established the COVID-19 Relief Fund to subsidise the wages of businesses that were impacted by the pandemic. In addition, CBT enterprises benefited from the P16 million donated by the German government through the Kavango-Zambezi Transfrontier Conservation Area. Furthermore, as a way of encouraging domestic tourism, BTO embarked on the Re-Discover Botswana Expedition, a campaign that saw many tourist facilities including CBT enterprises attracting domestic travellers. The OECD points out that post-COVID-19 there is a likelihood of increased travel, particularly for safari tourism where travellers prefer destinations with open spaces, remoteness, clean air, and fresh water (OECD, 2020). As result, places such as the Okavango Delta where most of the CBT enterprises are located have a high possibility of receiving more visitors and reviving CBT.

## Conclusion

Underlying the various conflicts in rich biodiversity areas such as the Okavango Delta is the fact that they contain numerous biotic and abiotic elements that could be valued as natural resources by one or more groups. Traditional stakeholders see the area as their patrimony, and their livelihoods mostly depend on using wildlife resources and veld products. Pastoralist and agro-pastoralist (traditional) communities want control of wildlife resources as well as the Moremi Game Reserve and the Chobe National Park, as they consider them to be an integral part of their territorial land. They see the potential value of the national parks and game reserves for settlement, grazing, and arable agriculture. The government of Botswana and the private-sector interest groups (which include the Batswana economic and political elites) see the area's wildlife resources as a potential source of wealth from hunting and tourism. Conservationists, both expatriate and local, regard the game parks and reserves highly for their biodiversity and aesthetic value. Each of these social groups thus constructs a different image of the wildlife areas, and a different set of natural resources, depending on how they perceive and value the different elements of the natural system.

Through the CBNRM programme, the Botswana government aims to address resource conflicts in the country. Conflicts between local communities indicate that partnership between local communities and stakeholders such as government is critical. For example, partnership between local communities and protected area management agencies can benefit both protected areas and biodiversity. What is needed is to encourage private and community investment in the area through the CBNRM programme, which has the potential to create employment and other wildlife tourist benefits for local people. The local communities in Botswana appreciate and support the implementation of the CBNRM programme, knowing they can derive meaningful benefits from the natural resources around them. To do this, they will be obliged to ensure the sustainability of these resources.

## References

Africa Outlook. (2020). *Coronavirus and the impact on Africa tourism*. https://www.africaoutlookmag.com/industry-insights/article/1174-coronavirus-and-the-impact-on-african-tourism

Anderson, T. L. & Leal, D. R. (2001). *Free market environmentalism*. New York: Palgrave.

Bakker, K. (2005). Neoliberalizing nature? Market environmentalism in water supply in England and Wales. *Annals of the Association of American Geographers*, 95(3): 542–565.

Bolaane, M. (2003). The impact of game reserve policy on the river Basarwa/Bushmen of Botswana. *Social Policy and Administration*, 38(4): 399–417.

The Botswana Gazette. (4 April, 2018). No Batswana land for Branson. Retrieved from: https://www.thegazette.news/latest-news/no-batswana-land-for-branson/#.YeFG8dJBzIU

Braun, V. & Clarke, V. 2006. Using thematic analysis in psychology. *Qualitative Research in Psychology*, 3: 77–101.

Brockington, D. (2002). *Fortress conservation: The preservation of the Mkomazi Game Reserve, Tanzania*. Bloomington, IN: Indiana University Press.

Butler, R. (1980). The concept of a tourist area cycle of evolution: Implications for management of resources. *Canadian Geographer*, 24(1), 5–12.

Cassidy, L. (2020). Power dynamics and new directions in the recent evolution of CBNRM in Botswana. *Conservation Science and Practice*, 3(1): e205.

Castree, N. (2008). Neoliberalising nature: The logics of deregulation and reregulation. *Environment and Planning*, 40: 131–152.

Ceballos-Lascurain, H. (1996). *Tourism, ecotourism and protected areas*. Gland, Switzerland: International Union for the Conservation of Nature and Natural Resources.

Dowie, M. (2009). *Conservation refugees: The 100-year conflict between global conservation and native peoples*. Cambridge, MA: MIT Press.

Dressler, W., Büscher, B., Schoon, M., Brockington, D., Hayes, T., Kull, C. A., McCarthy, J. & Shrestha, K. (2010). From hope to crisis and back again? A critical history of the global CBNRM narrative. *Environmental Conservation*, 37(1): 5–15.

Glasson, J., Godfrey, K. & Goodey, B. (1995). *Towards visitor impact management: Visitor impacts, carrying capacity and management responses in Europe's historic towns and cities*. Aldershot, UK: Ashgate Publishing Limited.

Government of Botswana. 2013. *Revised wildlife conservation policy*. Gaborone: Government Printers.

Hambira, W. L. (2020). Reviving the Botswana tourism industry after COVID-19. https://www.thecairoreview.com/covid-19-global-crisis/reviving-botswanas-tourism-industry-after-covid-19/

Harvey, D. (2005). *A brief history of neoliberalism*. Oxford: Oxford University Press.

Hitchcock, R.K. (2020) The plight of the Kalahari San:hunter-gatherers in a globalized world. *Journal of Anthropological Research*, 76: 164–184.

Hoon, P. (2014). Elephants are like our diamonds: Recentralizing community based natural resource management in Botswana, 1996–2012. *African Studies Quarterly*, 15(1): 55–70.

Kalabamu, F. T. (2019). Land tenure reforms and persistence of land conflicts in Sub-Saharan Africa: The case of Botswana. *Land Use Policy*, 81: 337–345.

LaRocco, A. (2016). The comprehensive hunting ban: Strengthening the state through participatory conservation in contemporary Botswana. In: Ramutsindela, M., Miescher, G. & Boehi, M. (eds.) *The politics of nature and science in Southern Africa* (pp. 179–207). Basel: Basler Afrika Bibliographien.

LaRocco, A. (2018). Memory as Claim-Making in Kalahari Socio-environments. In: Vikas Lakhani and Evelinede Smalen (eds.) *RCC Perspectives: Transformations in Environment and Society* (pp. 27–32). Munich: Rachel Carson Center for Environment and Society.

Marobela, M. N. (2010). The state, mining and the community: The case of the Basarwa of Central Kalahari Game Reserve. *Labour, Capital and Society*, 43(1): 138–153.

Massé, F. & Lunstrum, E. (2016). Accumulation by securitization: Commercial poaching, neoliberal conservation, and the creation of new wildlife frontiers. *Geoforum*, 69: 227–237.

Mbaiwa, J. E. (2005). Enclave tourism and its socio-economic impacts in the Okavango Delta, Botswana. *Tourism Management*, 26(2): 157–172.

Mbaiwa, J. E. (2015). Community-based natural resource management in Botswana. In: Van der Duim, R., Lamers, M. & Van Wijk, J. (eds.) *Institutional arrangements for conservation, development and tourism in Eastern and Southern Africa: A dynamic perspective* (pp. 59–80). Dordrecht, the Netherlands: Springer.

Mbaiwa, J. E. (2018). Effects of the safari hunting tourism ban on rural livelihoods and wildlife conservation in northern Botswana. *South African Geographical Journal*, 100: 41–61.

Mbaiwa, J. E. & Hambira, W. (2020). Enclaves and shadow state tourism in the Okavango Delta, Botswana. *South African Geographical Journal*, 102(1): 1–21.

Mogende, E. & Ramutsindela, M. (2020). Political leadership and non-state actors in the greening of Botswana. *Review of African Political Economy*, 47(165): 399–415.

Mmegi (2016, June 24). Moremi fights for inheritance. Retrieved from https://www.mmegi.bw/ampArticle/194072

Murphree, M. W. (1993). *Communities as resource management institutions*. London: International Institute for Environment and Development.

Nelson, F. (2010). *Community rights, conservation and contested land: The politics of natural resource governance in Africa*. London: Earthscan.

Neumann, R. P. (2004). Moral and discursive geographies in the war for biodiversity in Africa. *Political Geography*, 23: 813–837.

OECD. (2020). The future of tourism in natural areas: Impact, governance and financing. https://www.oecd.org/regional/leed/tournat.htm

Prosser, R. (1994). Societal change and the growth in alternative tourism. In E. Cater & G. Lowman (eds.), *Ecotourism: A sustainable option?* (pp. 19–37). Chichester: John Wiley.

Sapignoli, M. (2015). Dispossession in the age of humanity: Human rights, citizenship, and indigeneity in the Central Kalahari. *Anthropological Forum*, 25(3), 285–305.

Snyman, S. (2014). Partnership between a private-sector ecotourism operator and a local community in the Okavango Delta, Botswana: The case of the Okavango Community Trust and Wilderness safaris. *Journal of Eoctourism*, 13(2–3): 110–127.

Swatuk, L. A. (2005) From project to context: Community based natural resource management in Botswana. *Global Environmental Politics*, 5(3): 95–124.

Thakadu, O. T. (2005). Success factors in community based natural resource management in northern Botswana: Lessons from practice. *Natural Resource Forum*, 29(3): 199–212.

Twyman, C. (2000). Participatory conservation? Community-based natural resource management in Botswana. *Geographical Journal*, 166(4): 323–335.

Twyman, C. (2017). Community-based natural resource management. *International Encyclopaedia of Geography*.

van de Walle, N. (2001). *African economies and the politics of permanent crisis, 1979–1999*. New York: Cambridge University Press.

Vidal, J. (2014). Botswana Bushmen: If you deny us the right to hunt, you are killing us. *Guardian*, 18 April.

# 10 COVID-19, conservation, and tourism in Namibia's Conservancies

## Socioeconomic and land-use impacts

*Eduard Gargallo and Jona Heita*

### Introduction

One of the effects of the COVID-19 pandemic has been the near-collapse of international tourism. In Southern Africa, many Community Conservation programmes developed since the 1990s were based on the income generated from ecotourism and trophy hunting and have, therefore, been greatly impacted by the new situation. Recent research has started to explore the pandemic's impact on both tourism and conservation worldwide (Fletcher et al., 2020a, b; Lindsey et al., 2020; Musavengane et al., 2020). This chapter wishes to contribute to this emerging scholarship by responding to the calls made by Simula et al. (2020: 2) for "focused studies of particular settings" as well as for an analysis of COVID-19's repercussions on pastoralist communities. In our case studies, agropastoralists are also involved in tourism and conservation.

Namibia's programme of Communal Conservancies (CCs) has been depicted as one of the most successful in Africa and is often implemented through tourism business joint ventures between communities and private companies. Through the analysis of both the general evolution of Conservancies and of the specific cases of two of them, we will explore the effects of the pandemic on rural populations, placing special attention on three issues: the socioeconomic impact of declining revenues and employment, the effects on wildlife behaviour and human-wildlife relations, and, finally, the possible changes in land use in Conservancies. Regarding this last point, we will be exploring the possibility that a decrease in conservation-related incomes might lead to a modification in livelihood strategies: we will survey if an intensification of agricultural and pastoral activities and/or a change in rural-urban migration flows is taking place.

Data for this chapter essentially comes from fieldwork conducted in Anabeb and (to a lesser extent) Sesfontein Conservancies, where a total of 23 interviews were carried out in February 2021. Besides some Management Committee members, most interviews were conducted with ordinary Conservancy members. Secondary literature, government and NGO reports, and press articles were used to elicit additional evidence and to provide a wider context for the localised findings.

DOI: 10.4324/9781003188902-13

Although our data is still preliminary, it already suggests what may happen to community wildlife conservation schemes when tourism-generated income vanishes, and the way land use and agropastoralism may evolve when conservation loses ground.

## Community conservation and tourism in Namibia

Since the 1990s many African countries, in collaboration with international institutions, have developed a diversity of so-called Community-Based Natural Resources Management (CBNRM) programmes that are supposed to enhance the power of local communities over the management of wildlife and other natural resources, as well as to increase the revenue accruing to these populations from conservation-related economic activities. In most of these schemes, tourism – in the form of game viewing or sport hunting – is expected to provide the bulk of the new income. Academic and technical reviews of these initiatives have often highlighted, among other problems, the limitations of the benefits received by communities (Brockington et al., 2008: 87–111; Schnegg & Dimba Kiaka, 2018).

In 1996 the Namibian government introduced the Nature Conservation Amendment Act, which permitted rural communities to establish CCs on Communal Lands. They are awarded the right to manage wildlife within their boundaries, as well as an annual quota of trophy and consumption hunting, and can initiate communal tourism enterprises or joint ventures with private partners (Hohmann, 2003: 211–14, 219). The number of registered Conservancies rapidly increased, from the first four in 1998 to 83 in 2017. They amount, together with Community Forests, to 53% of all Communal Areas (NACSO, 2018: 7, 28).

To be officially recognised by the Ministry of Environment, Forestry and Tourism (MEFT), Conservancies need to have clear boundaries, a constitution, and an income-distribution plan. Normally, all adult residents within the Conservancy area become members. The governance system is based on a Management Committee (MC) elected by members that is responsible for the implementation of conservation measures, benefit distribution, and coordination of public-private partnerships. An Annual General Meeting of all members is expected to supervise the operation of the MC. Local Traditional Authorities have powers over communal land management and allocation and are, therefore, often involved or consulted in Conservancy projects (Gargallo & Kalvelage, 2020).

In Namibia, tourist visits reached 1,6 million in 2019 ("Over 1.6m tourists", 2020), and the presence of tourism companies is now widespread in the Conservancies. According to the Namibian Association of Community-Based Support Organisations' (NACSO) statistics, 62 CCs hosted a total of 171 enterprises "based on natural resources" and 38 CCs were directly involved with tourism activities. Fifty-four joint-venture tourism agreements with private companies had been signed and there were 56 conservation hunting concessions (NACSO, 2018: 13, 65).

In 2017, Community Conservation generated a total cash income and in-kind benefits to rural communities of over N$ 132.000.000 (7.762.000 €),[1] of which tourism generated N$ 80.117.640 and trophy hunting N$ 32.503.047. Conservancy residents earned a total cash income of N$ 65.828.264 from enterprise wages, of which N$ 42.081.247 was from joint-venture tourism, N$ 18.861.815 from conservancies, N$ 3.558.788 from trophy hunting, and N$ 1.326.414 from small and medium enterprises. In total, conservation created 5.350 jobs in 2017. Joint venture lodges employed 975 full time and 110 part-time workers, while the 56 conservation hunting concessions had 152 full time and 167 part-time employees. Conservancies themselves employed 831 workers. Trophy hunting also plays a significant role in the provision of meat to communities, and game meat worth N$ 12.566.280 (738.000 €) was distributed to Conservancies' residents (NACSO, 2018: 13, 64–65). Revenues received by the Conservancies from tourism and hunting companies are mostly used to finance a diversity of community projects (such as water provision, support to schools, or infrastructures) and, in a few cases, to make individual cash payments to members.

One of the main shortcomings of the Conservancies programme, however, has been identified as the insufficiency of benefits accruing to rural populations (Deere, 2011: 26; Lindsey et al., 2007: 465). Most tourism companies in Namibia are in the hands of foreigners or white Namibians. Beyond the number of jobs created, several analyses have highlighted shortcomings in terms of wages and work conditions (Koot et al., 2019: 11–12; Lenggenhager, 2018: 192–193; Schnegg & Dimba Kiaka, 2018: 109). It is worth mentioning that Namibia's rural areas are notorious for their lack of employment opportunities (Delgado & Jauch, 2014), and that regular cash income provided by tourism enterprises may significantly improve the situation of households.

Conservation and conservation-related investments have effects on the interrelated issues of land access and land use. If conservation, as advocated by both the MEFT and Conservancies, has sometimes prevented the expansion of land concessions to private investors or the fencing of individual ranches by local and outside elites, it has also been on other occasions responsible for land-related conflicts. Local farmers have expressed their discontent when Conservancies have delimitated – in a process called 'zonation' – areas of communal land as wildlife areas, to be devoted to ecotourism or trophy hunting. Zonation is expected to follow a process of consultation with the different stakeholders, but this has not always been the case (Gargallo, 2020).

## COVID-19 and tourism in Namibia

Following general world practice, a state of emergency was declared in Namibia in March 2020, and the country went into a national lockdown. All ports of entry were closed. Travelling between different regions was also restricted and from 18 April to 5 May 2020, no tourists were allowed to visit National Parks. At the same time, social distancing measures, such as the banning of public gatherings, were introduced (Lendelvo et al., 2020: 3).

As was to be expected, retrenchments in tourism and hospitality quickly followed (Lendelvo et al., 2020: 3–4). In May, for instance, Safari Hotels announced the layoff of 177 out of its 219 employees (Ngatjiheue, 2020a). In April 2020 the International Air Transport Association was already warning of massive losses to airlines in Southern Africa (Musavengane et al., 2020: 11). Air Namibia, the national carrier, which was already in dire straits before the pandemic, was finally liquidated following a cabinet decision in February 2021. This liquidation caused up to six hundred employees to lose their jobs (Ngatjiheue, 2020b; Editorial Team, 2021).

The Government attempted to ease restrictions and revive the tourism sector shortly afterwards, by partially reopening business in May and announcing an 'international tourism revival' initiative in August. On 1 September, Hosea Kutako Airport was reopened to foreign travellers and soon afterwards, the limited quarantine applied to tourists was removed as, according to the Minister of Environment, Forestry and Tourism, Pohamba Shifeta, restrictions were still preventing tourist arrivals (Bayer, 2020; "Government announce", 2020; Imbili, 2020). None of these measures, though, had any meaningful impact in the number of tourist arrivals.

## Socioeconomic effects on Conservancies

The collapse of tourism and the general economic downturn obviously impacted Conservancies, where conservation sometimes "provides the greatest source of cash income to households" (Lendelvo et al., 2020: 3–4). Conservancies quickly stopped recruiting and training staff and retrenchments and salary cuts of up to 50% were imposed. Private companies experienced difficulties paying the fees included in the joint venture agreements, and CCs had to suspend the distribution of cash payments to communities, social benefits, and meat distribution. The little income still available had to be used for "core operational costs", and savings started to be spent (Lendelvo et al., 2020: 7, 10; interview, Namibia Nature Foundation [NNF] programme coordinator). In the NNF-supported Conservancies in Erongo, Omaheke, Kunene South, and Kavango East and West, trophy hunting, mostly by US and UK hunters, all but ceased, while crafts and joint-ventures contributed below-average income. Some CCs found themselves with "no income at all" (interview, NNF programme coordinator).

Many of these processes were in operation in the two Conservancies where our research was carried out. One is Anabeb, located in the Kunene region and established in 2003. It occupies an extension of 1.570 square km and is inhabited by around 1.500 people. The environment is mostly arid, with less than 100 mm average annual rainfall. Significant numbers of wildlife are to be found in the area, including species attractive to tourists and trophy hunters, such as elephants, leopards, or lions. The Conservancy has a joint venture tourism agreement with Ongongo Camp as well as a community rest camp. It also has a share in the neighbouring Palmwag Tourism Concession. Trophy, shoot-and-sell, and own-use hunting are practiced (www.nacso.org.na/conservancies/anabeb). Benefits are mostly used for community projects such as a kindergarten, water supply to households, funeral assistance, or scholarships. The Conservancy employs eight people and a further 49 are employed by the Lodge (23 of them women) (Anabeb Institutional Report, 2019, http://www.nacso.org.na/sites/default/files/Anabeb%20Audit%20Report%202019.pdf).

The other Conservancy is Sesfontein, also in the Kunene region and established in 2003. It is bigger (2.465 square km) and even more sparsely populated (1.835 inhabitants) than Anabeb. Climate is equally arid, although with a slightly higher rainfall. Besides the attractive wildlife present in Anabeb, the highly endangered black rhino is also present. A joint venture tourism agreement was signed with Fort Sesfontein Lodge, and there are two community campsites. Sesfontein has also a share in the Palmwag Tourism Concession and enjoys trophy, shoot-and-sell, and own-use hunting quotas (http://www.nacso.org.na/conservancies/sesfontein). The Conservancy employs fifteen people and 59 are employed by the Lodge (31 of them women) (Sesfontein Institutional Report, 2019 http://www.nacso.org.na/sites/default/files/Sesfontein%20Audit%20Report%202019.pdf). Both Anabeb and Sesfontein are among the highest-earning group of Namibian Conservancies, with an annual income of between 1 and 5 million N$ (MEFT/NACSO, 2021: 33).

In both Conservancies, Herero and Damara are the main ethnic communities, although smaller groups of Himba are also present. The livelihoods of most residents are based on a mix of livestock herding (cattle and small stock) and small-scale crop cultivation. Pensions, wages derived from the limited local employment opportunities, and remittances by people working outside provide additional income to many households. In the arid environment, boreholes are used for the basic supply of water, despite being costly to maintain. Around Sesfontein (Six Fountains) settlement, water is easier to access and in the Sesfontein valley the density of livestock is higher (Pellis, 2011; NACSO, 2012).

Following the national pattern, interviews with Conservancy members in Anabeb and Sesfontein revealed that staff in local and outside tourism enterprises had been retrenched from work. Others still lost income because employers reduced their monthly salaries, in some cases up to a 25% of the usual wage. All this had a severe impact on livelihoods, as tourism employees often "were the breadwinners of the respective families". In other instances, "parents cannot afford [school] registration fees" anymore (interview, Anabeb Management Committee member [MCm] 1). Reduced salaries now provided "only for food" (interview, Sesfontein Conservancy member [Cm] 5). People also lost access to credit at shops, which was obtained using wages as a guarantee (interview, Sesfontein Cm 4).

COVID-19 not only negatively impacted those community members who were employed in tourism businesses but, according to almost all respondents, it also affected craft producers who depended on selling their products to tourists. Producers started generating below-average incomes and many found themselves with no revenue at all. Trophy hunting operations were equally affected, leading not only to a loss of income but to reductions in game meat distribution (interviews, Anabeb Cm 10; Sesfontein Cm 4). As one resident put it: "there is no meat now" (interview, Anabeb female Cm 3).

In view of the situation, Conservancies "started approaching NGOs for support" (interview, Tourism Supporting Conservation Trust [Tosco] representative 2). The MEFT issued Essential Services Permits that allowed mobility to NGOs' and CCs' staff (interview NNF programme coordinator). Initially, funding from donors such as WWF, EU, and IRDNC was also expected to fall amidst the massive international economic crisis, but soon some relief measures were implemented. In May 2020 the MEFT announced the Conservation Relief, Recovery and Resilient Facility (CRRRF) to maintain "core activities and core staff" of Conservancies and prevent further retrenchments, under which Conservancies received quarterly payments (interviews, NNF programme coordinator; Tosco representative 1). This "one-off emergency fund of around N$26 million" was established with contributions from Nedbank Namibia, Environmental Investment Fund of Namibia, Namibian Chamber of Environment, WWF, and the German Cooperation (Lendelvo et al., 2020: 11–13).

Government, Conservancy, and private support was evident in our case studies. Government funds assisted Anabeb in distributing food to its members and in avoiding retrenchments of Conservancy staff (interview, female MCm 2). Official aid also went into providing seeds for crop farmers and feed for cattle (interview, Anabeb MCm 1).

More significant, though, was that in April 2020, the Namibian government announced a one-off payment of N$ 750 (approximately 41 €) as an economic stimulus and relief package grant for unemployed Namibians between the ages of 18 and 60. In addition, through the Social Security Commission, the State also provided a further one-off payment of N$ 3.000 (approximately 166 €) as a national employment and salary protection scheme for COVID-19. This scheme was targeted at employed Namibians whose salaries were affected by the crisis. According to our interviews, many Conservancy members in Anabeb and Sesfontein received the N$ 750 and/or N$ 3.000 grants, although it seems that not all those entitled to the payments actually received them. The general feeling among interviewees was positive towards these government efforts to assist citizens.

Anabeb Conservancy focused on food distribution (interviews, Cm 2; female Cm 8; Cm 9; Cm 16) but also paid registration fees for students going to University (interview, Anabeb MCm 1) and bought and distributed soap and disinfection material for each homestead in the Conservancy (interviews, Anabeb female MCm 2; Cm 10; Cm 16). Sesfontein delivered food to unemployed members as well (interview Sesfontein Cm 1). Finally, Wilderness Safaris contributed food to residents in both Conservancies (interviews, Sesfontein Cm 1; Cm 2; Cm 3; Cm 4; and Anabeb female Cm 3; female Cm 4; Cm 10; Cm 13).

We also asked Conservancy members if they could identify any positive impacts that COVID-19 had brought to their communities. Firstly, they highlighted improvements in hygiene, as people started washing their hands more regularly to reduce the chances of contracting the virus. Other positive impacts of the pandemic that were mentioned included family reconnections: people who used to work in different towns and other places had to return home after losing their jobs. Lastly, interviews also revealed some satisfaction with the night-time curfew. This measure has allegedly diminished alcohol consumption, especially among the youth, and, consequently, night noise is reduced, and people can sleep well (interview, Anabeb Cm 17). It is also supposed to have caused a reduction in road accidents. As one respondent commented: "The curfew is a good thing. It has also reduced the number of accidents in the country because people are only allowed to travel at certain times of the day. Drivers most of the time are sober and not exhausted at all. That has really helped a lot" (interview, Anabeb Cm 1). In Sesfontein, it was also reported that "there has been a drop in the alcohol consumption" among youngsters (interview, Sesfontein Cm 2).

## Impact on wildlife behaviour, human-wildlife conflict, and poaching

Following in the line of the more 'positive' effects of COVID-19, first reports of its environmental impact have mentioned alterations to "humans' physical interaction with wildlife and natural spaces on a massive scale". In many areas of the world, lockdowns "have led to mass [human] withdrawal from many spaces", leading to "a widely documented proliferation of wildlife in rural as well as urban areas" (Fletcher et al., 2020a: 202–203).

Some such instances have also been detected in Namibia. Tourism's collapse has afforded a "huge relief for wildlife", with lower stress levels (interview NNF programme coordinator) and animals are said to "get much closer to the road" than before (interview, Tosco representative 1). The September 2020 game counts detected more animals drinking at water points as the human presence declined (interview, Tosco representative 2). Animals were described as enjoying tranquillity in Anabeb, repeating the idea that "you will find springboks just standing next to the road" (interviews Anabeb Cm 13; Cm 16). On the other hand, a significant number of respondents in both Anabeb and Sesfontein were convinced that wildlife was not under stress before (interviews, Anabeb Cm 1; female Cm 3; Cm 6; female Cm 8; female Cm 11; Sesfontein Cm 5; Cm 3).

Regional evidence also points towards more negative impacts. The very same absence of tourists and trophy hunters, together with the reduced presence of game guards patrolling and monitoring wildlife, contributed to higher levels of human-wildlife conflict (HWC) (Lendelvo et al., 2020: 7; Musavengane et al., 2020: 8–9).

Anabeb registered around 100 incidents of HWC in 2019, part of a growing trend. Most cases involved predators such as hyenas, cheetah, leopards, or lions attacking livestock (Anabeb Natural Resource Report, 2019). In Sesfontein, although HWC is below the highest point of 2013, predators, especially hyenas, continue to cause damage (Sesfontein Natural Resource Report, 2019). Some respondents stated that current HWC levels cannot be attributed to COVID-19. The problem was already present before, due to the cycle of repeated droughts experienced during the 2010s that led predators closer to farming and herding areas (interview Anabeb MCm 1). Others did detect recent changes, though: the absence of cars and people make wildlife "no longer afraid of going anywhere" and closeness to humans is increasing (interview, Anabeb female MCm 2). In Sesfontein, lions have settled "at the staff village" of the local Lodge, which is empty because of the lack of activity. "They are resting there", and this could create trouble when employees come back (interview, Sesfontein Cm 5).

At the same time, "less pairs of eyes" in Conservancies makes poaching easier (interview, Tosco representative 1). This has been confirmed in places like King Nehale Conservancy (Lendelvo et al., 2020.,: 8) or in Kunene North, where rhinos have been affected (interview NNF programme coordinator). It must be highlighted, though, that official statistics recently displayed by the MEFT claim fewer incidents of wildlife poaching in 2020, including a marked decrease in rhino killings compared to 2019 (Shikongo, 2021). It is also clear that wildlife was already decreasing throughout the extremely dry 2010s.

Despite reluctance from some respondents to discuss the subject, poaching seems to have already been present in Anabeb and Sesfontein. Some local people were killing animals to sell their meat. Those involved "are not doing it in public, when you are seen" (interview, Anabeb Cm 1; female Cm 3). In Sesfontein, one male lion was poisoned after killing some livestock, although this was described as also happening before COVID-19 (interview, Sesfontein Cm 2).

Both conservation NGOs and the METF implemented measures to combat poaching and HWC. In May 2020 the Community Conservation Fund's Human-Wildlife Conflict Field Team was registered as an essential service and authorised to continue its work despite the lockdown ("CCF's Human-Wildlife Conflict", 2020). The company B2Gold began the 'B2Gold Rhino Gold Bar' in January 2020: The scheme provided funds from gold sales to keep rangers from all 13 rhino range CCs in the northwest in the field for 12 months, as well as salaries and support for field staff from conservation NGOs. By July 2020, some N$3 million had been disbursed ("B2Gold supports", 2020).

## Possible changes in people's attitudes towards wildlife

Some analysts have warned that the reduction in tourism-related income may diminish rural populations' support for conservation (Lendelvo et al., 2020:

4; Lindsey et al., 2020: 1304). According to Fletcher et al., (2020a: 204–205) "this stakeholder strategy has always been a dangerous gamble, since basing conservation support on such 'extrinsic' motivation (rather than an 'intrinsic' sense of care for biodiversity) could obviate this support were the revenue fueling this motivation to disappear".

Interviews in Anabeb and Sesfontein revealed that some respondents supported the argument that people's attitudes towards wildlife could potentially change in the event that conservation-based benefits disappear. HWC and lack of compensation – either direct or through tourist-generated income and employment – were the main reasons behind these hardening attitudes. HWC increases in Namibia are said to have "left a bitter taste" in Conservancies. The governmental compensation system[2] is receiving more incident reports and cannot keep up with these claims, as income is decreasing. As a result, "people are frustrated" (interview, NNF programme coordinator). In Anabeb, a Management Committee member declared that compensation had already been "totally affected" while, before, "even if they were getting a small amount they appreciated", and he added that "one reason why we were taking care of predators" was income, otherwise "us as farmers we'll take the law into our hands" (interview, Anabeb MCm 1). Several respondents indicated that they would be forced to take retaliatory actions against wildlife causing damages to their livestock, their only hope in a context of struggle to overcome the consequences of drought. "Some will kill" in retaliation for HWC or to access meat, if both drought and COVID-19 continue (interview, Sesfontein Cm 5). You will see springboks in front of you and will think "that's my dinner now" (interview, Anabeb female Cm 11).

On the other hand, some Namibian conservation NGOs keep expecting that conservation will be valued. The link between less income and loss of interest for conservation is not seen as 'straightforward', as conservation finds support among local communities in rural areas per se and rural residents have an interest in preserving wildlife for "future generations" (interview, Tosco representative 1). Some CBNRM programmes have allegedly "been looking at balancing the two", i.e. economic and non-economic value of wildlife (interview NNF programme coordinator). These views can also be found in Anabeb and Sesfontein, where part of our respondents were convinced that people's interest in and liking of wildlife will not vanish (interviews, Anabeb Cm 5; Sesfontein Cm 5). Optimistic outlooks, though, were clearly in the minority: 64% of respondents predicted more hostile reactions towards wildlife, 23% maintained that no substantial change would occur, and 13% were unsure over future developments.

## Livelihood strategies of Conservancy residents

Once conservation-related income decreases occurred, the possibility that livelihood strategies might change had to be considered. This is especially so, as we indicated in the introduction, with the potential intensification of agropastoral activities or shifts in rural-urban migration. The actual impact of COVID-19 at this level in Namibia's Conservancies, however, remains limited or contradictory. After tourism stopped, some NGOs explain that "there hasn't been such effort to shift to agriculture", as many Conservancies are located in non-"agricultural-friendly environments" (interview, NNF programme coordinator). For the moment, no "drastic move towards livestock" is apparent either, and it was already common that people earning money from tourism maintained agricultural or pastoral activities (interview, Tosco representative 1). As a matter of fact, Conservancies and NGO projects in support of agriculture existed before.

Some changes occurred, though. In the Kavango regions, where 'efforts' to improve agriculture predated COVID-19, a slight increase in people's participation in the "NNF programme of conservation agriculture" was reported (interview NNF programme coordinator). In Na Jaqna Conservancy, the 2020 AGM witnessed requests for more project and food security support, and plans were made to start a small-scale garden and spades and seed distributed to enable each village to start their own food security initiative ("EU and MEFT support", 2021).

It is clear from numerous responses that gardening has expanded in Anabeb and Sesfontein. Most of the gardens are small, devoted to vegetable production, and both men and women seem to be involved (interview, Anabeb MCm 1; Cm 1; Sesfontein, Cm 1; Cm2, among many others). Investment in livestock is not also widespread. Some respondents used the money from retrenchment packages to buy goats (interview, Anabeb Cm.9), but several others remained sceptical, mostly for lack of funds in a context of deepening economic crisis: "Where do we get the money to buy goats?", asked one Anabeb resident (interview, female Cm 15), and the same concern could be found in Sesfontein (interview, Cm 1). Environmental difficulties were also mentioned. One herder had a "few cattle, goats and sheep" but he kept them in another area, near Opuwo (further north), because drought made it difficult to feed them in Sesfontein (interview, Cm 2).

It has been suggested that a reduction in urban and tourism-based employment may lead people to return to their rural homes (Lindsey et al., 2020: 1304), but in our research areas no significant change in rural-urban migration trends were apparent, and diverse and contradictory evidence emerged. As an example, one respondent explained that in his village some people had indeed moved back from towns, but he quickly added: "we cannot just sit here", "we are having babies to feed", and some other residents were going to urban areas (interview, Anabeb MCm 1). Another resident went to Walvis Bay to work as a security guard until he was called back to the tourist lodge where he used to be employed (interview, Anabeb Cm 6), while a respondent assured that "they know they cannot live without money" (interview, Anabeb Cm 16).

On the other hand, it was common to find respondents reluctant to migrate to cities as an alternative to the jobs lost in tourism. Reasons ranged from the higher cost of living in towns, to poor perspectives of finding employment and fear of higher urban rates of COVID-19 contagion (diversity of interviews). For example, an Anabeb resident stated that, "I cannot support the idea of going to towns. At least people should remain where they are then they start with small projects like cultivation. When you cultivate, you will get something that you can sell. In town, there are still the same problems since Covid-19 is everywhere. People should remain where they are and start small businesses" (interview, female MCm 2). Globally, 71% of our respondents did not consider migrating to towns as a viable or desirable economic alternative.

Evidence from other areas confirmed the complexity of the rural-urban nexus in pandemic times. Press reports on Himba residents in the coastal town of Swakopmund described a situation "worse off at the town than back home at their villages" after they left their home areas in the Kunene region expecting to find jobs and benefit from the tourism industry. COVID-19 led to the disappearance of tourists and made job-seeking harder. As in the city life is more expensive, many have been forced to return to their homes. But the option to go back to the rural areas does not look promising either. Local sources of employment or cash are scarce, and the recent droughts have hampered both livestock herding and crop growing. As one of the Himba stated: "there is nothing back home either", or another was sure that "we will come back again" (Hartman, 2021).

A significant number of our respondents' advanced plans, if the economic crisis continues, is to establish small businesses, almost all of them devoted to selling or reselling meat, sweets, fat-cake, and a variety of consumer products (interviews, female Cm 3; female Cm 4; Cm 5; female Cm 7; female Cm. 8; Cm 10; female Cm 15). Obviously, it is difficult to assess the viability of a large number of very small-scale sellers offering basically the same items.

The possibility of developing a craft production aimed at international markets whereby income would then be distributed among craft makers was valued by residents in Anabeb and Sesfontein, but some of them expressed concerns about trusting Conservancy officials to handle the whole process. They feared that, due to possible corruption among officials, craft producers may end up not getting their rightful income share (interviews, Anabeb Cm 6; Cm 10; female Cm 12; female Cm 15; Sesfontein Cm 16). One respondent showed clearly the failure of previous Conservancy work in building community confidence: "you do not trust anyone" (interview, Anabeb Cm 9).

## Conclusion

When evaluating the effects of COVID-19 on tourism and conservation, it is difficult to reach definite conclusions, assess medium-term impacts and, even less, make predictions towards a more distant future. Time is essential here, as the situation is evolving as we write. So it is the need to pay attention to variations across a myriad of local environments. This being said, the Namibian experience allows us to explore, albeit in limited form, wider issues relating to conservation and livelihoods in rural areas where conservation played a significant role before the pandemic.

It is obvious that African conservation was experiencing problems before COVID-19, and the pandemic has led it to a crisis point, with massive reductions of revenue for both governments and the private sector (Lindsey et al., 2020: 1302–1303). In this context, Namibia shows that in a country with a well-developed tourist industry and a reasonably well-managed Community Conservation programme, the impact of COVID-19 and the practical disappearance of tourism revenue can be contained. Conservancies' infrastructure and services have not collapsed, and they have been able to provide some support to residents. Donor funding has assisted in the maintenance of core activities and the government has been able to aid Conservancies and, more importantly, individuals and households through grants and one-off payments. But all this is temporary. Should the absence of tourism income persist, many of the measures will be unsustainable.

Some 'positive' environmental outcomes have been also detected in general assessments, such as 'reduced air pollution' due in part to the decrease in international travel, or the provision of 'respite' for Protected Areas suffering from 'tourist congestion' (Lindsey et al., 2020: 1302). It is very difficult, however, to predict how long this situation will prevail. In Namibian Conservancies, the reduction in animal 'disturbance' has also taken place, but it is not always evaluated equally by local authors, and few Conservancies could be described as 'congested' before COVID-19. It is likely that both the sudden and severe fall of revenues and the need to increase access and use of natural resources, including wildlife, will have a more relevant impact.

Calls have been made to avoid a simple return to business as usual when the pandemic situation improves (Fletcher et al., 2020b: 45–46). It is certain that, as we have just stated above, conservation practices in Africa needed to be reformed even without COVID-19. How to implement changes is less clear. African countries, for instance, have been criticised for an "overreliance on international tourism to support conservation", and calls have been made to "foster domestic tourism" (Lindsey et al., 2020: 1305, 1308). The turn towards domestic tourism, however, is problematic, to say the least. In Namibia, the MEFT called locals to visit national parks once the more restrictive measures were lifted (Bayer, 2020) but shortly afterwards the Minister himself acknowledged that "the survival and re-growth of the tourism sector depends mainly on our ability to attract international tourists" ("Government announce", 2020). In Anabeb and Sesfontein, the domestic tourism option was also received with scepticism. International travellers are described as willing to pay higher rates and to spend more money on site. They also used to arrive throughout the year, while Namibians tend to travel only in specific holiday seasons (interviews, Anabeb Cm 1; Cm 9; Cm17). In Sesfontein, cutting rates failed to attract meaningful numbers of national visitors (interview, Sesfontein Cm 2).

On a wider level, the crisis of the tourism sector has (re)opened the discussion over the need to diversify livelihood strategies in areas where conservation is very present, possibly through a reinforcement of agricultural activities, and to reduce dependence on tourism-related incomes (Lendelvo et al., 2020: 14). In Namibia's Conservancies, we have seen an incipient move towards gardening and calls for more attention to be paid to crops and livestock. But this is not, for now, a significant break with the past, as conservation programmes were already supporting small-scale agricultural projects, and residents in Conservancies are often farmers and/or herders in any case. Environmental and climatic conditions in arid or semi-arid lands make agricultural intensification difficult, as the recent cycle of drought exemplifies. In our research areas, gardening or goat herding was seen more as a survival strategy to cope with the present crisis than as an alternative source of income capable of replacing salaries and benefits derived from tourism and conservation. It is also possible that the very same COVID-19 crisis may hamper all other economic initiatives. In case of a rise in contagion rates, further lockdowns might restrict access to agricultural and livestock markets, something that has already been highlighted in recent analysis elsewhere (Simula et al., 2020: 8, 18–19). Up to now, the fall in tourism revenue has led to a restriction in the sources of livelihood rather than to its diversification. Migration does not appear as a clear alternative either. Respondents are divided between those favouring a move to cities in search of jobs and those opting for a return to the rural area or remaining there, and in neither case are future economic expectations high. For all these reasons, no dramatic changes in land-use strategies have been detected. Up to now, COVID-19 has foregrounded some of the shortcomings of the Community Conservation model, but it has also called attention towards some of its benefits – now that they are gone.

## Acknowledgements

Research for this chapter has been carried out as part of the research projects *COVID 19 in African and Asian Drylands*, included in the Social Science Extreme Event Research Network funded by the United States National Science Foundation (NSF Award 1841338), and *Imagining and Building Post-Covid-19 Futures: Tourism, Conservation and Dryland Communities in Africa* (Quick Response Research Award supported by the National Science Foundation, NSF Award #1635593, and by the Natural Hazards Center at the University of Colorado Boulder). We have benefited greatly from the work and views of our fellow researchers in these projects, and we thank Joana Roque de Pinho and Angela Kronenburg Garcia for their comments on earlier drafts of the chapter. We are also grateful to all individuals that agreed to be interviewed. We gratefully acknowledge the support provided by Mr Steve Kaisuma as research assistant and translator of some of the interviews. Finally, we thank an anonymous reviewer for comments and suggestions on an earlier draft. Any opinions, findings, conclusions, or recommendations expressed in this material are those of the authors and do not necessarily reflect the views of the NSF or Natural Hazards Center.

## Notes

1 Exchange rate at 22 May 2021. The totals have been rounded up.
2 In 2009 the MET set up the Human Wildlife Self Reliance Scheme, which contemplates the payment of compensation for damages reported under specific conditions and validated by Ministry officials or Conservancy guards. Funding is basically provided by MET and the scheme compensates for livestock and crop losses "at rates that do not cover the full value" (MET, 2009: 1–3, 6, 9–10, 12, 17, 22–24).

## References


B2Gold supports community-backed rhino conservation efforts. (2020). Retrieved from http://www.nacso.org.na/news/2020/07/b2gold-supports-community-backed-rhino-conservation-efforts

Bayer, R. (2020, May 15). Hospitality, tourism sector can now open. *The Namibian.*

Brockington, D., Duffy, R. & Igoe, J. (2008). *Nature unbound. Conservation, capitalism and the future of protected areas.* London: Earthscan.

CCF's human-wildlife conflict field team is back in action. (2020). Retrieved from http://www.nacso.org.na/news/2020/06/ccf%E2%80%99s-human-wildlife-conflict-field-team-is-back-in-action

Deere, N.J. (2011) Exploitation or conservation? Can the hunting tourism industry in Africa be sustainable?. *Environment: Science and Policy for Sustainable Development*, 53(4), 20–32.

Delgado, G. & Jauch, H. (2014). *Trade unions at the crossroads? Reflections on the challenges and opportunities facing Namibia's labour movement.* Windhoek: Sociology Department of the University of Namibia (UNAM) & Namibia Office of the Friedrich Ebert Stiftung (FES).

Editorial Team. (2021, February 12). Air Namibia: It's now or never. *The Namibian.*

EU and MEFT support for Na Jaqna AGM critical during this difficult time. (2021). Retrieved from https://www.nndfn.org/eu-and-meft-support-for-na-jaqna-agm-critical-during-this-difficult-time

Fletcher, R., Büscher, B., Massarella, K. & Koot, S. (2020a). Close the tap! COVID-19 and the need for convivial conservation. *Journal of Australian Political Economy*, 85, 200–211.

Fletcher, R., Büscher, B., Massarella, K. & Koot, S. (2020b). Ecotourism and conservation under COVID-19 and beyond. *ATLAS Tourism and Leisure Review*, 2020-2, 42–50.

Gargallo, E. (2020). Community conservation and land use in Namibia: Visions, expectations and realities. *Journal of Southern African Studies*, 46(1), 129–147.

Gargallo, E. & Kalvelage, L. (2020). Integrating social-ecological systems and global production networks: local effects of trophy hunting in Namibian conservancies. *Development Southern Africa.* DOI: 10.1080/0376835X.2020.1835608

Government announce new implementation protocol for international tourism revival. (2020). Retrieved from https://www.met.gov.na/news/192/government-announce-new-implementation-protocol-for-international-tourism-revival

Hartman, A. (2021, February 16). Covid-19 eats away Ovahimba livelihoods at Swakop. *The Namibian.*

Hohmann, T. (2003). We are looking for life. We are looking for the conservancy. Namibian Conservancies, Nature Conservation and Rural Development: The N‡a-Jaqna Conservancy. In T.Hohmann (Ed.), *San and the State: Contesting land, development, identity and representation* (pp. 209–11). Köln: Rudiger Köppe Verlag.

Imbili, F. (2020). Seven days' tourist isolation protocol removed. Retrieved from https://www.met.gov.na/news/194/seven-days-tourist-isolation-protocol-removed

Koot, S., Hitchcock, R. & Gressier, C. (2019). Belonging, indigeneity, land and nature in Southern Africa under Neoliberal Capitalism: An overview. *Journal of Southern African Studies*. 45(2), 1-15 DOI: 10.1080/03057070.2019.1610243

Lendelvo, S., Pinto, M. & Sullivan, S. (2020). A perfect storm? The impact of COVID-19 on community-based conservation in Namibia. *Namibian Journal of Environment*, 4 B, 1–15.

Lenggenhager, L. (2018). *Ruling nature, controlling people. Nature conservation, development and war in North-Eastern Namibia since the 1920s*. Basel: Basel Afrika Bibliographien.

Lindsey, P.A. Roulet, P.A. & Romañach, S.S. (2007). Economic and conservation significance of the trophy hunting industry in Sub-Saharan Africa. *Biological Conservation*, 134, 455–69.

Lindsey, P. et al. (2020). Conserving Africa's wildlife and wildlands through the COVID-19 crisis and beyond. *Nature Ecology and Evolution*, 4, 1300–1310.

MEFT/NACSO (2021). *The state of community conservation in Namibia (Annual Report 2019)*. Windhoek: MEFT/NACSO.

Ministry of Environment, Tourism (MET) (2009). *National policy on human wildlife conflict management*. Windhoek: MET.

Musavengane, R., Leonard, L. & Mureyani, S. (2020). Doing tourism in Southern Africa amid the coronavirus pandemic: Navigating political, socio-economic and environmental inequalities. *Development Southern Africa*. DOI: 10.1080/0376835X.2020.1829459

NACSO (2012). *Living with wildlife: The story of Sesfontein conservancy*. Windhoek: NACSO.

NACSO (2018). *The state of community conservation in Namibia: A review of communal conservancies, community forests and other CBNRM activities (Annual Report 2017)*. Windhoek: MET/NACSO.

Ngatjiheue, Ch. (2020a, May 13). Safari looks to Govt to save jobs. *The Namibian*.

Ngatjiheue, Ch. (2020b, July 3). AirNam needs N$7 billion. *The Namibian*.

Over 1.6m tourists visited in 2019. (2020). Retrieved from https://namibiatourism.com.na/industrynews/over-1-6m-tourists-visited-in-2019

Pellis, A. (2011). *Access to Benefits from Community Based Tourism. A discursive ethnography of conflict over benefits in Anabeb Conservancy, Namibia*. (MSc Thesis). Wageningen University.

Schnegg, M. & Dimba Kiaka, R. (2018). Subsidized elephants: Community-Based resource governance and environmental (in)justice in Namibia. *Geoforum*, 93, 105–115.

Shikongo, A. (2021, February 5). Less poaching, more arrests in 2020. *The Namibian*.

Simula, G., Bum, T., Farinella, D., Maru, N., Mohamed, T.S., Taye, M. & Tsering, P. (2020). COVID-19 and pastoralism: Reflections from three continents. *Journal of Peasant Studies*. DOI: 10.1080/03066150.2020.1808969

# 11 Conflicts between conservation and community livelihoods

## Lessons from KwaNibela and iSimangaliso Wetland Park, KwaZulu-Natal, South Africa

*Zwelakhe Thulasizwe Mascot Maseko and Inocent Moyo*

### Introduction

Protected areas (PAs) are increasingly being created, managed, and owned by private actors, leading to land grabs that frequently jeopardise local control of the land, livelihoods, and biodiversity. Changes in land use and ownership result in new governance arrangements that are riddled with contradictions and cause clashing of viewpoints on how nature should be valued and utilised (Busscher et al., 2018). Land grabbing alters patterns of land ownership and use while also encouraging new modes of land regulation and governance (Brent, 2015). Companies' exploitation of land and land-based resources also causes socioenvironmental conflict, inequality, and environmental degradation (Busscher et al., 2018). Land grabbing can be defined as "the capturing of control of relatively vast tracts of land and other natural resources through a variety of mechanisms and forms involving large-scale capital that often shifts resource use to that of extraction, whether for international or domestic purposes" (Busscher et al., 2018, p. 573). The consequences of land grabbing are varied, and in many cases struggles over land lead to increasing political marginalisation of groups of people living nearby (Busscher et al., 2018). Land grabbing further leads to the displacement of indigenous people from their territorial land thus creating inequality (Busscher et al., 2018). From a social standpoint, the community of KwaNibela recognised that the consequences of land grabbing include violations of human rights, disregard for customary land rights, changes in livelihood, forced evictions, and prosecution of local people who take action to protect their ancestral land (Busscher et al., 2018). Land grabbing can thus be seen as a strategic way in which the elite gains control and ownership of land and resources at the expense of poor marginalised groups (Busscher et al., 2018).

Peoples' rights to access land constitute basic building blocks for enhancing and sustaining their food security .The dispossession of land due to the establishment of PAs leads to indigenous communities having less access to natural resources to carry on ancestral activities and further poses risks to food security and to indigenous livelihoods (Paredes & Kaulard, 2020). The restriction of natural resource harvesting may force communities to acquire market goods or

DOI: 10.4324/9781003188902-14

labour extensively in agriculture for a living thus altering their traditional ways of survival (Paredes & Kaulard, 2020). This restriction further leads to tensions between park rangers and local communities, as well as unlawful harvesting of natural resources. PAs are primarily established for the conservation of natural resources, but on the contrary, conservation policy has been seen to reproduce ethnic inequalities through the disempowerment of indigenous peoples' land rights (Paredes & Kaulard, 2020). In some instances, indigenous groups that reclaim legal rights over land that is conserved tend to be outlawed. This often results in indigenous communities getting caught up in legal messes, despite both national and international recognitions of the rights of indigenous peoples (Paredes & Kaulard, 2020). This shows that land disputes have far-reaching negative effects on the certainty of land markets, food security, economic production, and poverty alleviation (Paredes & Kaulard, 2020).

Environmental threats within and outside boundaries of PAs from tourism, human use, and resource development pressures have sparked conflicts and tensions between land managers and local people (Wiersma et al., 2015). Local communities rely on natural resources and land-use decisions for their fundamental necessities and livelihoods. Planning and implementing procedures for administering PAs that exclude local communities and other stakeholders have resulted in a variety of conflicts and concerns, including dislocation, violence, poaching, and poverty among indigenous populations (Afriyie et al., 2021). Tourism revenue from nature and wildlife is a major component of national economies in Africa but the exclusion of indigenous people in the management of land and natural resources has sparked conflict between the management of PAs and indigenous groups (Defries et al., 2007). This is the context within which this chapter explores the conservation-based conflict between the community of KwaNibela and iSimangaliso Wetland Park, KwaZulu-Natal, South Africa. The rest of the chapter includes a brief discussion on PAs and then the historical background on iSimangaliso Wetland Park and co-management approaches. There is then a discussion of the context of the study and the study area, and then the theoretical framework and data collection and analysis procedures. What follows after that is a discussion of the results and the conclusion. In the conclusion, the point is emphasised that the people of KwaNibela feel as if iSimangaliso Wetland Park has done very little to improve the livelihoods of the indigenous communities.

## On protected areas, conservation, and indigenous communities

The establishment of PAs is seen by some authors as an attempt to protect biodiversity and the environment, thus preventing the exploitation of valuable natural resources (Soliku & Schraml, 2018). The International Union for Conservation (IUCN) describes PAs as "clearly defined geographical areas committed and maintained through legal or other successful means to achieve long-term conservation of nature with its associated ecological services and cultural values" (Soliku & Schraml, 2018, p. 136). The objectives for setting up PAs varies from region to region. In North America, policymakers, communities, rulers, and other stakeholders normally set aside land for its cultural significance, religious purposes, aesthetic beauty, and the protection of natural resources (Soliku & Schraml, 2018). The driving force behind the creation of PAs and game parks in Africa is to safeguard the beautiful landscapes and attract visitors/tourists, protect the landscapes, and prevent valuable resources from being over-exploited (Soliku & Schraml, 2018). It is posited that PAs encourage the use of natural resources in a sustainable way, thus minimising the over-extraction of such resources and providing cultural and livelihood benefits (Ward et al., 2018). Other purported positive effects of PAs relate to development through tourism expenditure, job creation, and trade opportunities (Zafra-calvo & Moreno-Peñaranda, 2018).

However, substantial costs such as the lack of access to arable and subsistence agricultural production, crop destruction, and animal predation from PAs by wildlife adversely affect the local livelihoods (Zafra-calvo & Moreno-Peñaranda, 2018). Many marginalised communities residing along PAs depend on subsistence and livestock agriculture for survival. Therefore, the restrictions on access to land can be seen as a catalyst for conflict. This is because indigenous groups are likely to have an emotional attachment to their ancestral land, and once they are restricted access to their traditional land they feel as if their basic fundamental rights and sense of identity have been taken away (Zafra-calvo & Moreno-Peñaranda, 2018). Conflicts can also arise when protected wildlife has an impact on people and their activities, such as predating farm crops and livestock, resulting in retaliatory killings (Soliku & Schraml, 2018).

The basic challenge of conservation is the recognition of conservation measures that can protect natural resources and biodiversity while reducing natural resource restrictions and negative impacts on livelihoods. This challenge can be tackled through the inclusion of local people in conservation initiatives and by improving their benefits from conservation, so that livelihoods can be maintained (Zafra-calvo & Moreno-Peñaranda, 2018). Studies such as that carried out by Mizrahi et al. (2019) have found that, unless alternative livelihood activities are available, PAs that restrict access to natural resources can have negative impacts on households that rely on natural resources as their main source of livelihood. In South Africa, the 2017 study by Fairer-Wessels shows that the failure of PAs to improve poor and disadvantaged rural communities' socioeconomic situation is a sign that indigenous communities do not always benefit from conservation programmes in PAs (Fairer-Wessels, 2017). The unequal participation in PA governance between the indigenous communities and the so-called conservationists can lead to elite leadership capture by the latter, which can increase the unfair share of the related advantages of PAs (Ward et al., 2018). Many studies in Africa show an increasing lack of local decision-making ability, which could lead to limited contributions from local communities to decisions taken on conservation of natural resources in their region (Saunders, 2014).

As PAs continue to grow in scope and size, they are more likely to face challenges in achieving their conservation objectives due to conflicting interests which may develop over time (Bixler et al., 2016). Effective delivery of conservation projects includes the alignment of social structures, political viability, and complete support for its affected communities. The involvement of local citizens in environmental projects ensures that people are closely involved in life-influencing economic, social, cultural, and political processes (Njuguna & Deisser, 2016). The enforcement of strict conservation laws in PAs puts pressure on people's livelihoods and social welfare because they can obtain little to no conservation benefits whatsoever (Chechina et al., 2018). Some scholars (Brockington & Wilkie, 2015, Lamsal et al., 2015) argue that the centre of conservation is corporate, and elimination of poverty is not its main mandate. This is because at times conservation agencies prioritise profit generation over the wellbeing of local people. Such conservation agencies seek to maximise self-interests at the expense of poor and marginalised communities. The economic exclusion of rural people in conservation by profit-oriented conservation agencies also shows that at times, conservation may be used by the elite to secure their pockets at the expense of the poor.

In developing countries with high priorities for food security and poverty reduction rather than conservation, communities find the importance of PAs and the notion of conservation difficult to understand (Lamsal et al., 2015). The eviction of people from their ancestral land in Africa in the name of conservation further perpetuates rural poverty (Tang & Gavin, 2016). The migration of local populations away from their traditional regions has resulted in a reduction in access to resources and the absence of indigenous groups in the design, execution, and decision-making regarding conservation programmes (Kaplan-Hallam & Bennett, 2018). An example of such a scenario occurred in Ghana where the establishment of the Mole National Park resulted in the forced displacements of whole communities from within the park. Enclosure of traditional hunting grounds, farmlands, and sacred sites by the Park resulted in the loss of livelihoods and homes, fuelling resentment of the Park's authorities (Soliku & Schraml, 2018). Such situations are likely to trigger tensions and failure of the conservation goals between indigenous communities and conservation agencies. This background on the supposed benefits of PAs and their negative impacts on indigenous communities in many parts of the world and Africa generally and South Africa specifically is important. This chapter explores conflict arising from conservation between iSimangaliso Wetland Park and the community of KwaNibela because it provides a context of the discussions which will follow in the next sections. KwaNibela was considered as an ideal area to conduct this study due to its unique history, where the community was forcefully removed from their traditional land which is within the Park.

## The historical background on iSimangaliso Wetland Park and co-management approaches

The iSimangaliso Wetland Park, previously known as the Greater St Lucia Wetland Park, was first established in 1895, making the Hluhluwe-Umfolozi

Park the oldest conservation area in South Africa. Further moves to protect wildlife took place in 1944, and this led to the extension of the park through the addition of the False Bay park to the list of PAs in the country (Department of Environment, Forestry, & Fisheries, 2021). Both iSimangaliso Wetland Park and the Hluhluwe-Umfolozi Park were previously used as King Shaka's private hunting grounds (Department of Environment, Forestry, & Fisheries, 2021). iSimangaliso and the Hluhluwe-Umfolozi Park contribute a lot to the economy of KwaZulu-Natal through tourism activities that attract a large number of both national and international tourists to the area, who in turn contribute to the local economy through tourism expenditure (Department of Environment, Forestry, & Fisheries, 2021). In 1975 South Africa signed the international Ramsar Convention, a treaty providing the framework for the conservation and protection of wetlands and their resources. It was then that the Greater St Lucia Wetland Park was formally declared as a PA. The area was then proclaimed as the first UNESCO World Heritage Site in South Africa in December 1999 for its natural beauty and unique biodiversity (Department of Environment, Forestry, & Fisheries, 2021). In November 2007 the Park was renamed to iSimangaliso, which means miracle and wonder. Before the Park was established, the area was home to the Tsonga people who utilised the land for hunting, gazing, and cultivation since the early 14th century (Department of Environment, Forestry, & Fisheries, 2021). The establishment of the park in the 19th century led to the eviction of these indigenous people, and as a result they were driven away from their ancestral land for conservation purposes (Department of Environment, Forestry, & Fisheries, 2021).

Due to the unlawful eviction of people from their land during the apartheid era, the South African democratic government implemented a land reform programme in 1994 to address previous injustices (Department of Land Affairs, 1997). This programme has three pillars, which are land restitution, land redistribution, and land tenure reform (Department of Land Affairs, 1997). Land restitution involves the return of land that was forcefully taken from people by racially discriminatory laws. Its sole aim is to restore land and provide remedies to people who were dispossessed of their land through discriminatory legislation and practice. Land redistribution, on the other hand, has been set up to make it possible for the poor and the disadvantaged to buy land through the assistance of settlements/land acquisition grants. It seeks to provide the poor with land for residential and productive purposes to improve and sustain their livelihoods (Department of Land Affairs, 1997). Land tenure reform aims to bring all individuals occupying land under a unitary and legally accepted system of land ownership. It is meant to assist in resolving tenure disputes and provide alternatives for people who have been displaced. Land tenure reform also seeks to address the difficult land problems that were created in the past. The solution to such problems may lead to new systems of land holdings, land rights, and forms of ownership (Department of Land Affairs, 1997).

KwaNibela is a land restitution case, in which after 1994, the people applied to get their land back from where they were removed. This led to co-management agreements between land claimants and neighbouring PAs being established. This is evident in that "after the establishment of the land reform programme, people launched claims for hectares of land within the Park, so we signed a co-management agreement with the land claimants in order to make the management of natural resources more inclusive by involving the community in decision-making processes that involve the management of resources" (Interview with iSimangaliso Wetland Park official, September 2019). The land claimants from KwaNibela and surrounding communities established a claimant community trust which allows for various benefit-sharing opportunities between iSimangaliso Wetland Park and land claimants from KwaNibela and neighbouring communities (iSimangaliso Wetland Park, 2017).

Co-management is a collaborative method that combines the concepts of collaborative resolution of problems and sustainable management of the environment. It is thought to be a platform to tackle the depletion of natural resources and to monitor natural resources mismanagement. State officials involve the community in the design of natural resource management laws. Co-management also helps to decentralise decision-making and to satisfy local resource users (Miles, 2013). This implies that the community of KwaNibela is entitled to access the benefits from conservation which accrue from the iSimangaliso Wetland Park. This is because co-management entitles them to play a role in decision-making with regard to the conservation of natural resources, to access the financial benefits of conservation, and to participate in ongoing conservation initiatives and programmes (Miles, 2013). Thus, the community must contribute to conservation decision-making processes that may affect their livelihoods and socioeconomic wellbeing. In general, the co-management agreement between iSimangaliso and KwaNibela signifies that the community has the right to participate and mutually share responsibilities in the conservation of natural resources in the area. Therefore, theoretically, co-management should decentralise decision-making powers to accommodate local communities and resource users and form partnership between local resource users and government agencies (Archeson, 2013). Whether or not this happened in practice is further discussed in this chapter.

## Study area

KwaNibela is located in the uMkhanyakude District Municipality, which has four local municipalities, namely, Big Five Hlabisa (which combined the previous Big Five False Bay and Hlabisa local municipalities), Jozini, Mtubatuba, and uMhlabuyalingana. KwaNibela is located in the Big Five Hlabisa Local Municipality.

## Theoretical consideration: Social conflict theory

Conflict can be described as a situation in which an actor feels impairment from the behaviour of another actor because of differences in perceptions, emotions, and interests (Soliku & Schraml, 2018). In general, the conflict theory aims to scientifically explain the broad aspects of conflict in society, including how conflict begins and evolves, as well as the consequences of conflict. The conflict theory is concerned with the unequal distribution of scarce resources and power (Allan, 2013). According to Allan (2013) conflict may be ignited by absolute and relative deprivation. Absolute deprivation is the state of being impoverished, living considerably below the poverty line, and living a life dictated by uncertainty over necessities (food, shelter, and clothing).

Relative deprivation, on the other hand, refers to a sense of being disadvantaged in comparison to another person or group. The fundamentals of life are not under dispute here; rather, there is a feeling that a certain group is doing better than the other (Allan, 2013). People in this case have the emotional and material resources to become involved in conflict and social change (Allan, 2013). The case of KwaNibela is that of both absolute and relative deprivation since most residents are poor and live below the poverty line and suffer from food insecurity. In addition, some felt that they were disadvantaged by the manner in which resources were governed in the PA under consideration. It should be remembered that environmental legislation and programmes have a considerable impact on the social relations surrounding land and natural resources (Peters, 2004). In the case of KwaNibela, the establishment of the iSimangaliso Wetland Park has caused land disputes since the indigenous people of KwaNibela were evicted from their ancestral land. In Africa, land has been commodified, making it difficult for the poor to have access to land resources due to their low socioeconomic status (Peters, 2004). As previously mentioned, KwaNibela is dominantly populated by poor people, due to their low socioeconomic status, as they do not have the financial resources to regain control of their land. Even though a co-management agreement was signed, the community feels neglected by iSimangaliso Wetland Park since they (the community) are often excluded from decision-making processes related to conservation. The community further receives little to no monetary benefits from the park. This has sparked conflict between the management of the park and the community.

Due to the lack of access to land for subsistence and small-scale agriculture, many rural households have seen their livelihood options as constricted. Thus, they have been forced to diversify their income strategies to keep up with survival demands. Many people in KwaNibela depend on subsistence agriculture. Lack of access to land for agriculture and grazing has resulted in land conflict in the area. In the African context, people with authority over land such as chiefs/Amakhosi are by no means immune from the state and its representatives, who take advantage of opportunities to alienate land to their own advantage (Peters, 2004). In KwaNibela, people feel as if the chiefs/Amakhosi are the only individuals who benefit from conservation as they may be paid off by government officials, and this has further perpetuated conflict in the area (Interview with community member, September 2019).

Sometimes, competition over land leads to efforts to exclude some users through various types of enclosure (Peters, 2004). The enclosure of arable land suitable for agriculture and grazing livestock by iSimangaliso Wetland Park is another factor which has led to a conflict of interest between the park and the community. The community seeks to use the land for agriculture in order to escape poverty while the iSimangaliso Wetland Park finds it critical to conserve the land and natural resources, thus leading to conflict. In the case of KwaNibela, people are trying to gain access to land for subsistence agriculture and also benefit from the conservation of natural resources. To this extent, the social conflict theory assists in understanding why and how there is conflict between the community of KwaNibela and iSimangaliso Wetland Park (conservation-based conflict between the community of KwaNibela and iSimangaliso Wetland Park). To this extent, the conflict illustrates two things: firstly, disgruntlement by the indigenous community, and secondly, an attempt to improve their condition. The second issue is amplified by Allan (2013), who states that when people engage in a conflict, that signifies a struggle in an attempt to achieve a particular goal, which in this case is inclusion of the community in the exploitation of the resources in the PA under study.

## Methods

This study adopted the qualitative approach. According to Creswell (2014), qualitative research seeks to explain some aspects of life. The method is predominantly thematic and explanatory, instead of numerical. The method is used to describe actions and attitudes to a certain phenomenon broadly. The qualitative approach does not inherently imply that many participants should be chosen (Creswell, 2014). As a result, this study utilised simple random sampling to select people (from the community of KwaNibela) who participated in the research. A simple random sample is a randomly selected subset of a population. In this sampling method, each member of the population has an exactly equal chance of being selected (Creswell, 2014). This method is the simplest of all probability sampling methods because it only includes a single random selection and requires little advanced knowledge of the population. Because randomisation is used, any research conducted on this sample has great internal and external validity (Creswell, 2014). In this regard, 50 individuals from the community were selected through simple random sampling to participate in this study in order to collect information on natural resource conservation and the conflict it may have sparked between iSimangaliso Wetland Park management and the community of KwaNibela. One-on-one interviews were conducted with the assistance of a questionnaire. This helped the researcher to ask questions which are relevant to the topic. In order to enrich the study, three officials from the iSimangaliso Wetland Park were also selected to participate in the study through purposive sampling. Purposive sampling relies on the judgement of the researcher when selecting the units that are to be studied. The key benefit of purposive sampling is that it can give the researcher the reason for generalising the studied sample (Rai & Thapa, 2015). The officials of the iSimangaliso Wetland Park were chosen based on their knowledge, connections, and experience in the research subject (Langos, 2014). Thus, in-depth interviews were conducted with the relevant officials with the assistance of a questionnaire. The main advantage of personal interviews in this study is that they involved personal and direct contact between the researcher and participants, in the form of conversations, which lasted between 10 and 15 minutes each.

Purposive sampling was sufficient for the study because it helped to gather relevant information and views from different persons who have relevant information and experience on the research subject without any discrimination. The actual data collection utilised was in-depth interviews. According to Langos (2014), in-depth interviews are personal and unstructured interviews which aim to identify the participant's emotions, feelings, and opinions regarding a particular research subject. This assisted the researcher in successfully understanding the socioeconomic influence of iSimangaliso Wetland Park on the community of KwaNibela, KwaZulu-Natal, South Africa. The collected data was analysed following a thematic approach (content analysis) which involved reading through the collected data and categorising it into themes and subthemes in order to make comparisons (Langos, 2014). The main advantage of content analysis is that it helps in reducing and simplifying collected data.

Qualitative research involves an interpretive and naturalistic approach to its subject matter. This means that researchers study things in their natural setting and attempt to interpret the phenomena in terms of the meanings people assign to them (McLeod, 2019). Qualitative research is a method for investigating and understanding the meaning that individuals or groups ascribe to a social problem. The research involves questions and procedures, data collection in the participant's environment, data analysis inductively building from broad themes, and the researcher making interpretations of the collected data (Creswell & Creswell, 2017). The structure of the final written report is flexible. Researchers who engage in this type of inquiry support a research approach that prioritises an inductive manner, a focus on individual meaning, and the importance of rendering the complexity of a situation (Creswell & Creswell, 2017). In the final analysis, the qualitative research approach was the most fitting to the nature of this study, which is aimed at understanding how people see the protection of natural resources and conflict which may be associated with conservation.

## The socioeconomic influence of iSimangaliso Wetland Park on the community of KwaNibela, KwaZulu-Natal, South Africa

During the interview sessions, officials from iSimangaliso Wetland Park were asked whether the KwaNibela community can take part in conservation programmes such as the protection of natural resources and whether they (the community) have access to natural resources. The officials reacted by saying that through decision-making processes that affect natural resources and biodiversity, the community gets to be involved in conservation. The officials further stated that the community is consulted through kings and traditional leaders if decisions about conservation of natural resources must be taken (Interview with iSimangaliso Wetland Park official, September 2019). The officials of iSimangaliso Wetland Park further revealed that the Park also enabled community members to engage in its inclusive conservation projects, such as arts and crafts production, hospitality, tourism, and land rehabilitation (Interview with iSimangaliso Wetland Park official, September 2019). This may have a positive influence on the socioeconomic wellbeing of the local residents, since exposing them to such projects may allow them to gain skills that may enable them to generate income by realising opportunities within the tourism sector. However, the community did not believe that it had completely benefitted from the resources conserved by the Park. Therefore, one community member stated that, "in no way do we benefit from the iSimangaliso Wetland Park, because they have taken our ancestral land from us in order to gain control of our natural resources" (Interview with the Community Member, September 2019). They (the community) also did not feel that they had been adequately and/or thoroughly consulted during conservation decision-making processes. Thus, the complaint by the community may be taken to mean that the conservation programmes by iSimangaliso Wetland Park were not effective to the extent of meeting the goals of co-management and including the community in environmental conservation programmes.

iSimangaliso Wetland Park officials further confirmed that the iSimangaliso Wetland Park has given bursaries and grants to local learners wishing to pursue careers in environmental management and conservation. After completing their studies, some of the bursary and scholarship beneficiaries were further trained by the iSimangaliso Wetland Park. This may contribute to the socioeconomic wellbeing of the community since an investment in the local people's education may allow them to become skilled, thus boosting their chances of securing formal employment to financially support their families and households. This confirms the view that investments in education (human capital) assist people in meeting their basic needs (Munanura et al., 2018). Unfortunately, not all the beneficiaries are employed since iSimangaliso does not have the capacity to employ many people at the moment (Interview with iSimangaliso official, September 2019).

A further analysis of this study revealed that the community benefits from conservation through tourism expenditure. This occurred when eco-tourists bought their items, such as craftwork which tourists buy as souvenirs, thus contributing to the community's socioeconomic wellbeing through monetary exchange. In this regard, one community member stated that, "most of us are able to generate income and maintain a living by selling craftwork to visitors who come to visit the park. But it is hard because during the peak season we make money when many tourists come to iSimangaliso but do not raise enough money during the off season to fulfil our everyday needs" (Interview with community member, September 2019). This is supported by Suich's (2010) assertion that one of the ways in which communities can benefit from the conservation of natural resources is through job creation and income from eco-tourism. Further, the iSimangaliso Wetland Park is optimistic that local business owners can produce income and satisfy the living and financial needs of their families and provide increased job opportunities through its financial and skills development assistance programmes such as the Rural Entrepreneurship Accelerator Program (REAP), which aims to offer monetary and capital resources to local entrepreneurs. One official of the PA stated that, "as iSimangaliso, our training workshops help local entrepreneurs and train them to develop their business management skills. These workshops are of utmost value because local entrepreneurs create jobs in the community" (Interview with community member, September 2019).

Notwithstanding the above, conservation may negatively influence the socioeconomic wellbeing of local communities through the lack of direct benefits from conservation. The predation of livestock by wild animals adversely affects the socioeconomic wellbeing of local livestock subsistence farmers as they depend on their livestock to sustain a living and generate income. In this regard, one farmer stated that "predators escape from the park and prey on our livestock, the worst part is that one is not allowed to harm the predator that has destroyed our livelihood, but we have to call the iSimangaliso officials to come and fetch the predator. In cases where community members harmed the predator they were arrested which I find unfair since we are not compensated for the loss of our livestock" (Interview with community member, September 2019). This strengthens Khan, Awan, and Begum's (2018) argument that conservation could adversely affect the wellbeing of individuals through the predation of livestock by wild animals. This further supports the statement made by Soliku and Schraml (2018) asserting that conflicts also arise when protected wildlife has an impact on people and their activities, such as predating farm crops and livestock, resulting in retaliatory killings. As a result, communities suffer economic losses because most rural poor households depend on livestock to produce revenue. As livestock loss can have a negative economic impact on households that rely on animal livestock to generate income, some indigenous communities go as far as poisoning wild animals that prey on their livestock. This leads to the loss of conserved biodiversity which is on the verge of extinction and further sparks conflict between PAs and local communities (Kaplan-Hallam & Bennett, 2018).

Furthermore, the fact that some people believe that only the elite profit from conservation suggests that there may be some social inequality in the allocation of conservation benefits. Some of the reasons KwaNibela residents feel that conservation does not benefit their livelihoods is due to the lack of jobs and a limited access to natural resources. Hence, it was argued that "iSimangaliso has driven us away from our land and has taken control of our resources, but in return they do not employ people in our community, but one finds out that people from other regions are employed" (Interview with community member, August 2019). The restrictions placed on natural resources also make it hard for the community to access plants for medicinal purposes. For example, "as a traditional healer, the lack of access to natural resources makes it hard for me to find certain herbs I use to heal people in the community" (Interview with community member, August 2019). This gives justification to the statement made by Lamsal et al. (2015) that the restriction on people's access to natural resources that sustain their livelihood may lead to local communities being against conservation. Prohibition of hunting practices has adversely affected the livelihoods of the community, as some participants claimed that they relied on hunting for food security prior to conservation. Thus, one member of the community asserted that:

> We used to hunt and share what we catch with community members before hunting was declared illegal. This has caused food insecurity in the community. The banning of hunting was not necessary because, through indigenous knowledge systems which have been passed on from our forefathers, we used to hunt in a sustainable manner that allowed the population of the species we hunted to repopulate.
>
> (Interview with community member, August 2019)

The eviction of indigenous people from their traditional land has also led to lack of arable land for farming and livestock grazing. This has become a major issue since people's livestock are forced to graze on land which they regard as unsustainable for livestock and agriculture, as subsistence farmers are also forced to cultivate and farm on plots that are not fertile enough. The community members also argued that insufficient community participation in conservation is the reason why they thought that conservation did not fulfil their needs. Hence, one community member asserted that "although conservation is a good thing that it attempts to prevent the depletion of natural resources, we have lost livelihoods in the process because we depended on the rich fertile land and other natural resources that are within the park" (Interview with community member, August 2019). This shows that, although indigenous communities try to regain access to their land through land restitution, PAs remain controlled by the government and private landholders (Watts & Faasen, 2009). One community member argued that "the community has no say in the management of natural resources; iSimangaliso Wetland Park has never consulted the community when designing and implementing conservation programmes that can meet our needs" (Interview with community member, August 2019). The community also felt that the main reason that the benefits of conservation are unequally allocated is because they believe that conservation only benefits the Chiefs/Amakhosi, traditional leaders, and individuals who are politically connected (Interview with community member, September 2019). This shows that conservation may sometimes enrich the elite at the expense of the poor who are often subjected to economic exclusion. This leads to local people engaging in alternative livelihood activities such as craftwork, agriculture, and forestry to make ends meet. This is the basis of Coulthard et al. (2017)'s argument that politics will directly or indirectly affect cashflows and the distribution of conservation-based benefits. In all this, one sees that the co-management agreement between the community of KwaNibela and iSimangaliso Wetland Park was not working well for the benefit of the community. In other words, there was no co-management because it was the park which made decisions without even consulting the community. This assaulted the co-management principles as discussed in the preceding parts of this chapter, and this is problematic to the extent that it shows us the source of the lack of socioeconomic development in KwaNibela. If this is seen through the prism of social conflict theory, it then becomes evident that the community of KwaNibela were not happy because they felt that the PA unfairly benefitted from the natural resources at their expense. They therefore blamed their poverty and limited livelihood opportunities on the PA. Until this sentiment (whether it is true or not) that the PA unfairly benefits at the expense of the community is addressed, the animosity between the latter and former may persist into the future.

## Conclusion

The results of this study suggest that conservation may negatively influence the socioeconomic wellbeing of local communities through the lack of access to natural resources which they depend upon to secure their livelihoods. Given that co-management seeks to strengthen the capacity of local communities to manage their own resources (Zhu et al., 2014), the scenario described in the preceding section shows that the iSimangaliso Wetland Park falls short in achieving the goals of co-management. However, the park does try to empower local business owners through its Rural Enterprise Accelerator Programme (REAP). The banning of hunting activities also adversely affects the socioeconomic wellbeing of local people since they are now forced to buy meat from local retailers, rather than using the money for other livelihood needs. The predation of livestock by predators that escape from the park also causes economic losses to the livelihoods of households in the area. This confirms the observation by Khan et al. (2018) that conservation may have detrimental effects on people's livelihoods through attacks on livestock, thus leading to economic losses since the poorest rural households depend on their livestock for income generation. The restricted access to fertile land for farming also has a negative influence on the local socio-economy since local people depend on agriculture to secure a living and earn an income by selling their surplus agricultural produce.

Based on the findings of this study, it is suggested that proper consultations with local communities by PAs may go a long way in preventing the adoption of conservation strategies that may adversely affect the socioeconomic wellbeing of local communities. iSimangaliso Wetland Park should support local small-scale farmers and subsistence agricultural practitioners through agricultural workshops. Farmers will get to be equipped with skills and methods which may enable them to be successful in farming and offer the farmers necessary farming equipment to increase their success rate in terms of agricultural production. This may be effective since most of the people in KwaNibela depend on agriculture to sustain their living and for food security and income generation. The park should also engage with communities through organising community meetings to allow the community to raise their concerns and grievances with regards to the conservation methods that may threaten their socioeconomic wellbeing. The park should also reimburse families who lose their livestock because of predators escaping the park. This should be done by means of a formally structured procedure by the affected families to allow them to lay formal complaints with the assistance of the local traditional authority. After receiving complaints, the park should evaluate the damage and get to decide on a fair amount which can be compensated to the owners who have lost their livestock due to predation. The park should further support local craft workers by building a formal craft market where craft workers can sell their craftwork to tourists who visit the park, thus enabling them to generate income and sustain their livelihoods.

## References


Afriyie, J. O., Asare, M. O., Danquah, E., & Pavla, H. (2021). Assessing the management effectiveness of three protected areas in Ghana. *Conservation & Society, 19*(1), 13–24.

Allan, K. (2013). *The social lens: An invitation to social and sociological theory.*, North Carolina: Sage Publications

Archeson, J. M. (2013). Co-management in the Maine lobster industry: A study in factional politics. *Conservation and Society, 11*(1), 60–71.

Bixler, R. P., Wald, D. M., Ogden, L. A., Leong, K. M., Johnston, E. W., & Romolini, M. (2016). Network governance for large-scale natural resource conservation and the challenge of capture. *Frontiers in Ecology and the Environment, 14*(3), 165–171.

Brent, Z.W. (2015). Territorial restructuring and resistance in Argentina. *Journal of Peasant Studies, 42*(3–4), pp.671–694.

Brockington, D., & Wilkie, D. (2015). Protected areas and poverty. *Philosophical Transactions of the Royal Society B: Biological Sciences, 370*(1681), 1–5.

Busscher, N., Parra, C., & Vanclay, F. (2018). Land grabbing within a protected area: The experience of local communities with conservation and forestry activities in Los Esteros del Iberá, Argentina. *Land Use Policy, 78*, 572–582.

Chechina, M., Neveux, Y., Parkins, J. R., & Hamann, A. (2018). Balancing conservation and livelihoods: A study of forest-dependent communities in the Philippines. *Conservation and Society, 16*(4), 420–430.

Coulthard, S., Evans, L., Turner, R., Mills, D., Foale, S., Abernethy, K., ... & Monnereau, I. (2017). Exploring 'islandness' and the impacts of nature conservation through the lens of wellbeing. *Environmental Conservation, 44*(3), 298–309.

Creswell, J. W. (2014). *A concise introduction to mixed methods research.* SAGE publications.

Creswell, J. W., & Creswell, J. D. (2017). *Research design: Qualitative, quantitative, and mixed methods approaches.* Sage publications.

DeFries, R., Hansen, A., Turner, B. L., Reid, R., & Liu, J. (2007). Land use change around protected areas: Management to balance human needs and ecological function. *Ecological Applications, 17*(4), 1031–1038.

Department of Environment, Forestry, & Fisheries. (2021, January 12). People and Parks National Conference 2010. Retrieved from https://www.environment.gov.za/sites/defualt/files/docs/site_visits

Department of Land Affairs. (1997). *White paper on South African land policy*. Department of Land Affairs.

Fairer-Wessels, F. A. (2017). Determining the impact of information on rural livelihoods and sustainable tourism development near protected areas in Kwa-Zulu Natal, South Africa. *Journal of Sustainable Tourism*, *25*(1), 10–25.

iSimangaliso Wetland Park. (2017). *iSimangaliso Wetland Park Integrated Management Plan (2017-2021)*. iSimangaliso Wetland Park.

Kaplan-Hallam, M., & Bennett, N. J. (2018). Adaptive social impact management for conservation and environmental management. *Conservation Biology*, *32*(2), 304–314.

Khan, M. Z., Khan, B., Awan, M. S., & Begum, F. (2018). Livestock depredation by large predators and its implications for conservation and livelihoods in the Karakoram Mountains of Pakistan. *Oryx*, *52*(3), 519.

Lamsal, P., Pant, K. P., Kumar, L., & Atreya, K. (2015). Sustainable livelihoods through conservation of wetland resources: a case of economic benefits from Ghodaghodi Lake, western Nepal. *Ecology and Society*, *20*(1), 1-3.

Langos, S. (2014). *Athens as an international tourism destination: An empirical investigation to the city's imagery and the role of local DMO's*. (MSc in Marketing Management). University of Derby.

McLeod, S. A. (2019, July 30). *Qualitative vs. quantitative research*. Simply Psychology. https://www.simplypsychology.org/qualitative-quantitative.html

Miles, J. D. P. (2013). Designing collaborative processes for adaptive management: four structures for multistakeholder collaboration. *Ecology and Society*, *18*(4).

Mizrahi, M. I., Diedrich, A., Weeks, R., & Pressey, R. L. (2019). A systematic review of the socioeconomic factors that influence how marine protected areas impact on ecosystems and livelihoods. *Society & Natural Resources*, *32*(1), 4–20.

Munanura, I. E., Backman, K. F., Hallo, J. C., Powell, R. B., & Sabuhoro, E. (2018). Understanding the relationship between livelihood constraints of poor forest-adjacent residents, and illegal forest use, at Volcanoes National Park, Rwanda. *Conservation and Society*, *16*(3), 291–304.

Njuguna, M., & Deisser, A. M. (2016). *Conservation of Natural and Cultural Heritage in Kenya* (p. 272). UCL Press.

Paredes, M., & Kaulard, A. (2020). Fighting the climate crisis in persistently unequal land regimes: Natural protected areas in the Peruvian Amazon. *Journal of Cleaner Production*, *265*, 121605.

Peters, P. E. (2004). Inequality and social conflict over land in Africa. *Journal of Agrarian Change*, *4*(3), 269–314.

Rai, N., & Thapa, B. (2015). *A study on purposive sampling method in research*. Kathmandu: Kathmandu School of Law.

Saunders, F. (2014). The promise of common pool resource theory and the reality of commons projects. *International Journal of the Commons*, *8*(2) 637–650.

Soliku, O., & Schraml, U. (2018). Making sense of protected area conflicts and management approaches: A review of causes, contexts and conflict management strategies. *Biological Conservation*, *222*, 136–145.

Suich, H. (2010). The livelihood impacts of the Namibian community based natural resource management programme: A meta-synthesis. *Environmental Conservation*, *37*(1), 45–53.

Tang, R., & Gavin, M. C. (2016). A classification of threats to traditional ecological knowledge and conservation responses. *Conservation and Society*, *14*(1), 57–70.

Ward, C., Stringer, L. C., & Holmes, G. (2018). Protected area co-management and perceived livelihood impacts. *Journal of Environmental Management*, *228*, 1–12.

Watts, S., & Faasen, H. (2009). Community-based conflict resolution strategies for sustainable management of the Tsitsikamma National Park, South Africa. *South African Geographical Journal*, *91*(1), 25–37.

Wiersma, Y. F., Duinker, P. N., Haider, W., Hvenegaard, G. T., & Schmiegelow, F. K. (2015). Introduction: Relationships between protected areas and sustainable forest management: Where are we heading? *Conservation and Society*, *13*(1), 1–12.

Zafra-calvo, N., & Moreno-Peñaranda, R. (2018). Exploring local people's views on the livelihood impacts of privately versus community managed conservation strategies in the Ruvuma landscape of North Mozambique-South Tanzania. *Journal of Environmental Management*, *206*, 853–862.

Zhu, T., Krott, M., & Chen, H. (2014). Co-management implementation in forested national reserves: Contradicting cases from China. *Forest Policy and Economics*, *38*, 72–80.

# 12 The partially transformed frontier

## Aspirations, limitations, and tensions of transfrontier conservation in the Maloti-Drakensberg

*Oscar Mthimkhulu and Adrian Nel*

### Introduction

The concept of transboundary conservation areas is internationally acclaimed and is common practice across the globe (Büscher, 2013; Neumann, 2014; Saarinen, 2016). According to Mugadza (2019), Transfrontier Conservation Areas (TFCAs) originated from the concept of establishing conservation areas across international borders for biodiversity conservation, economic development, and poverty alleviation. The practice of transfrontier conservation has been hailed internationally as the preferred holistic approach to conservation, with multiple wins despite its associated shortcomings and contradictions (Büscher, 2013; Neumann, 2014; Saarinen, 2016). Typically, a transfrontier conservation initiative boasts and canvasses local community support and advocates environmentally responsible stewardship and sustainable development that advance a country's commitment to its development agenda (Mugadza, 2019). This is ostensibly achieved by responsible nature-based ecotourism and Payment for Ecosystem Services (PES) as a sustainable income-generating mechanism to support local communities' livelihoods and improve catchment management. However, this approach has limitations which are not clearly articulated and understood by local communities; this creates significant expectations, grave tensions, and hostile relationships amongst stakeholders in contexts where no real and tangible benefits are generated for the local communities.

Notably, within the Southern African Development Community (SADC), TFCAs are defined as "areas of large ecological regions that straddle the boundaries of two or more countries – encompassing one or more protected areas, and multiple resource use areas" (Mugadza, 2019, p. 2). Within the SADC, nature-based tourism is a key driver of economic development and poverty alleviation in TFCAs (Ahebwa et al., 2012). Ramutsindela (2007) and Saarinen (2016) suggest that nature conservation and nature-based tourism development initiatives in TFCAs demonstrate certain features of neoliberal conservation. These are the monetisation and privatisation of natural resources (for example, PES); the establishment of capitalistic markets; and the decentralisation of state governance of natural resources to local authorities. Ramutsindela (2007) and Saarinen (2016) indicate that establishing TFCAs has become a fashion which

DOI: 10.4324/9781003188902-15

at times disregards local communities. Similar studies on TFCAs in Southern Africa within the past decade have focused on the marginalisation of local communities, the evolution and progression of TFCAs in Southern Africa, and the challenges they face (Hanks & Myburgh, 2015; DeMotts, 2017).

The Maloti-Drakensberg TFCA (MDTFCA) between the Republic of South Africa and the Kingdom of Lesotho is the area discussed in this chapter. The MDTFCA has a documented history of a contentious relationship between South Africa and Lesotho, in part related to the need to protect important water catchments from the Maloti-Drakensberg mountains between the two countries. The emergence of a TFCA in the area is well-documented in the book *Transforming the Frontier* by Bram Büscher (2013), who detailed the importance of consensus and marketing as neoliberal conservation tools to create legitimacy for the MDTFCA. He further addressed the hybridisation of the postcolonial socioeconomic conservation approach, which seeks to obtain stakeholder buy-in and support. Apart from this political ecology intervention, there is scant literature on transfrontier conservation in the MDTFCA, and there is a need for further updates and practitioner perspectives on the area which reflect on the disconnection between conservation rhetoric and practice. The dynamics of environmental management governance across international boundaries, such as the limitations and challenges associated with the implementation of PES and tourism, should also be investigated. Accordingly, this chapter draws on practitioner research engagement, wherein the first author, previously park manager for the South African side of the protected area (a World Heritage site), employed a critical political ecology perspective on key aspects such as dissensus, aspirations, neoliberal conservation, political ecology, transfrontier conservation, and PES. The chapter also navigates the strained relationship between the two countries' Project Coordination Units (PCUs) and how it affected the implementation of the MDTFCA's programme, and argues that the MDTFCA is only partially transformed, with little likelihood of the process being completed.

## Perspectives on transfrontier conservation: The Maloti-Drakensberg in context

Transfrontier conservation in Southern Africa first implicates colonial conservation and territorialisation. Owing to the impact of colonialism and political partitioning in Africa and its far-reaching consequences, the African landscape was fragmented (Ramutsindela, 1999). The politico-geographical map of Africa was annotated by the outcome of the 1884–1885[1] Berlin Conference (Wang, 1998), which laid down ground rules for the annexation of African territory by European powers (Phimister, 1992, p. 18) as different ethnic groups were forced together in different colonial territories (Büscher, 2013).

The fragmentation of a natural geographic continuum led to the establishment of Lesotho within the enclave of South Africa, or what Büscher (2013, p. x) refers to as "the historical accident in the middle of South Africa".

Due to mere proximity, Lesotho and South Africa have similar political and historical roots, and arguably influence each other's political economies and socio-political stance to a certain degree. Their historical commonalities range from colonialism in 1652–1961 in South Africa, the Mfecane 1810–1830[2], the Great Trek 1835–1840, the apartheid system 1948–1994, and transfrontier conservation from 2008 to the present (Büscher, 2013). These historical events played a significant role in each country's political and socioeconomic affairs, where native tribes fought for land and were later exploited for cheap labour[3] (Skelcher, 2003). Despite the similarities between the two countries in terms of political and economic turmoil, geography, ecosystems, and ethnic groups, Lesotho has maintained its independence as a constitutional monarchy with very distinct conservation and development approaches which are influenced by their internal politics, economic growth, and development aspirations.

While transfrontier conservation has come to significantly impact the Maloti-Drakensberg landscape, the concept did not originate within the African continent; it was introduced in the early 1920s by the creation of binational parks on the border of the United States and Canada (Duffy, 2005). By 1997 the idea had gained significant momentum, with 136 TFCAs established and 85 in the pipeline across 112 international borders (ibid.), including in Southern Africa. Terminology synonymous with TFCAs is found in international literature, such as 'peace parks' and 'transborder conservation areas' in Indonesia and Malaysia. Internationally and within Southern Africa, the common primary goals of TFCAs tend to be conserving important fauna and flora across national boundaries; preserving important natural resources; preserving genetic diversity amongst species; and maintaining essential ecological processes (Iskandar, 2008). According to Stoldt et al. (2020), the establishment of TFCAs is an attempt to reduce poverty and an alternative conservation management style to the colonial 'fences and fines' approach which alienated local people from nature.

Internationally, transfrontier conservation is considered a panacea for challenges such as alleviating poverty, empowering rural communities, and healing the wounds of conflict (Büscher, 2013; Neumann, 2014). According to Mugadza (2019, p. 2), TFCAs might contribute to enhanced cooperation between local communities and state agencies, and TFCAs in the SADC have the potential to overcome the "socio-economic marginalisation that is associated with the isolation of border areas". However, critical research indicates that, at times, TFCAs disregard local communities (Ramutsindela, 2007; 2009; Saarinen, 2016); one example is the Great Limpopo TFCA (GLTFCA), a flagship TFCA that was formed in 2002. It primarily sought to provide employment opportunities for indigent communities through sustainable tourism. However, since its introduction it has been reported that people living on the boundary of the GLTFCA "are often forgotten and potentially marginalised" (Chiutsi & Saarinen, 2017, p. 2) – thus threatening the sustainability of conservation and the GLTFCA itself.

In contextualising critical views on transfrontier conservation, Büscher (2013) considers TFCAs as a local form of neoliberal conservation. Büscher et al. (2012, p. 4) describe neoliberal conservation as a process which "shifts the focus from how nature is used in and through the expansion of capitalism, to how nature is conserved in and through the expansion of capitalism". The premise of neoliberal conservation is based upon commodifying and commercialising nature to the benefit of its direct constituents (local communities and relevant stakeholders) and nature itself (Büscher et al., 2012; Andersson et al., 2017). This results in natural assets with high monetary value being, ostensibly, well taken care of. Consensus and marketing are neoliberal conservation tools used to create legitimacy (Büscher, 2013). Büscher further argues that consensus and marketing are not fundamentally neoliberal, but they fit well within the neoliberal political economy because they are exploited to restructure and legitimatise the process as the by-products of the neoliberal approach (ibid.).

However, varying views of neoliberal conservation tell a different story. Suarez (2015) indicates that the international conservation community now refers to biodiversity conservation in terms of both market and solution, which is an attempt to develop a tool which is politically unassailable and a chimera of logic. Sagoff (2004) warns that environmental economics fails as a science of valuation. He argues that the valuation process is inefficiently attributed to market prices being based on supply, which does not necessarily correlate with consumer benefits. Similar concerns are documented by Vatn (2000), who states that commodity fiction[4] misconstrues ethical values and disregards ecosystem interdependencies within the environment. Interestingly, Holmes (2012) and Mugadza (2019) believe that TFCAs appeal to transnational elites and developers because they increase the potential for conservation–business partnerships and corporate sponsorship for the management of protected areas for profit – hence multiple wins.

The Maloti-Drakensberg can be approached as a contested transfrontier landscape. The Lesotho Highlands Water Project established in 1987 stemmed from South Africa's interest in obtaining water from Lesotho to supply the industrial Pretoria–Witwatersrand–Vereeniging area. The aggressive attempt to control Lesotho's water resources was to buttress the racist regional political economy and guarantee inputs for white industrial development (Büscher, 2013; Skelcher, 2003). The most recent transfrontier project between the two countries is the Maloti-Drakensberg Transfrontier Programme (MDTP), which was presented as an opportunity for collaboration and better cooperation amongst different actors. The resulting formation is formally known as the Maloti-Drakensberg TFCA (MDTFCA), according to a Memorandum of Understanding between the governments of Lesotho and South Africa signed in December 2008. The MDTFCA was the result of the Giant's Castle Declaration, which was agreed upon on 04 September 1997 at Giant's Castle Game Reserve in KwaZulu-Natal, South Africa. The case study area in this study is the MDTFCA. Lesotho and South Africa agreed to form joint management initiatives pertaining to biodiversity, catchment areas, and cultural heritage for sustainable development and poverty alleviation. The programme is conducted through a corresponding country-specific PCU, which is implemented by a 20-year strategy with a five-year action plan.

In his 2013 book *Transforming the Frontier*, Büscher (2013) rekindled interest in transfrontier conservation in the MDTFCA in scholars such as Balsiger, Middlemass (2014), Bocchino (2014), Neumann (2014), Saarinen (2016), and Suarez (2015). The authors' views ranged from TFCAs being fashionable, to tourism development being dubbed "neoliberal governance of conservation". There were signs of a strained relationship between the PCUs of Lesotho and South Africa, which were riddled with racial undertones, inequality, and conflicting interests. Büscher's (2013) critique identified three political strategies – consensus, anti-politics, and marketing – used to obtain desired outcomes against the dissenting voices of actors with divergent interests in the MDTFCA. These differences, which this chapter further examines, include safety and security, job creation, and the flow of tangible benefits to local communities. Büscher also identifies consensus as a political tool of neoliberal conservation to create legitimacy, and a means to an end if exercised in influential hands. Anti-politics, for its part, is defined as "the mediation and contestation of different interests and power struggles … and the act of doing away with politics" (Büscher, 2013, pp. 20–21).

More directly, for Büscher (2013) marketing includes advertising enclosed natural spaces (parks and private lodges) and product offerings and services as high-end 'tourist destinations' which are categorised as nature-based tourism. He concludes that in the MDTFCA nature-based tourism initiatives provide job opportunities but tend to be selective and do not always employ or prioritise local community members. Büscher (2009, p. 91) aptly termed this "induced self-marginalisation" where people are lured by the golden promise of multiple-wins neoliberal conservation. Büscher (2013, p. 53) and Andersson et al. (2017) refer to this as exclusive access. Büscher (2009) also views nature-based tourism as a strategy to broker harmony between capitalism and nature. Scholars such as Büscher (2009) have long alluded to the fact that environmental conservation is always viewed as a bulwark of capitalism. However, Ramutsindela and Shabangu (2013) indicate that there is a growing relationship between capitalism and the environment. This makes it difficult for local communities to participate in the mainstream tourism value chain. This study draws on and unpacks these findings using practitioner critical research, as described below.

## Practitioner critical research engagement with the MDTFCA

A qualitative case study design was adopted for the study. Yazan (2015) indicates that case studies are one of the most frequently used research methodologies for investigating, analysing, and understanding the complexities of an entity. According to Stake (1995), case study research is the study of the uniqueness and complexity of a single case to understand its workings. The

MDTFCA was chosen for its unique and complex leadership and governance. This research was conducted using a practitioner critical research approach, wherein the researcher is both doing research and practising conservation within his or her place of work. The political ecology theory framework was applied to reinforce research application and enhance understanding of various power relations.

The impetus to function as a well-rounded practitioner lies in adopting a holistic view and alternative perspectives[5] on conservation research; this can be aided by critical research insight. The discerning conservation researcher challenges the inherent goldfish-bowl view and questions the status quo to bridge the gap between conservation practice and applied research. However, insights garnered from the positionality of the practitioner–researcher can also influence critical research. A potential shortcoming of the aforementioned research approach and framework is the possibility that a practitioner–researcher will be considered too conflicted to objectively review a programme within their own backyard (Coupal, 2004). However, the rationale for using political ecology is justified by Robbins (2011), in his definition of political ecology as an epistemological project to bring to an end a comfortable and simple truth about the relationship between the society and its natural environment.[6] Therefore, critical research supported by the political ecology framework is appropriate for researching TFCAs, including findings about the MDTFCA as a political breeding ground, as it encompasses cross-border political dynamics and environmental issues.

Merriam (2002, p. 6) defines qualitative research as "an attempt to understand and make sense of a phenomenon from a participant's perspective". It is a holistic approach that unfolds in a natural setting and assists the researcher to understand the meaning of social experiences and human dimensions (Williams, 2007). Qualitative research can also be used to investigate how social and political elements influence people's reality (Merriam, 2002). This made qualitative research appropriate for studying the MDTFCA due to the inherent socio-political forces at play in the project area.

Data collection by fieldwork began in July 2018 and was concluded in November 2018. Primary data were collected in semi-structured interviews with key informants using a questionnaire to obtain information about leadership and governance intricacies. The five key informants included current and former Ezemvelo KZN Wildlife and MDTP employees. Data were collected by purposive sampling once relevant and knowledgeable participants had been identified. Snowball sampling, in which the researcher was referred to other people by the initial respondents, was also employed. All the research interviews were transcribed. The data was compared to current literature on transfrontier conservation within the SADC region, in search of similar and dissimilar management strategies, and analysed qualitatively by systematic content analysis. The research findings were grouped according to emergent themes such as institutional relations and capacity, natural resource management, and workplace representation, which informed the interpretation of the results.

## Findings and analysis: Traversing rigid frontiers

The historical background of the MDTFCA is presented below, followed by discussion of the dissensus, aspirations, tensions, limitations, and contradictions in transfrontier conservation. It is natural to expect that a transfrontier initiative will traverse political boundaries and thus unearth complexities. Transfrontier projects invite a variety of stakeholders with different motives, which may lead to disparities between the project objectives and the actual deliverables when benchmarked against reality and people's needs. However, to the benefit of other actors involved such as the ecotourism industry, the MDTFCA has encouraged and facilitated a paradigm shift to exclusive ownership and enclosures, which create private territories. Ecotourism has become a luxury for the elite that is not available to local actors (Büscher, 2013; Saarinen, 2016; Mugadza, 2019). This kind of exclusive land use for self-proclaimed lovers of nature has little impact on the receiving environment, including local communities, compared to extractive land use. Such high-end tourist destinations were nevertheless established at the expense of traditional access to natural resources for local communities, disturbing aspects of their livelihoods such as access to grazing land, medicinal plants, wood for fuel, and hunting.

Disparities in tourism offerings around the Maloti-Drakensberg Park World Heritage site are a cause for concern. There are tourism businesses that were established before the park was designated a World Heritage site by the United Nations Education, Science and Culture Organisation (UNESCO) World Heritage Centre. However, one questions whether Lesotho (which forms part of the park's western border) can match South Africa's well-established tourism businesses (such as at Underberg and Cathkin). Again, we suspect that establishing more high-end ecotourism businesses in Lesotho would entail traversing entrenched rigid boundaries to the concern of conservation practitioners, who are keen to maintain the pristine natural spaces of Lesotho at the expense of socioeconomic development. Obviously, because of a significant difference in the strength of both countries' economies and resultant development, the playing field is not level. The South African/Lesotho frontier is only partially transformed, as Lesotho's tourism infrastructure is underdeveloped compared to South Africa's.

Upon closer inspection, it appears there was non-alignment amongst those who initially championed the MDTFCA programme. The motives of those involved were questioned by the likes of Büscher (2013) and the World Bank during project implementation; this study found that stakeholder power relations and rigid political frontiers resulted in tension between the two countries' PCUs. A further complexity was the decision of the South African PCU to opt for the instrumental anti-political approach that prefers systematic conservation planning,[7] arguing that any decision made in the absence of proper planning and sufficient data would be irrational (Büscher, 2013). K. Zunckel (personal communication, July 20, 2018) mentions that following the South African systematic conservation planning outcome, the Bilateral Steering Committee adopted a 'bioregion map' which effectively became the 'new MDTP boundary'.

South Africa has a history of a paternalistic relationship with Lesotho, which did not help the MDTFCA programme to achieve its intended goals. According to informants from South Africa, the strained relationship between the two PCUs was caused by, among other things, Lesotho's apparent resistance to South Africa's "big brother approach" and their lead role in systematic conservation planning. It was an "unspoken perception" (R. Porter, personal communication, July 12, 2018) that the South African PCU was overbearing and did not recognise the sovereign independence of Lesotho. The new MDTP boundary or bioregion map illustrated that half of Lesotho would fall within the programme area and therefore could be subject to stringent land-use regulations, creating a key tension between the two PCUs. The polarisation of the two units potentially threatened the future of the project. The unspoken perceptions and the 'imposed' introduction of resource economics and PES resulted in unexpected dissensus between the PCUs.

## Payment for Ecosystem Services

PES in the MDTFCA appears to have been elusive. PES is regarded as a form of neoliberal conservation as it commercialises natural resources; it is also viewed as an innovative way to avoid environmental degradation and improve the yield of environmental services through incentive payments to the custodians of the natural environment. A feasibility study was conducted by the South African PCU in and around the Mnweni/Cathedral Peak and the Eastern Cape Drakensberg areas, in which a consultant assessed the feasibility of developing an ecosystem services trading model. According to the MDTFCA PES report (Maloti-Drakensberg Transfrontier Project, 2007), the research team engaged more than 536 people and institutions and reported that there were no legal impediments to trading water resources. Yet when the research was completed, there were no real and tangible benefits for the local communities.

The recognition and endorsement of the concept of PES has been hailed as a "strong success story" for the MDTFCA in which South Africa bought into PES as a viable concept (K. Zunckel, personal communication, July 20, 2018). PES is a market-based approach to environmental management that makes cash payments or other compensation to land stewards to encourage ecosystem conservation and restoration (Milder et al., 2010). It aims primarily to protect the quality of environmental services provided, whilst incentivising local communities to support nature conservation initiatives. The MDTFCA programme resorted to PES as a potential mechanism to improve local community livelihoods (improved grazing and better water yield from the catchment area). These benefits included direct payments from ecosystem service beneficiaries to land stewards, and increased value placed on services provided by land under the custodianship of normally poor and rural communities (ibid). PES would have been ideal for the MDTFCA programme because low-income households and rural communities control much of the ecologically sensitive land (ibid.). However, in reality, material benefits to rural local communities from PES have been elusive and strong criticism has been levied against the concept by some actors. Poor communities often fail to benefit from PES because in the South African context it ignores the social ills of the past and primarily services private landowners and large-scale commercial farmers. Certain eligibility criteria such as requirements for legal land title (Milder et al., 2010) immediately disqualify rural black communities as beneficiaries of PES, whereas South African rural areas are infamous for insecure land tenure systems.

## Aspirations, consensus, and limitations

The establishment of the MDTFCA brought hope to local communities in the form of an enabling environment that would improve the confidence of investors and translate into employment opportunities through tourism due to increased capital investment (Büscher, 2009). Tourism development was viewed as neoliberal conservation governance, and this is supported by Balsiger (2014). Unfortunately, MDTFCA implementation strategies of devolved governance and leadership appear to have strongly limited the programme's success. The current MDTP boundary is still the old original boundary and the programme's work is confined within this boundary. As such, the Maloti-Drakensberg frontier remains partially transformed, calling for an extraordinary effort and understanding of ostensibly uncharted political terrain. Seemingly, adopted consensus was effectively dissensus in practice.

Desirable political cooperation for economic integration and legal cooperation for sustainable development have not been fully embraced by conservation and development practitioners. The lack of acceptance stems from previous social and economic injustices, including past and present racial discrimination, especially where protected areas were established as a social construct.[8]

TFCAs create a new market within a global neoliberal political economy and are potentially areas for ecotourism development and hubs for economic growth. As a result, Büscher (2013) and Andersson et al. (2017) advocate local community partnerships with private and public enterprises to manage and develop capital gains projects. Despite the MDFTCA's limited success, we found that the partnership between Transfrontier Parks Destinations (a private company) and the Batlokoa community in the Free State province of South Africa, with a capital injection of over R20 million from the national government to manage and develop Witsieshoek Mountain Lodge, may indeed be a classic example of neoliberal conservation efforts in practice; it is also one of the most promising private and community tourism joint ventures. The MDTFCA needed support and a sense of ownership from affected authorities and actors within the programme area to succeed. It resorted to using political strategies of consensus such as marketing and instrumental anti-political strategies, which are powerful ways to garner support in neoliberal conservation. The following section reflects on dissensus, tensions, and contradictions in the project.

## Dissensus, tensions, and contradictions

There appears to be a continuous struggle to reconcile conservation and development goals. There is limited success with simultaneous growth for both conservation and development because both factors have the potential to give more.[9] To substantiate this view, Büscher et al. (2012) state that the neoliberal conservation approach can either manage or overcome contradictions by avoiding or ignoring them and focusing purely on conservation management. Ramutsindela and Shabangu (2013) note that reconciling land reform and biodiversity conservation is a complex undertaking. Based on the MDTFCA project, the ability, wisdom, and experience to reconcile conservation and development goals are still lacking because every conservation and development situation is different. To present and defend their territories, conservation, and development practitioners in the MDTFCA are using a 'positional' approach which is based on an 'incompatibility' mindset. It is common for conservation and development practitioners to be entangled in a push-and-pull manoeuvre, trying to maintain their mandates at the expense of local community's aspirations, whereas the aim should be to meet the needs of people while maintaining or enhancing conservation goals.

The needs and aspirations of mountain communities have not been met. Black community-owned tourist establishments are a rare occurrence and promises made to local communities never materialise. Yes, menial job opportunities for low salaries were created, and a few opportunities for tourism initiatives were facilitated, but none of the real benefits and opportunities have really changed hands or expanded from previously advantaged groups to previously disadvantaged individuals. Real benefits would mean that local people own and manage their own tourism facilities, to the extent that they are able to employ other people from their own community. Stock theft, tourist attacks, struggles over limited resources, and illegal natural resource harvesting have not completely abated, partly because of superficial legitimacy, lack of resources, and limited benefits. This affirms the tensions in discursive consensus, which in reality is dissensus in disguise and an invincible contradiction.

The establishment in the 1970s of Sehlabathebe National Park (SNP) in Lesotho within the MDTFCA demonstrated interesting aspects of consensus, contradiction, and struggle. The area was desirable to many pastoralists as it was believed to have good pastures and plenty of water. As a result, its transition to a national park was met with ferocious opposition from the local people (Rakotsoane, 2015) because it translated into loss of grazing land. However, the transition also meant that a communal grazing area became a potential place of employment by creating opportunities to benefit the community (ibid.). However, it could also be argued that local herdsmen from the same community would lose the income or livelihood they had derived from herding. This shows how a landscape without people is a man-made concept that has been entrenched in society to benefit project proponents who may overlook the needs of the local community. The natural environment and local communities are still perceived by some as two separate entities in one landscape, which conveniently neglects local socioeconomic reality.

As can be expected, the implementation of the MDTFCA gave rise to conflict among the different implementing structures and potentially hampered the success of the programme. At the forefront were the skills requirements and equitable representation of various racial groups on the respective PCUs. First, the World Bank's recruitment and funding conditions neither stipulated nor advocated equitable racial representation in institutional structures such as the PCUs. Within the South African context, the lack of equitable representation of different racial groups within the PCU was justified by a perceived shortage of black professionals in the scientific and technical field of biodiversity studies due to an excessive skills shortage in science. However, historically, highly skilled, and technical jobs in South Africa were only accessible to, and dominated by, whites and Indians (Reddy et al., 2016), creating a skills imbalance between black and white scientists. This reflects the profound consequences of apartheid. Although a failed attempt to traverse the rigid MDTFCA frontiers, PES was viewed as a possible way to restore the degraded environment in the Maloti-Drakensberg catchment area and generate income to sustain the MDTP.

Initially, both countries agreed to use systematic conservation planning (K. Zunckel, personal communication, July 20, 2018). Inconsistencies subsequently became apparent, although the Lesotho PCU was reluctant to change the project log frame. Project log frame is a planning term aligned to the logic model. Project log frames are meant to reflect each country's priorities, so there is room for practitioners to influence the agenda on natural resource management. The South African PCU addressed the matter with the World Bank, and the World Bank accepted and changed the South African log frame to introduce resource economics and include PES. Lesotho was reluctant to change the log frame; the South African PCU's request for a change was perceived by some members as undermining and disregarding the Lesotho PCU since the matter was not resolved before the South African PCU engaged with the World Bank. However, both countries were allowed to make work changes at their discretion. It could be said that the Lesotho PCU ignored the South African PCU's wish to amend the project log frame.

With diverse stakeholders in both countries coupled with different expectations and skillsets, it would have been extremely difficult to deliver project objectives using one coordinating structure. Citizens of both countries would also suspect that project implementation was inherently biased if the project functioned through one structure. Furthermore, it should be noted that having two country-specific PCUs was necessary because the World Bank had issued each country a separate grant, to be accounted for through a formal structure such as a PCU. According to an informant, South Africa was stronger than Lesotho in terms of resource base, level of funding, and skills within their agencies, particularly in natural resource management. It is interesting to note that the PCUs were both on par, following very similar terms of reference.

Unfortunately, inconsistencies in project implementation of the same PCUs created tensions which resulted in dissensus and polarisation of the programme.

## Conclusion

Attaining sustainable transformational environmental change is a difficult, but not insurmountable, task despite contradictions. Critical research through the lens of political ecology provides a platform for practitioners to view conservation challenges and consider social-based solutions, thus expanding their range of focus from their familiar territories. Considering the past and present challenges of the MDTFCA, it appears that frontier boundaries are indeed partially transformed but still very rigid. PES, stakeholder power relations, and rigid political frontiers resulted in tension between the two countries' PCUs, hence the evidence of rigid frontiers. Matters of sovereignty between the two countries contributed to the tensions. A dearth of real and tangible benefits from PES versus tourism is evident. The idea of community involvement and a substantial flow of benefits to communities is still an elusive concept for many conservation practitioners. Land tenure, ownership, leadership, and capacity seemed to have had a strong influence on the programme's limited success. The actors' diverse interests and priorities contributed to the MDTFCA's challenges. However, an important landmark and the greatest achievement in the history of the MDTFCA is the extension of uKhahlamba Drakensberg Park to include SNP in Lesotho, which thus became the first transboundary World Heritage site in both countries.

## Notes

1 Following colonial rivalries that had intensified in West Africa, the Berlin Conference took place from 15 November 1884 to 26 February 1885. It involved 14 countries (Wang, 1998).
2 The Mfecane (1810–1830) is a period of warfare between indigenous communities in Southern Africa (Eldredge, 1992).
3 Cheap labour could also be referred to as a dispossessed labour force. Most black African labourers came from rural 'Bantustan' homelands and were dispossessed of their land (with the exception of Lesotho in the case study area) by the racially discriminatory laws of apartheid.
4 This is the constructed or inflated value of natural resources, whereas their value depends on many other interdependent natural aspects.
5 Adopting a holistic view of conservation research entails overcoming the incompatible mindset of conservationists, such as the notion that conservation is exclusive of people, particularly local communities, and the thinking that conservation means minimal to no use of space (wilderness areas) and exclusivity of nature.
6 Adams and Hutton (2007) state that social and environmental conditions are indistinguishably interrelated. Previous approaches practised "ecology without politics" and ignored the fact that political ecology is essentially about political influence on environmental change (Vayda & Walters, 1999, p. 168).
7 A scientific method for identifying priority areas of biodiversity importance, including mapping biodiversity features (such as ecosystems, species, spatial components of ecological processes); mapping a range of information related to these biodiversity features

and their ecological condition; and setting quantitative biodiversity targets for biodiversity features (SANBI, 2016; SANBI and UNEP-WCMC, 2016).

8 Protected areas were established for the enjoyment of certain ethnic groups only and local communities were denied access (Neumann, 1998; Carruthers, 2013).

9 Both have the potential to make a tangible difference in the lives of local people. There is room for more conservation initiatives that are people-centred and for local community upliftment through development initiatives.

## References


Adams, W.M. & Hutton, J. (2007). People, parks and poverty: Political ecology and biodiversity conservation. *Conservation and Society*, 5(2):147–183.

Ahebwa, W.M., Van der Duim, V., & Sandbrook, C.G. (2012). Private–community partnerships: Investigating a new approach to conservation and development in Uganda. *Conservation and Society*, 10(4):305–317.

Andersson, J.A., Dzingirai, V., & Cumming, D.H. (2017). TFCAs and the invisible peoples. In *Transfrontier conservation areas*. New York: Routledge:12–24.

Balsiger, J. (2014). Transforming the frontier: Peace parks and the politics of neoliberal conservation in Southern Africa and Parks, peace, and partnerships: Global initiatives in transboundary conservation. International Mountain Society. *Mountain Research and Development*, 34(1):71–73.

Bocchino, C. (2014). Transforming the Frontier: Peace parks and the politics of neoliberal conservation in Southern Africa by Bram Büscher. *Journal of Development Studies*, 50(7):1038–1039. DOI: 10.1080/00220388.2014.922267

Büscher, B. (2009). Letters of gold: Enabling primitive accumulation through neoliberal conservation. *Human Geography*, 2(3):91–93.

Büscher, B. (2013). *Transforming the frontier*. London: Duke University Press.

Büscher, B., Sullivan, S., Neves, K., Igoe, J., & Brockington, D. (2012). Towards a synthesized critique of neoliberal biodiversity conservation. *Capitalism Nature Socialism*, 23(2):4–30. DOI: 10.1080/10455752.2012.674149

Chiutsi, S. & Saarinen, J. (2017). Local participation in transfrontier tourism: Case of Sengwe community in the Great Limpopo Transfrontier Conservation Area, Zimbabwe. *Development Southern Africa*, 34(3):260–275.

Carruthers, J. (2013). The Royal Natal National Park, Kwazulu-Natal: Mountaineering, tourism and nature conservation in South Africa's first national park c. 1896 to c. 1947. *Environment and History*, *19*(4): 459–485.

Coupal, L. (2004). Practitioner research and the regulation of research ethics: The challenge of individual, organizational, and social interests. *Forum Qualitative Sozialforschung / Forum: Qualitative Social Research*, 6(1):Art 6. Retrieved from: http://nbn-resolving.de/urn:nbnde:0114-fqs050163

DeMotts, R. (2017). *The challenges of transfrontier conservation in Southern Africa: The park came after us*. Lanham, MD: Lexington Books.

Duffy, R. (2005). The politics of global environmental governance: The powers and limitations of transfrontier conservation areas in Central America. *Review of International Studies*, 31(2):307–323.

Eldredge, E.A. (1992). Sources of conflict in Southern Africa, c. 1800–30: The 'Mfecane' reconsidered. *Journal of African History*, 33(1):1–35.

Hanks, J. & Myburgh, W. (2015). The evolution and progression of transfrontier conservation areas in the Southern African Development Community. In Van der Duim, R., Lamers,

M. & Van Wijk, J. (eds.) *Institutional arrangements for conservation, development and tourism in Eastern and Southern Africa*. Dordrecht: Springer:157–179.

Holmes, G. (2012). Biodiversity for billionaires: Capitalism, conservation and the role of philanthropy in saving/selling nature. International Institute of Social Studies. *Development and Change*, 43(1):185–203. DOI: 10.1111/j.1467-7660.2011.01749.x

Iskandar, J. (2008). Transborder environmental and natural resource management: Case studies of transfrontier protected areas in Indonesia and Malaysia. In De Jong, W. (ed.) *Transborder environmental and natural resource management*. Kyoto University: CIAS, Kyoto, Japan.

Maloti-Drakensberg Transfrontier Project. (2007). Payment for ecosystem services: Developing an ecosystem services trading model for the Mnweni/Cathedral Peak and Eastern Cape Drakensberg areas. In Mander (ed.) *INR Report IR281*. Development Bank of Southern Africa, Department of Water Affairs and Forestry, Department of Environment Affairs and Tourism, Ezemvelo KZN Wildlife, South Africa.

Memorandum of Understanding between the Government of the Republic of South Africa and the Government of the Kingdom of Lesotho. (2008). In respect of the Maloti-Drakensberg transfrontier conservation and development area. Unpublished document.

Merriam, S.B. (2002). Introduction to qualitative research. *Qualitative Research in Practice: Examples for Discussion and Analysis*, 1(1):1–17.

Middlemass, J. (2014). Transforming the frontier: Peace parks and the politics of neoliberal conservation in Southern Africa. *International Journal of Environmental Studies*, 71(4):582–583. DOI: 10.1080/00207233.2014.930225

Milder, J.C., Scherr, S.J., & Bracer, C. (2010). Trends and future potential of payment for ecosystem services to alleviate rural poverty in developing countries. *Ecology and Society*, 15(2):4.

Mugadza, A.T. (2019). *Sustainable tourism development in transfrontier conservation areas: A legal perspective*. (PhD thesis. Name of faculty). Potchefstroom: North-West University.

Neumann, R.P. (1998). *Imposing wilderness: Struggles over livelihood and nature preservation in Africa* (Vol. 4). Los Angeles and Berkeley, CA: University of California Press.

Neumann, R.P. (2014). Transforming the frontier: Peace parks and the politics of neoliberal conservation in Southern Africa. *AAG Review of Books*, 2(2):51–53. DOI:10.1080/2325548X.2014.901858

Phimister, I. (1992). *Unscrambling the scramble: Africa's partition reconsidered*. Unpublished Report. Johannesburg.

Rakotsoane, F.C.L. (2015). *Sehlabathebe National Park oral history*. Unpublished Research Report. Lesotho.

Ramutsindela, M. (1999). African boundaries and their interpreters. *Geopolitics*, 4(2):180–198. DOI: 10.1080/14650049908407646

Ramutsindela, M. (2007). *Transfrontier conservation in Africa: At the confluence of capital, politics and nature*. CABI. United Kingdom.

Ramutsindela, M. (2009). Crossing paths: Diplomacy and the neoliberalisation of the environment. *Geopolitics*, 14(3):570–575. DOI: 10.1080/14650040802694067

Ramutsindela, M. & Shabangu, M. (2013). Conditioned by neoliberalism: A reassessment of land claim resolutions in the Kruger National Park. *Journal of Contemporary African Studies*, 31(3):441–456. DOI: 10.1080/02589001.2013.811791

Reddy, V., Bhorat, H., Powell, M., Visser, M., & Arends, A. (2016). *Skills supply and demand in South Africa*. Pretoria: Human Sciences Research Council.

Robbins, P. (2011). *Political ecology: A critical introduction* (Vol. 16). Hoboken, NJ: Wiley.

Saarinen, J. (2016). A review of "Transforming the Frontier: Peace Parks and the Politics of Neoliberal Conservation in Southern Africa" by Bram Büscher. *Journal of Sustainable Tourism*, 24(6):926–928. DOI: 10.1080/09669582.2015.1013357

Sagoff, M. (2004). *Price, principle, and the environment*. Cambridge: Cambridge University Press.

SANBI. (2016). *Lexicon of biodiversity planning in South Africa*. Pretoria: South African National Biodiversity Institute.

SANBI & UNEP–WCMC. (2016). *Mapping biodiversity priorities: A practical, science-based approach to national biodiversity assessment and prioritisation to inform strategy and action planning*. Cambridge: UNEP–WCMC.

Skelcher, B. (2003). Apartheid and the removal of black spots from Lake Bhangazi in KwaZulu-Natal, South Africa. *Journal of Black Studies*, 33(6): 761–783.

Stake, R.E. (1995). *The art of case study research*. Thousand Oaks, CA: SAGE Publications.

Stoldt, M., Gottert, T., Mann, C. & Zeller, U. (2020). Transfrontier conservation areas and human–wildlife conflict: The case of the Namibian component of the Kavango–Zambezi (KAZA) TFCA. *Scientific Reports*, 10(1):1–16.

Suarez, D.C. (2015). Transforming the frontier: Peace parks and the politics of neoliberal conservation in Southern Africa. *Journal of Peasant Studies*, 42(2):452–456. DOI: 10.1080/03066150.2015.1006457

Vatn, A. (2000). The environment as a commodity. *Environmental Values*, 9(4):493–509.

Vayda, A.P. & Walters, B.B. (1999). Against political ecology. *Human Ecology*, 27(1):167–169.

Wang, S.T. (1998). The Conference of Berlin and British. 臺大歷史學報, 22:191–230.

Williams, C. (March 2007). Research methods. Grand Canyon University. *Journal of Business & Economic Research*, 5(3): 65–72.

Yazan, B. (2015). Three approaches to case study methods in education: Yin, Merriam, and Stake. *The Qualitative Report*, 20(2):134–152. Retrieved from http://www.nova.edu/ssss/QR/QR20/2/yazan1.pdf.

# Part 4

# Conclusion

# 13 The future of community-based tourism amid socioeconomic and political conflicts in Southern Africa

*Llewellyn Leonard and Regis Musavengane*

## Snapshot

Land is at the core of development in Africa and a backbone for major economic activities. The tourism sector, in particular community-based tourism, ecotourism, and adventure tourism, heavily relies on land and associated resources ranging from wildlife to water. As we have pointed out, the quest for land and the associated natural resources led to the exploitation of Africans through colonisation, which in turn framed the current conflicts. In contemporary society, issues regarding natural resource governance such as land tenure continue to underpin evolving relationships between states and citizens, but also with the private sector. Inequalities relating to land use and access have been and remain to be the key reason for land conflicts in Southern Africa. The United Nations Sustainable Development Goal 15: Life on land (SDG15) encourages people to "protect, restore and promote sustainable use of terrestrial ecosystems, sustainably manage forests, combat desertification, and halt and reverse land degradation and halt biodiversity loss" (UNDP, 2015). Attaining this goal requires collaborative efforts from a number of sectors, including agriculture and tourism. Tourism has been recognised as one of the sectors that have enhanced conservation efforts while improving community livelihoods. This current book agrees with such sentiments and propositions; Southern Africa should not be known for grabbing the land violently and destroying any economic activity, including tourism. To re-emphasise: This volume focused on Sub-Saharan Africa because of the widespread concerns over the intensity of the competition around land. This competition is the result of not only the global 'land rush' and the prevalence of land tenure insecurity in Africa but also the need to bridge the scholarships around 'development' and 'conflict'. Hence, the book navigates the pertinent issues on the nexus between land conflicts and tourism in Southern Africa. The chapters in this volume have demonstrated the complexities surrounding land in the tourism industry. The main land conflicts highlighted in the chapters emanate from socioeconomic and political issues.

The first theme (*Land governance and sustainable tourism management*) explored the role of governance in natural resource management and tourism.

DOI: 10.4324/9781003188902-17

Governance consists of systems, mechanisms, processes, relationships, and institutions through which groups and citizens articulate their interests, perform legal rights, recognise obligations, and resolve differences. Proponents of good governance in the African tourism sector argue that macro and micro tourism benefits can easily be realised equally if all actors follow principles of good governance (Nunkoo, 2017; Robbins, 2016; Siakwah et al., 2020).

In Chapter 2, Leonard discussed an alternative governance approach towards addressing the intersection between mining developments and impacts on tourism and conservation sites in Southern Africa. The author highlighted that Southern Africa has been endowed with an abundance of minerals and natural resources. The former has been viewed as a 'resource curse' due to multinational corporations and African governments viewing it as an opportunity for wealth generation and economic development. However, due to poor governance, this development largely amounts to the destruction of the natural environment, which is essential for local tourism, which in turn serves as a revenue generator and ensures sustainable livelihoods. Although governance is important in ensuring sustainable development, there is tension between the governance of capitalist political economies and governance directed at environmental protection and land use. This results in conflict between communities and civil society on the one hand and government and multinationals on the other. By examining secondary data on mining developments and contestation over land use in Southern Africa, the chapter shed light on the governance mechanisms that may fuel land conflict and favour capitalist mining political economies over the conservation of land use and the protection of tourism. Using data drawn from South Africa, the chapter argued that governments need to engage in an ecological reflexive governance approach that emphasises solidarity, accountability, and networking. This may be reached via the African Union, which is centred on the ideals of Pan-Africanism, African socialism, and promoting African unity. The African Union Commission will be required to revisit its position on mining development on the continent and educate African governments on mining and land-use conflicts.

In Chapter 3, Kamuti explained the deepening challenge of the governance of wildlife ranching and land issues in South Africa in the context of rising citizen participation. This kind of land conflict is based on the contention between a minority of private landowners and stakeholders from the wildlife ranching sector, including the state and citizens. An institutional approach inherently linked to governance was used to reflect upon critical developments in major sectors related to the private wildlife ranching sector in KwaZulu-Natal Province, South Africa, over the last decade. Kamuti argued that the persistent skewed ownership of land within the post-1994 democratic dispensation witnessed through tension on privately owned land under wildlife-based production justifies the questioning of the state's role in confronting those challenges of inequality and slow transformation. Rising tension on the back of the populist citizens' call for rapid economic transformation is deepening the challenge of land and wildlife governance in South Africa, especially in the rural spaces that bear the remnants of historical processes which have alienated the majority of the population from their land and wildlife resources.

In Chapter 4, Mthimkhulu and Nel, using a case of Somkhanda Game Reserve in South Africa, expounded on the intricacies of leadership and governance in communally owned protected areas. Protected area management in Southern Africa has evolved from a preservationist and protectionist approach towards integrated biodiversity conservation management. Modern-day biodiversity conservation management has had to work parallel with land reform objectives and acknowledge the need for 'community' beneficiation. Communally-Owned Protected Areas (COPAs) on restituted land have raised expectations of generating substantial benefits for the new dispensation of previously disadvantaged landowners. The chapter presented the leadership and governance intricacies at Somkhanda Game Reserve (SGR) as a COPA established in 2005 after a successful land claim by the Gumbi community in northern KwaZulu-Natal. SGR is now a proclaimed protected area co-managed by the landowning Emvokweni Community Trust (ECT) and Wildlands Conservation Trust. The study found that a tripartite power struggle between the local iNkosi (traditional leader), the ECT, and the land-stripped former labour tenants created havoc and disorder in the management of SGR and the Gumbi community. The chapter concluded that a harmonious relationship between traditional leadership and community trusts is essential to the effective management of COPAs in rural areas.

The second theme (*Managing natural disasters and land reform tourism crises*) explored uncertainty issues to enhance management approaches during disasters and crises. In Chapter 5, Virtanen, Cristóvão, and Mourinho argued that for protected areas to be sustainable, they must bring concrete benefits to local populations who suffer from the restrictions imposed for conservation. Natural disasters, such as major floods, bring additional challenges to conservation efforts and related support activities, notably nature-based tourism. They highlighted that those disasters often intensify the conflict between conservation objectives and local community needs, but they may also bring some mutual benefits. Reduced income from decreased nature-based tourism can, for example, lead to the expansion of agricultural fields to protected forests and subsequent land-use conflicts. Yet, disasters can also strengthen feelings of solidarity and result in additional investment in the area for both income-generating activities and production of services. Using comparative analysis, the chapter sheds light on the contrast in the management of the challenges posed by Cyclone Idai on the communities in two COPAs in Mozambique, namely the national parks of Chimanimani and Gorongosa. The comparative setup of the study provided an excellent opportunity to examine the complex ways in which such unexpected challenges may change the prospects of different types of ecotourism ventures – and the situation of local populations.

In Chapter 6, Zhou and Nyahunzvi enlightened the readers on the challenges and prospects of community-based tourism after Zimbabwe's land reform programme in the Midlands Province. Zimbabwe's land reform programme spawned several challenges for community-based tourism (CBT) projects. This chapter unpacked the challenges using predominantly interpretive research methods involving CBT proprietors, local community residents, and institutions selected through snowball sampling. Their thematically analysed findings suggested low CBT prospects after land reform due to the withdrawal of critical funding, looting of CBT infrastructures, and disruption and the demise of CBT activities as a result of the land reform programme. These findings are crucial in policymaking to enhance inclusive community-based natural resources management.

In Chapter 7, Muzirambi, Naylor, and Mearns reviewed post-restitution land rights agreement conflicts and their resolution at &Beyond Phinda Private Game Reserve in KZN, South Africa. The chapter reported on achievements and areas of disagreement relating to land ownership and community participation in management at &Beyond Phinda Private Game Reserve post 2016. Some of the challenges identified include exclusion from decision-making, breakdown in communication between management and community, power relations, employment opportunities, equity issues, and concerns relating to governance. The chapter provided an opportunity for stakeholders around the game reserve to consider existing and potential threats to conservation using the Bending the Curve Model proposed by Muzirambi. This model is based on the use of problems as a springboard for the generation of robust and progressive solutions. The research was conducted with &Beyond Phinda Game Reserve and the Makhasa and Mnqobokazi communities in the Umkhanyakude District in KwaZulu-Natal. Leadership development, employment of more of the local residents, skills development and transfer and, to a lesser extent, revenue and social development projects were some of the positive developments illustrated by the Bending the Curve Model. Lack of active participation in decision-making, poor communication, and lack of skills transfer for decision-making positions were identified as persistent obstacles. As an important tool within the community engagement framework for both the private sector and state authorities, the Bending the Curve Model has the potential to make a valuable contribution by providing an insight into difficulties affecting community-based conservation and tourism and potential avenues for their resolution.

In Chapter 8, Musavengane concluded the second theme by focusing on Environmental Operational Research (EOR) to enhance conflict management in community-based natural resources management. Within the tourism sector, managing operations and the associated natural resources tend to be complex during episodes of land conflict and other crises. The chapter reviewed conceptual and methodological approaches for EOR associated with participatory community-based natural resource management (CBNRM) in tribal communities. The analysis focused on research that uses a socio-ecological learning approach to study community participation in CBNRM. Firstly, the methodological choices reported in the current EOR and social learning literatures were deconstructed to map out the prevailing epistemological orientation of eco-social research in participatory CBNRM. Data were drawn from the Gumbi and Zondi communities located in the uPhongolo and Umvoti municipalities of KwaZulu-Natal in South Africa, respectively. The chapter proposed systemic–resilience thinking as a methodological imperative for conflict management in CBNRM to enhance EOR practices in tribal communities.

The third theme (*Managing land use, access, and benefit-sharing conflicts*) focused on issues that are seemingly fluid and often cause diverse conflicts. Mbaiwa and Mogende, in Chapter 9, demonstrated the linkages between the state, community-based tourism, and wildlife user rights in tourism concessions in Botswana. The CBNRM programme is the backbone of CBT in Botswana. The chapter analysed how state control of CBNRM has created conflict between the state and its citizens and how this undermines the growth of CBT in Botswana. It argued that CBT in Botswana faces a set of political and economic constraints that determine the performance of their business model and their engagement with people in conserving environmental assets. Although CBNRM puts a strong emphasis on devolving rights over land and wildlife resources to local communities, the increased state involvement in CBT ventures and projects results in the poor performance of the CBNRM programme in Botswana. State decisions such as financial control of CBT revenue, hunting bans, the Land Bank, and displacement of local communities from conservation areas reflect state dominance in CBT. This has forged new relations and deepened the existing conflict over user rights to wildlife resources between the state and its citizens. The implementation of neoliberal policies and the emergence of an elite class in the wildlife-based tourist industry in Botswana have reduced local autonomy over wildlife resources and deepened the dominance of foreign-owned multinational companies in this sector. For CBT to succeed in Botswana, the principles of devolving user rights to communities and forming joint venture partnerships between communities and the private tourism sector must be adhered to.

In Chapter 10, Gargallo and Heita focused on the socioeconomic and land-use impacts posed by COVID-19 in the conservation and tourism sectors in Namibia's Conservancies. The authors noted that Namibia's programme of Communal Conservancies has been depicted as one of the most successful in Africa and is often implemented through tourism business joint ventures between communities and private companies. One of the main effects of COVID-19 and its preventive measures, though, has been an almost total collapse of international tourist visits to Namibia, leading to a sharp fall in income to conservancies and communities. By analysing the general evolution of conservancies and two specific cases, the chapter investigated how the crisis in the tourism sector has impacted populations in conservancy areas. Special focus was placed on three issues: the socioeconomic impact of declining revenue and employment on the people, the effects on wildlife behaviour and human-wildlife conflict, and finally, the possible changes in land use in conservancies.

Although the data are still preliminary, it already suggests what may happen to community wildlife conservation schemes when tourism-generated income vanishes and how land use and agropastoralism may evolve when conservation loses ground.

Maseko and Moyo, in Chapter 11, assessed conflicts arising from conservation between the iSimangaliso Wetland Park and the community of KwaNibela, KwaZulu-Natal, South Africa. The findings in the chapter suggest that iSimangaliso Wetland Park conservation strategies have a negative impact on the socioeconomic wellbeing of the people in KwaNibela due to limited access to natural resources and a lack of economic opportunities. This has led to conflicts between the stakeholders of iSimangaliso Wetland Park and the community. iSimangaliso Wetland Park generates income from tourists who visit the park, while the community of KwaNibela receives little to no benefits from both tourism and conservation. This resulted in conflict since the community of KwaNibela feels that iSimangaliso is generating income from their traditional land and natural resources while they (the community) are left poverty-stricken. To achieve conservation that caters for the needs and livelihoods of local people, it is suggested that iSimangaliso Wetland Park include the community of KwaNibela in their conservation efforts and create economic opportunities for the same community through conservation and tourism.

Finally, Mthimkhulu and Nel discussed the aspirations, limitations, and tensions of the Maloti-Drakensberg Transfrontier Conservation Area (MDTFCA). Transfrontier conservation has been internationally acclaimed as the preferred holistic approach to conservation with multiple wins despite its associated shortcomings. The formation of a Transfrontier Conservation Area between the Kingdom of Lesotho and the Republic of South Africa was framed as an opportunity to address historical injustices that are geographically and ecologically evident. While the initiative has been lauded and criticised alike for its impact, this chapter argued that the political boundaries of transfrontier initiatives can be rigid and are anchored in the complexities found in different political economies of both countries. The dynamics of transfrontier initiatives include disparities between intended project objectives and actual deliverables, the continuous struggle to reconcile conservation and development, and tensions and dissensus arising from divergent implementing authority interests and aspirations. The political ecology theory framework was applied to reinforce research application and enhance understanding of various power relations. It nuances and updates current understandings of neoliberal conservation and the role of the state, which is under-appreciated in the literature on conservation (emphasises understandings of neoliberalism that are not dismissive of the continuing role of the state) and contributes towards the enhancement of local knowledge in the Maloti-Drakensberg Transfrontier Conservation and Development Programme. The findings suggest that international boundaries and processes in the transfrontier conservation area can be durable and rigid or partially transformed through interventions.

## The future of tourism amid land conflicts

The near future of Africa is enshrined in the African Union's Agenda 2063: The Africa We Want (African Union Commission, 2015). Thus, the future of the tourism sector was mirrored in Agenda 2063 to have a better understanding of the nexus between land conflicts and tourism development in Southern Africa. The Agenda 2063 blueprint aims for Africa to be the "global powerhouse of the future" (African Union Commission, 2015). Almost every chapter in this volume addresses at least one of the seven priority areas of Agenda 2063 (see Table 13.1). It will be interesting for scholars to look into linkages between Agenda 2063, the SDGs, land conflicts, and tourism in Africa.

The chapters in this volume emphasised to varying degrees the need for good governance approaches to prevent and reduce land conflicts. Such approaches must include non-state stakeholders in tourism development planning and decision-making to reduce and eliminate land conflicts whilst emphasising state accountability and transparency. Barriers to tourism planning, such as the state relying on technocratic and bureaucratic processes that may increase land conflicts, must be removed. Collaborative management was generally highlighted as a key element for implementation by governments and other leaders to facilitate the participation of community members in making decisions regarding their resources and in taking ownership of these resources for sustainable tourism development and control over natural resources. Such social-ecological approaches can create more ecological resilient communities and improved livelihoods. They would assist in enshrining the Agenda 2063 goals and priorities, particularly those promoting a more prosperous Africa, based on inclusive growth and sustainable development. It would be an effective strategy for realising some important SDGs of the United Nations, such as SDG15, to protect, restore, and promote sustainable use of natural resources and to halt and reverse land degradation and biodiversity loss. Researchers embracing the work on land conflicts and tourism development would need to do the following:

1. Explore how power relations unfold over land conflicts and between governments, the private sector, and local communities, and at the same time understand that land conflicts and SSA tourism places are distinct, and development trajectories are not similar.
2. Examine social dimensions (i.e. class, caste, gender, religion, age, race, and ethnicity) that influence and may determine accessibility and ownership of land since these dimensions have been the major sources of land conflict in the region.
3. Bridge the scholarship around 'development' and 'conflict' considering Africa's relative underdevelopment. This would also entail encouraging research collaboration among scholars from different subregions on the continent for comparison of land conflict dynamics and to provide more

*Table 13.1* Goals and priority areas of Agenda 2063

| *Aspirations* | *Goals* | *Priority areas* |
| --- | --- | --- |
| 1) A prosperous Africa, based on inclusive growth and sustainable development | (1) A high standard of living, quality of life and wellbeing for all citizens | • Incomes, jobs, and decent work<br>• Poverty, inequality, and hunger<br>• Social security and protection, including persons with disabilities<br>• Modern and liveable habitats and basic quality services |
| | (2) Well-educated citizens and skills revolution underpinned by science, technology, and innovation (STI) | • Education and STI skills-driven revolution |
| | (3) Healthy and well-nourished citizens | • Health and nutrition |
| | (4) Transformed economies | • Sustainable and inclusive economic growth<br>• STI-driven manufacturing/ industrialisation and value addition<br>• Economic diversification and resilience<br>• Hospitality/tourism |
| | (5) Modern agriculture for increased productivity and production | • Agricultural productivity and production |
| | (6) Blue/ocean economy for accelerated economic growth | • Marine resources and energy<br>• Port operations and marine transport |
| | (7) Environmentally sustainable and climate-resilient economies and communities | • Sustainable natural resource management and biodiversity conservation<br>• Sustainable consumption and production patterns<br>• Water security<br>• Climate resilience and preparedness for and prevention of natural disasters<br>• Renewable energy |

| | | |
|---|---|---|
| 2) An integrated continent, politically united and based on the ideals of Pan-Africanism and the vision of African Renaissance | (8) A united Africa (federal or confederate)<br>(9) Established and functional continental financial and monetary institutions<br>(10) World-class infrastructure criss-crossing Africa | • Framework and institutions for a United Africa<br>• Financial and monetary institutions<br>• Communication and infrastructure connectivity |
| 3) An Africa of good governance, democracy, respect for human rights, justice, and the rule of law | (11) Democratic values and practices, universal principles of human rights and justice, and an entrenched rule of law<br>(12) Capable institutions and transformative leadership | • Democracy and good governance<br>• Human rights, justice, and the rule of law<br>• Institutions and leadership<br>• Participatory development and local governance |
| 4) A peaceful and secure Africa | (13) Peace, security, and stability<br>(14) Stability and peace<br>(15) A fully functional and operational African Peace and Security Architecture (APSA) | • Maintenance and preservation of peace and security<br>• Institutional structure for AU instruments on peace and security<br>• Fully operational and functional APSA pillars |
| 5) An Africa with a strong cultural identity, common heritage, values, and ethics | (16) Pre-eminent African Cultural Renaissance | • Values and ideals of Pan-Africanism<br>• Cultural values and African Renaissance<br>• Cultural heritage, creative arts, and businesses |

(*Continued*)

*Table 13.1* Continued

| *Aspirations* | *Goals* | *Priority areas* |
|---|---|---|
| 6) An Africa whose development is people-driven, relying on the potential offered by African people, especially women and youth, and caring for children | (17) Full gender equality in all spheres of life<br>(18) Engaged and empowered youth and children | • Empowerment of women and girls<br>• Violence and discrimination against women and girls<br>• Youth empowerment and children |
| 7) An Africa as a strong, united, resilient, and influential global player and partner | (19) Africa as a major partner in global affairs and peaceful coexistence<br>(20) Africa taking full responsibility for financing its development | • Africa's place in global affairs<br>• Partnership<br>• African capital market<br>• Fiscal system and public sector revenue<br>• Development assistance |

Source: African Union Commission (2015)

informed African perspectives on land conflict and tourism development. There is a need for Africans to learn from one another as they largely share similar backgrounds.

4. Frame research questions that aim to discuss land conflicts and tourism development constructively while celebrating successes about positive developments and learning from disappointments to enhance sustainable tourism development practices.
5. Provide a more thorough understanding of how the pandemic has proliferated land conflicts over natural resources and affected sustainable tourism development livelihoods. As highlighted in Chapter 1, COVID-19 resulted in social conflict in the tourism sector with deterioration of security both inside and outside protected areas across Africa, causing loss of natural resources and loss of livelihoods for communities. There is no doubt that the pandemic will have long-lasting repercussions over access to land and natural resources in the near future and years to come. Researchers will need to study these dynamics and provide critical recommendations for stakeholders to combat any unfolding crises.

Furthermore, to achieve Africa's Agenda 2063: The Africa We Want, it is important to robustly synchronise concepts of land conflicts, natural resources, sustainable tourism and conservation, environmental justice, human rights, democracy, and peace. This will help us understand the dynamics of land conflicts, move towards sustainable tourism development, and protect natural resources. Some of the goals of Agenda 2063 aim to ensure that peace, security, and stability are preserved (Goal 13) and that Africa becomes a major partner in global affairs and peaceful coexistence (Goal 19). Specifically, Aspiration 3 of Agenda 2063 envisages an Africa of good governance, democracy, and respect for human rights, justice, and the rule of law. These elements are vital in attaining protection for and development of natural tourism resources and combating land conflicts. It will, however, be the responsibility of African leaders to engage in good governance practices to ensure that land conflicts over natural resources are resolved to enable the development of sustainable tourism and the protection of natural resources for the benefit of the African people. African governments must ensure that good governance includes the appropriate use of land for the benefit of the society and reduces poverty and inequality, ensuring the implementation of adequate and robust land policies and land tenure security. This will also require African citizens to hold government and local leaders accountable for lack of action and appropriate interventions to avoid land conflicts. Essentially, all stakeholders must engage in a dialogue that will define relationships specifying their respective rights and responsibilities. Ultimately, land and natural resources are central to the livelihoods and cultures of African communities, and any interventions must ensure poverty reduction, sustainable livelihoods, and environmental sustainability.

## References

African Union Commission. (2015). Agenda 2063: The Africa we want. Online: Accessed 8 October 2021 at https://au.int/en/agenda2063/overview

Nunkoo, R. (2017). Governance and sustainable tourism: What is the role of trust, power and social capital? *Journal of Destination Marketing & Management*, 6, 277–285.

Robbins, B. G. (2016). What is trust? A multidisciplinary review, critique, and synthesis. *Sociology Compass*, 10(10), 972–986.

Siakwah, P., Musavengane, R., & Leonard, L. (2020). Tourism governance and attainment of the sustainable development goals in Africa. *Tourism Planning & Development*, 17(4), 355–383. DOI: 10.1080/21568316.2019.1600160

United Nations Development Programme (UNDP). (2015). Sustainable development goals (SDGs). Online: Accessed 18 October 2021 at https://sdgs.un.org/goals

# Index

Pages in *italics* represent figures, while page numbers in **bold** mark tables.